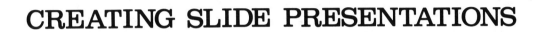

CREATING SLIDE PRESENTATIONS

CREATING SLIDE PRESENTATIONS

A Basic Guide

JOHN R. PODRACKY

Illustrated by the author

Prentice-Hall, Inc., Englewood Cliffs, New Jersey 07632

Library of Congress Cataloging in Publication Data

Podracky, John R.
  Creating slide presentations.

  Includes index.
   1. Slides (Photography) I. Title.
TR505.P64   001.55'34'028   82-7481
ISBN 0-13-191205-4   AACR2

Editorial/production supervision and
    interior design by Sonia Meyer
Layout by Bruce Kenselaar and Steven Frim
Cover design by Ray Lundgren
Cover photograph and all illustrations by the author
Manufacturing buyer: Ed O'Dougherty

Printed in the United States of America

10 9 8 7 6 5 4 3 2 1

ISBN 0-13-191205-4

Prentice-Hall International, Inc., *London*
Prentice-Hall of Australia Pty. Limited, *Sydney*
Editora Prentice-Hall do Brazil, Ltda., *Rio de Janeiro*
Prentice-Hall Canada Inc., *Toronto*
Prentice-Hall of India Private Limited, *New Delhi*
Prentice-Hall of Japan, Inc., *Tokyo*
Prentice-Hall of Southeast Asia Pte. Ltd., *Singapore*
Whitehall Books Limited, *Wellington, New Zealand*

A special thanks to Mr. Vincent V. Merlo,
Director of Media and Technology at
the Instructional Resource Center of
Kean College of New Jersey, for his
permission to photograph specialized
audio-visual equipment.

CONTENTS

PREFACE

In recent years there has been an explosion in the development and utilization of new media techniques in classroom teaching. Some of the factors in this proliferation of materials is undoubtedly due to the increased importance placed on thorough and efficient curriculums and the general increases in class size experienced in the school systems, as well as the necessity of ensuring that school budgets and funding provide the best possible education.

In light of this background, the ever increasing demand for audio/visual materials would indicate that their use has proven to be extremely valuable in many areas and subjects of instruction. So much so that currently in all types of educational institutions ranging from elementary through college, the establishment of audio/visual resource departments, media centers, and even libraries, is considered a necessity.

Audio/visual materials have found value in the industrial sector as well, and are being increasingly utilized in projects ranging from the presentation of advertising concepts, and the training of management personnel, to the application of specific industrial skills and processes.

One of the media areas in the audio/visual field that has produced great interest and demand traditionally, is the *sound-slide-system.*

These compact and easy to use materials are familiar to the classroom teacher as film strips, or slide sets that are accompanied by a record, cassette tape, or written script which explains and enlarges upon the visual information presented. A set of such materials focusing on a specific subject or instructional area is referred to as a module. Such modules are produced by a large number of companies, in a wide spectrum of interest areas, both in the United States and abroad.

However, despite the large number and variety of materials available, frequently the special instructional needs of a school, subject, or industrial training application cannot be met because they fall outside of the necessarily more general areas covered in mass-prepared materials designed for wide distribution. Another consideration is the price of professionally prepared sound-slide modules, and the very real problems of obtaining and maintaining these materials within a limited budget.

The purpose of this book, therefore, is to provide a body of information and step-by-step procedures to the establishment of the skills needed to produce audio/visual modules. Whether a one-person operation, a mini-production lab, or for the addition of a media department or center in a school or business, the planning and production of sound-slide systems with readily available equipment and, wherever possible, inexpensive materials that can give professional results, will be described and outlined. Such a set-up of production equipment, when made available to the teacher, instructor, or curriculum designer in school or industry, is an ideal medium for the growth and development of "customized" instructional materials. The possibilities are as wide as the experience and imagination of those who will design and use them.

A SPECIAL NOTE TO THE READER

The wide variety and profusion of mass communication media in the last fifty years has produced a generation that is the most visually sophisticated in history. As specialized knowledge in so many fields doubles and redoubles each decade, the need to find new and more efficient ways of presentation to larger audiences also increases.

Most persons today are aware of the interrelationship of the visual arts and the teaching process, even if they have not studied it as a separate discipline. From seeing countless photographs, magazines, illustrated books, and other pictorial and printed matter, a sense of graphic discrimination and sensibility develops rapidly. This sense of "knowing-what-I-like" is a valuable tool for the person who wishes to design visual teaching materials. Join this to an introduction to, and understanding of, the basic principles and rules of graphic design, and an application of the virtues of patience and care, and a good start in the field is assured. The requirement of talent, often linked to an undertaking of a visual project, is not always a necessity. A willingness to learn the foundations of graphic design, and the innate sense of design that every human being possesses, will serve you well.

This text is not meant to be the last word to all design needs, but as a body of information and procedures to be modified and built upon it can begin to suit your individual needs. Do not hesitate to experiment; try out your own variations and innovations of any process outlined in these pages, because such an attitude and approach is truly the basis of the creative teaching process. Good luck.

1
THE SCRIPT

THE SCRIPT

Audio-visual instructional materials should mirror the sequence of steps of the actual learning process. The most successful learning process starts at the logically simple and proceeds, step by step, to the logically complex. To produce a thorough and retainable learning experience for the student, each successive audio-visual frame should reinforce the information in the preceding one. A segment of new information should be added until, by the final frame, a coherent statement is the result.

The true instructional value of audio-visual materials lies in the visual portion of the presentation. Because human beings receive most of their abstract learning stimulus visually either through type or pictorial images, seeing information in addition to hearing it produces a maximum potential for retention. Therefore, if audio-visual materials are to have a maximum impact, they must be very will planned as to both *selective content* and *sequence*.

SELECTIVE CONTENT AND SEQUENCE

Selective content is essentially *focus*, the elimination of superfluous information from the subject of the module. The best way to ensure selective content is to prepare a script for each frame of the presentation (for both the audio and the visual portions).

The script is actually two sequences of information that fit together to form the learning objective of the module. The first step is the written script. A primary idea or unit of information is the desired end product. Having decided what this end product will be, the script must incorporate a series of steps to achieve it. The most difficult part of this process is not the information but the method by which it will be presented to form a coherent pattern when translated to visual images. The best way to achieve a script pattern is (1) write down the objective of the module (this can be the title as well) and then, as a continuous statement, all the information leading to the achievement of this objective; and (2) break down this written statement, literally sentence by sentence, and reconstruct it in terms of the visual images it presents. These complete images will eventually become the individual frames of the completed module. An example of this would be the following module script.

COMPLETE SCRIPT

Title (or objective of the module) *How To Change a Standard Light Bulb Socket*

When the light bulb socket of a lamp, such as a reading lamp, no longer switches properly or otherwise malfunctions, it can easily be replaced. You'll need the following tool and part: a screwdriver and a replacement socket of the same type that is now in the lamp. The first thing to do is to make sure that the lamp is unplugged to eliminate the chance of electrical shock. Next, remove the lampshade and bulb. Then press in the sides of the socket case above the base seam and gently rock and pull up to loosen and remove it. When the socket case shell is removed, it will expose the socket-switch assembly. Pull the socket-switch assembly up approximately two inches to expose the wiring and aid in removal. If necessary, feed a little wire up through the base of the lamp to allow the socket switch to be pulled up. Using a screwdriver, loosen the terminal screws as far back as they will go and pull out the two wire leads. At this point, the old switch can be thrown away. Twist the bare wire leads tight again, and wrap them around the terminal screws of the new switch in a *clockwise* direction (so that they will tighten around the screw shaft when the screws are retightened). Replace the socket case, pressing it down over the new switch until it "clicks" into place. The lamp is now ready to have its bulb and shade replaced and be plugged in for use.

END

This narrative suggests a process in descriptive steps, each of which should be separately illustrated in order to make a coherent instructional module. Therefore, the next step is to ascribe a picture or illustration of some kind to each verbal image. The script would appear as follows.

Title *How to Change Standard Light Bulb Socket*

FRAME 1
NARRATIVE When the light bulb socket of a lamp, such as a reading lamp, no longer switches properly or otherwise malfunctions, it can easily be replaced.

FRAME 1
VISUAL Illustration of a hand turning switch button on the lamp (which is unlit).

FRAME 2
NARRATIVE You'll need the following tool and part: a screwdriver and a replacement socket of the same type that is now in the lamp.

FRAME 2
VISUAL Illustration of a screwdriver and a new socket with switch.

FRAME 3
NARRATIVE The first thing to do is to make sure the lamp is unplugged to eliminate the chance of electrical shock.

FRAME 3
VISUAL Illustration of a hand pulling the plug from a wall socket.

FRAME 4
NARRATIVE Next, remove the lampshade and bulb.

FRAME 4
VISUAL Illustration of lamp with shade removed, and hand holding the removed bulb above the socket (as though having just unscrewed it).

FRAME 5
NARRATIVE Then press in the sides of the socket case above the base seam and gently rock and pull up to loosen and remove it.

FRAME 5
VISUAL Illustration of hand clasping the sides of the socket switch, with arrows indicating the rocking and pulling action.

FRAME 6
NARRATIVE   When the socket case shell is re-moved, it will expose the socket-switch assembly.

FRAME 6
VISUAL   Illustration (close-up) of switch assembly.

FRAME 7
NARRATIVE   Pull the socket-switch assembly up approximately two inches to expose the wiring and aid in re-moval. If necessary, feed a little wire up through the base of the lamp to allow the socket switch to be pulled up.

FRAME 7
VISUAL   Illustration of a lamp, with one hand pulling socket switch up while another hand feeds wire into the base of the lamp.

FRAME 8
NARRATIVE   Using a screwdriver, loosen the terminal screws as far back as they will go and pull out the two wire leads. At this point, the old switch can be thrown away.

FRAME 8
VISUAL   Illustration of socket with screw-driver unthreading one terminal. The other terminal is unscrewed and the lead is loose.

FRAME 9
NARRATIVE   Twist the bare wire leads tight again.

FRAME 9
VISUAL   Illustration of one hand holding the wire lead while the other twists the bare portion of the lead tight.

FRAME 10
NARRATIVE   And wrap the leads around the terminal screws of the new switch in a *clockwise* direction.

FRAME 10
VISUAL   Illustration (close-up) of socket switch and terminal with wire lead wrapped in a clockwise direction (indicated with an arrow) around the terminal screw.

FRAME 11
NARRATIVE   So that the leads will tighten around the screw shaft when the screws are retightened.

FRAME 11
VISUAL   Illustration (close-up) of a socket switch with a screwdriver tight-ening terminal screw with wire lead wrapped around it (use arrow to indicate turning of screwdriver).

FRAME 12
NARRATIVE   Replace the socket case, pressing it down over the new switch until it "clicks" into place.

FRAME 12
VISUAL   Illustration of a hand pressing down the socket case, holding it by the sides (use arrow to indi-cate pressing action).

FRAME 13
NARRATIVE   The lamp is now ready to have its bulb and shade replaced and be plugged in for use.

FRAME 13
VISUAL   Illustration of lamp with shade and bulb replaced and lit.

FRAME 14
VISUAL
*(No
narrative)*   *How to Change a Standard Light Bulb Socket*

END

Several important points regarding this script should be noted. First, in grammatically correct sentences, more than one image idea is often presented. For instance, in the sentence "Twist the bare wire leads tight again, and wrap them around the terminal screws in a clockwise direction . . ." it would be difficult for a single pictorial illus-tration to convey this complex process. The best thing to do in this type of situation is refragment the written image further into additional frames to make sure that the process is completely understood. (This has been done in the narrative-visual script.)

Second, note that this script is concerned with a *physical* process. The instructions in most of the frames are directly involved in the manipulation of the materials and the hands. The final cognitive goal is not abstract knowledge, but a new physical skill. As will be demonstrated, a module whose subject-goal is purely abstract information, or a learning process in itself, presents different, but not necessarily more difficult, image production obstacles.

A final, but rather important, factor to consider in the production of any audio-visual script is *prior-knowledge assumptions* of the author. All software materials, regardless of the subject matter, assumes some form of *prior knowledge on the part of the viewer.* Exactly how much prior knowledge to assume is one of the more difficult aspects of the production of the script. For example, in the light bulb socket replacement script, it was assumed that the viewer already knew how to remove the lampshade and light bulb or could manage this without actual instruction. It was also assumed that the viewer would examine the socket and procure a proper replacement and would know how to use a screwdriver. In frame 3, the viewer is instructed to remove the plug from the power source to avoid the chance of electrical shock while fixing the socket. Although this might seem unnecessary because the average person would be aware of that danger and would unplug the lamp, it can and should be included as a *reminder*, as well as being an integral part of the safe procedure to the final goal of the module. Information such as how or why a light switch works, although perhaps both interesting and valuable, is not something that the viewer has to know in order to complete the simple repair task successfully, which is

the goal. Nor is any information given as to what steps to take if the repair doesn't work. If the author believes that such kinds of information should be covered, they might be developed into separate modules by themselves. If included in a single module, all of this additional material would merely obscure the goal and confuse the viewer.

Therefore, in writing any script the author should first examine *all* possibilities and attendant factors, or prior knowledge that the viewer must have in order to reach the learning goal, and than carefully eliminate any superfluous or tangent information.

COMPOSING IN VISUAL TERMS

In audio-visual teaching systems, the audio, or spoken, portion of the module is subjugated to the visual image. Therefore, the script should be written with this in mind. The audio portion of the module, as it is presented in sequence to the viewer, can and should act as more than a mere explanation of the pictorial image. It is a key to the proper understanding of the internal structure of the individual frame. For example, when a module frame is projected on the screen in a classroom or on the screen of an audio-visual machine, it takes the viewer several seconds to encompass all the information. The eyes scan over the surface in "jumps" to build up a coherent mental image of the presented information. While this process is occurring (and if the audio-script portion is well planned and presented), a "leading" of the visual cognitive action can be put into effect. The viewer's eyes should be led through each individual frame, just as the learning process is led from beginning to end in the entire module.

When writing a script, the author should try to compose the narrative for each frame around a mental pictorial image. He or she should avoid using words that have unclear or multiple meanings as well as tangent or qualifying statements unless absolutely necessary. With a little practice, a clear, image-oriented working script can be produced.

The preceding script was primarily concerned with learning that involves a physical process. The following script is primarily concerned with learning that involves abstract information.

COMPLETE SCRIPT

Title *How the Place of a Decimal Point Changes the Value of a Number*

The learning objectives of this module are to review the decimal number system and to determine how the position of a decimal point changes the value of a number. Our number system is a decimal number system. It is based on the number 10. When a whole number that is more than nine is written, it is necessary to write two or more digits to express it. Each of these digits has a "decimal place value," which indicates its value in relation to the other digits. For example, the number four hundred and twenty-three is expressed in numbers 423. This means, quite simply, four hundreds plus two tens plus three ones. As the number is read from left to right, the digits are added to complete the whole number. The number four alone means four ones. The number forty means four tens and no ones (the zero is used as a place holder for the *one* value place). The number four hundred means four hundreds and no tens and no ones. Therefore, every whole number that is more than nine is expressed with digits that are placed in value columns for ones, tens, hundreds, thousands, ten thousands, and so on. Each decimal column has ten times the value of the column to its right.

The decimal point is also concerned with the value of a number and can change that value by where it is placed. The decimal point, like our number system, is based on the number ten or multiples of ten. In our decimal number system, the number one is the smallest whole number. However, we divide each *one* into ten equal parts called *tenths*. With this breakdown and the decimal point, we can very easily express fractions of one. For example, four-tenths is expressed as a fraction as four over ten. However, four-tenths can be expressed as a decimal fraction as .4—by placing the decimal point to the *left* of the number, we indicate that it is a fraction expressed in tenths. The fraction four-hundredths is expressed as four over one hundred. The decimal fraction four-hundredths is expressed .04. The zero is a place holder for the "tenths" value place. Four thousandths would be expressed as .004, meaning that the decimal value places to the right of the decimal point are multiples of ten and to the left of the decimal point are multiples of ten as well. This system is very useful in expressing whole numbers and fractions, which can then easily be added or multiplied or divided by other decimal fractions or whole numbers. For example, the whole number and fraction six and eight-tenths is expressed as the decimal combination 6.8, meaning six and eight-tenths. If we move the decimal point one digit to the right, we in effect multiply the number six point eight by ten, which gives us the whole number sixty-eight. In the next module, you will learn how to add and subtract decimal whole numbers and fractions.

END

This script is simply an example. The educator writing his or her own version of such a module would undoubtedly consider the students' vocabulary level, previous experience, and so on. However, a breakdown of the script into narrative and visual would be in the following format.

Title *How the Place of a Decimal Point Changes the Value of a Number*

FRAME 1
NARRATIVE

The learning objectives of this module are to review the decimal number system and to determine how the position of a decimal point changes the value of a number.

FRAME 1
VISUAL

Learning objectives:
1. Review the decimal number system
2. Determine how the position of a decimal point changes the value of a number

FRAME 2
NARRATIVE

Our number system is a decimal number system. It is based on the number ten.

FRAME 2
VISUAL

A solid color background with the number 10 printed in bright colors.

FRAME 3
NARRATIVE

When a whole number that is more than nine is written, it is necessary to write two or more digits to express it.

FRAME 3
VISUAL

The numbers 25, 185, 6,256 with the word *digits* printed above each and individual arrows pointing to each number.

FRAME 4
NARRATIVE

Each of these digits has a "decimal place value," which indicates its value in relation to the other digits.

FRAME 4
VISUAL

Same visual as frame 3, but with the words *decimal place value* in large letters over the word *digits*.

FRAME 5
NARRATIVE

For example, the number four hundred and twenty-three is expressed in numbers as four two three.

FRAME 5
VISUAL

The number 423 is the upper-middle part of the frame.

FRAME 6
NARRATIVE

This means quite simply, four hundreds plus two tens plus three ones. As the number is read from left to right, the digits are added to complete the whole number.

FRAME 6
VISUAL

The number 423 with arrows pointing to 4 (hundreds), 2 (tens), and 3 (ones).

FRAME 7
NARRATIVE

The number four alone means four ones.

FRAME 7
VISUAL

A large number 4, with an equal sign to four ones added together: $1 + 1 + 1 + 1$

FRAME 8
NARRATIVE

The number forty means four tens and no ones (the zero is used as a place holder for the *one* value place).

FRAME 8
VISUAL

The number 40 with arrows to the digits indicating "tens" place and "ones" place.

FRAME 9
NARRATIVE

The number four hundred means four hundreds and no tens and no ones.

FRAME 9
VISUAL

The number 400 with arrows pointing to the hundreds, tens, and ones columns.

FRAME 10
NARRATIVE

Therefore, every whole number that is more than nine is expressed with digits that are placed in value columns for ones, tens, hundreds, thousands, ten thousands, and so on. Each decimal column has ten times the value of the column to its right.

FRAME 10
VISUAL

The different decimal value

columns labeled with both numbers and words.

FRAME 11
NARRATIVE The decimal point is also concerned with the value of a number and can change that value by where it is placed.

FRAME 11
VISUAL Title "The Decimal Point," with an arrow pointing to a decimal point.

FRAME 12
NARRATIVE The decimal point, like our number system, is based on the number ten or multiples of ten.

FRAME 12
VISUAL The number 10 in the center of the frame.

FRAME 13
NARRATIVE In our decimal number system, the number one is the smallest whole number.

FRAME 13
VISUAL The number 1 on the left side of the frame.

FRAME 14
NARRATIVE However, we divide each *one* into ten equal parts called *tenths.*

FRAME 14
VISUAL The number 1 (from frame 13) on the left side with an equal sign and ten small circles each marked one-tenth, two-tenths, three-tenths, etc., to ten-tenths.

FRAME 15
NARRATIVE With this breakdown and the decimal point, we can very easily express fractions of one.

FRAME 15
VISUAL On the left side of the frame is "the decimal point" with an arrow to a decimal point. On the right side of the frame are the ten "tenth" circles used in frame 14. Between the two images, the word *and.*

FRAME 16
NARRATIVE For example, four-tenths is ex-

pressed as a fraction as four over ten.

FRAME 16
VISUAL The fraction $4/10$ placed on the left side of the frame.

FRAME 17
NARRATIVE However, four-tenths can be expressed as a decimal fraction as point 4—by placing the decimal point to the left of the number, we indicate that it is a fraction expressed in tenths.

FRAME 17
VISUAL (Frame 16 repeated) The fraction $4/10$ with an equal sign to point 4 on the right side of center frame.

FRAME 18
NARRATIVE The fraction four-hundredths is expressed as four over one hundred.

FRAME 18
VISUAL The fraction $4/100$ placed in left center of frame.

FRAME 19
NARRATIVE The decimal fraction four-hundredths is expressed as point zero four. The zero is a place holder for the "tenths" value place.

FRAME 19
VISUAL (Frame 18 repeated) The fraction $4/100$ with an equal sign to point zero four on the right side of center frame.

FRAME 20
NARRATIVE Four-thousandths would be expressed as point, zero, zero, four.

FRAME 20
VISUAL The fraction $4/1000$ = .004 placed in center of frame.

FRAME 21
NARRATIVE The decimal value places to the right of the decimal point are multiples of ten, and to the left of the decimal point are multiples of ten as well.

FRAME 21
VISUAL A decimal point (indicated by an

arrow and words) and the ones, tens, hundreds, and thousands value columns marked to the right and left of the point.

FRAME 22
NARRATIVE
This system is very useful in expressing whole numbers and fractions, which can then easily be added or multiplied or divided by other decimal fractions or whole numbers. For example, the whole number and fraction six and eight-tenths is expressed as the decimal combination six point eight, meaning six and eight-tenths.

FRAME 22
VISUAL
$6.8 = 6\frac{8}{10}$ Both mean 6 and 8 tenths.
(Place above in center of frame.)

FRAME 23
NARRATIVE
If we move the decimal point one digit to the right, we in effect multiply the number six point eight by *ten.*

FRAME 23
VISUAL
6.8. placed in left center of the frame with an arrow indicating the decimal point movement one place to the right.

FRAME 24
NARRATIVE
This gives us the whole number sixty-eight.

FRAME 24
VISUAL
$6.8. = 6.8 = 68$
$\times 10$

FRAME 25
NARRATIVE
In the next module, you will learn how to add and subtract decimal whole numbers and fractions.

FRAME 25
VISUAL
A plus and a minus sign in the center of the frame.

FRAME 26
VISUAL
(No narrative)
How the Place of a Decimal Point Changes the Value of a Number

END

MODULE QUESTIONS

Having written a script and processed it into narrative and visual segments, a decision can be made as to the necessity and value of asking questions as part of the module. Audio-visual modules can be divided into two main categories: passive and active. The term *passive module* refers to the role of the student or viewer; it does not refer to the information given in the module. In a *passive module,* the viewer is not asked to participate in any actual application of the information given except to comprehend and remember it. In an *active module,* the viewer is asked to perform exercises or apply newly acquired skills to the solution of problems at various selected points. Depending on the module's subject matter, this process can be a valuable tool in the reinforcement of the sequential learning method. The author, having decided to employ the *active* module, should keep several important points in mind. Unlike the usual procedure in classroom teaching, the student cannot ask questions of a sound-slide presentation. This is obviously why a coherent script is a necessity. This limitation also applies to asking questions that call for conclusions during the course of the presentation. Therefore, the type of questions, as well as their frequency and placement, is important.

First of all, the script and narrative-visual segments should be completed before the question segments are formulated. This practice ensures that *all* the information will be present in the module without side-tracking the author in the middle of the process of preparing the script. If questions are asked, it is a logical and necessary requirement to supply, in subsequent frames, the answers to the questions.

A second, but equally important, consideration is *where* to ask questions. Obviously a question cannot be asked before the viewer has received all of the information that will enable him or her to answer it. Therefore, questions should be asked at logical "pauses" in the script. For example, in the decimal system script presented earlier, a logical place to ask questions is during the "pause" between the description of the decimal number system (which is a review for the first half of the script) and the description of the use of the decimal point in number value changes (which constitutes the second half of the script). Questions for the second half of the script would logically be placed at the end. There are, perhaps, other places in the script where questions might be inserted, but the author of the script should realize that too many questions can dilute the purpose of the module.

Therefore, the third consideration regarding the question process is the *frequency* of the questions. Too many or poorly placed questions can be more counterproductive than not asking any at all.

FORMULATION AND FORMAT OF QUESTIONS

Questions, like the script itself, must be visually oriented. They will also function better, in terms of viewer comprehension, if they mirror the logical information steps given in the preceding frames.

The formulation of questions involves the same procedure as that used in the script—write down the question and answer as a continuous statement. For example, the following question should be placed between frame 10 and frame 11 (taking advantage of the logical break or pause in the information flow):

Question

Here is the number one thousand three hundred and fifty-four. Write this number down and indicate the value column that each digit falls into. When you have completed this, you may go on to the next frame.

Solution

Since the number given is a whole number, it will fit into the decimal value columns shown earlier. The first step is to write these columns down in their proper order—ones, tens, hundreds, and thousands. Then place the number given, with each of the digits falling into a column—starting with the ones. The answer, therefore, is that the number one thousand three hundred and fifty-four is made up on one "thousand" plus three "hundreds" plus five "tens" (or fifty) plus four "ones."

Having prepared the script for the question and answer or solution, the next step is to break it down into narrative and visual segments.

Question

FRAME (A)
NARRATIVE   Here is the number one thousand three hundred and fifty-four. Write this number down and indicate the value column that each digit falls into. When you have completed this, you may go on to the next frame.

FRAME (A)
VISUAL   The number 1,354 in the upper center portion of the frame.

Solution

FRAME (A)
NARRATIVE   Since the number given is a whole number, it will fit into the

decimal value columns shown earlier. The first step is to write these columns down in their proper order—ones, tens, hundreds, and thousands.

FRAME (A)
VISUAL

Columns are placed in the lower center of the frame, with names designating their values.

FRAME (B)
NARRATIVE

Then place the number given, with each of the digits falling into a column—starting with the ones.

FRAME (B)
VISUAL

The number 1,354 superimposed on the value columns—the 1 in the "thousands," the 3 in the "hundreds," etc.

FRAME (C)
NARRATIVE

The answer, therefore, is that the number one thousand three hundred and fifty-four is made up of one "thousand" plus three "hundreds" plus five "tens" (or fifty) plus four "ones."

FRAME (C)
VISUAL

The number 1,354 on left of frame with an equal sign to the value columns (in reduced size) on the right of the frame.

Using this system or your own adaptation, questions and answers can successfully be introduced to modules dealing with virtually any subject.

THE STORYBOARD

Whether the author of a module prepares the illustrations and art copy or the script is submitted to a graphic artist for production, the storyboard is a necessary and valuable tool. A *storyboard* is a series of sketches, or "roughs," that briefly outline the layout, or visual content, of each frame. These sketches can be done on small blank file cards or placed in a series on a large sheet of paper, or they can be done on a storyboard pad or "TV board" that is prepared for exactly this process (see Figures 1-1A and 1-1B). Storyboard sketches should not be confused with finished drawings or completed art copy. They are guides to an accurate preparation of the final art for each frame. They clarify the instructions and written information in the visual portion of the script.

Storyboard sketches supply valuable additional information about each

FIGURE 1-1A, B TV pads, or storyboard pads, provide the first link between the written script and the visuals that will illustrate it. The sketches should be kept simple. Notations for words appearing in the visual, arrows indicating direction, and other vital information can be positioned and mapped out as a guide when preparing the finished camera-ready art at a later point.

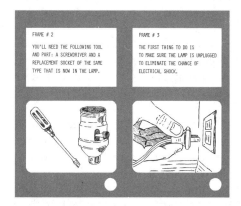

frame, such as emphasis on words or illustrations, color coding, graphic information (e.g., charts), and the proper positioning of print and pictorial matter within the frame. Information that is difficult to describe either verbally or in the written frame description—such as mathematical, electronic, and mechanical symbols, or arrows indicating direction—can also be clearly indicated in the storyboard sketches. For example, frame 5 of the *How to Change a Standard Light Bulb Socket* module contains the following narrative:

> Then press in the sides of the socket case above the base seam and gently rock and pull up to loosen and remove it.

This seemingly forthright and clear statement can be handled as a visual representation in a number of ways. A set of storyboard sketches can help you select the best frame format and illustrations to achieve maximum viewer impact. Figures 1-2, 1-3, and 1-4 show a series of possible frame layouts.

In Figure 1-2, the socket case is shown with arrows indicating where its sides should be pressed and the rocking-pulling motion needed to remove it. Although this layout fills the script requirements for this frame, all of these arrows indicating direction without ex-

FIGURE 1-2 Although this sketch meets the requirements of the script for that particular frame, all the arrows indicating direction without the proper sequence of what to do first are too confusing.

plaining what to do first can be very confusing. Remember that the actual time that the frame may be seen by the viewer while the narrative is being presented could be as little as six to ten seconds. The graphic material *must* be as clear as possible.

In Figure 1-3, a simple outline sketch of a hand has been added to help indicate the pressing, rocking, and pulling actions required. This clarifies the frame content while showing the proper hand movements and best position. Including a picture of a hand or a hand holding a tool can also be valuable in indicating the actual size of a mechanical or electronic part. Viewer recognition is improved when the information and processes outlined in the module are applied in an actual physical exercise later.

For example, a module might show a physical process such as the assembly or disassembly of small parts in a large machine. If just these parts are shown in a frame, the viewer will have no scale of reference to determine whether the parts are small or large. By showing a hand or a recognizable tool in the frame, *in a proper size relation to the part*, the viewer recognition is immensely improved.

Figure 1-4 uses a *split-screen* effect to break down and simplify the three physical movements required and des-

FIGURE 1-3 By adding a simple sketch of a hand holding the socket case in the proper position, the desired action is clarified.

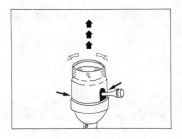

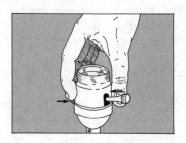

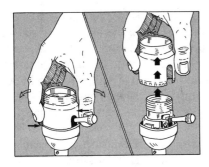

FIGURE 1-4 By using a split-screen image, the required actions for this frame are easily presented and clearly outlined. When this frame is shown with the proper accompanying verbal instructions, the viewer will have little or no trouble understanding it.

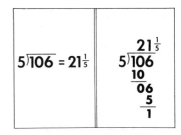

FIGURE 1-5 The split-screen effect allows immediate explanations of frame content, rather than forcing the viewer to remember information that is not explained until the next frame or later in the module.

cribed in the frame. This is accomplished by dividing the frame area in half and giving part of the information in each, allowing the viewer to combine the called-for action mentally. In this case, the pressing action and the rocking action are given in the *left* half of the frame. The *right* half of the frame shows the freed socket case held above the switch. Depending upon the subject matter, such a division of information can be extremely useful in clarifying the specific steps that the viewer must understand and accomplish.

Note that if the split screen is used, it should exactly reflect the script and verbal narrative. The split-screen frame is read from left to right, just like a written page. Therefore, the frame information should visually follow the logical sequence of the verbal narrative. The split-screen effect is also quite useful in depicting such processes as mathematics, especially when the placement or movement of a number must be emphasized.

In the simple division problem illustrated in Figure 1-5, the problem and answer are shown in the left half of the frame and the actual long-division process is shown in the right half. The split screen allows for immediate ex-

planations of the frame content, rather than forcing the viewer to remember information that is not explained until the next frame.

It is not advisable to break down the frame beyond the split-screen effect, that is, into three or more subdivisions. Too many breaks in the individual frame tend to confuse the viewer. The split-screen effect should be reserved for the occasional frame that contains information that is too complex to be explained in a normal series of frames.

Figure 1-6 shows a number of possible graphic formats for the split-screen frame. The separation between the halves of the frame can be accomplished by a simple line, or different-colored backgrounds can be used.

Obviously, the choice of whether to use a split-screen frame or frames, and what type of graphic format would be preferable, is very much determined by the subject of the module and the approach that the author takes in presenting the material. In any event, all

FIGURE 1-6 A selection of possible graphic formats for the split-screen frame.

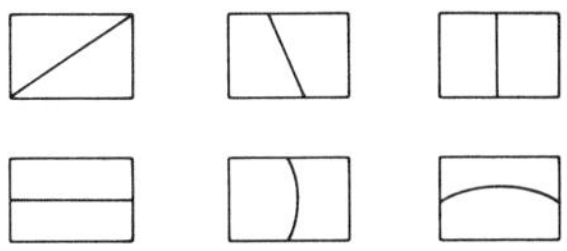

decisions with regard to the frame format and its graphic content should be indicated in the storyboard sketches.

Color for Emphasis

Along the other decisions about frame designs and content that are indicated in the storyboard, color is also important. Slide modules are a color medium, and color can be both a decorative and an instructional tool. Color can help focus the viewer's attention throughout a long or complex module, as well as providing valuable *keys* to emphasize places where special attention should be directed within the individual frame.

For example, in a module whose subject is mathematics, such as the decimal system module described earlier, color can play a major role in the viewer's understanding of several important items. In one of the frames, a decimal point is moved to change the value of a number, and this action is indicated by a small arrow. It is possible for the viewer to miss this decimal point even if the narrative describes it. However, if the small arrow were presented in bright *red* or another color that did not appear elsewhere in the numbers or words in the frame, the viewer's eyes would immediately focus on it (see Figure 1–7).

Therefore, the selective use of color for emphasizing key items in the frame can improve the viewer's understanding of the learning objectives of the module. Almost any subject that can be translated to a sound-slide format can utilize color emphasis in some way. Examples would include the flow of electrical currents through electronic components; graphs or charts of all kinds; specific locations on maps or other geographic information; and temperature or chemical variants in scientific experiments. Color can also be used in relation to meteorology, basic mathematics, and machinery adjustments or repair. The possibilities are virtually endless, and the author of the module script should realize that color is as important to the graphic content of the frame as words, numbers, or any pictorial illustrations that might be needed.

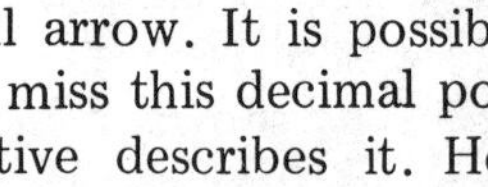

Color emphasis of any kind should be indicated in the storyboard sketches *in the actual color required.* Therefore, the author should have felt-tipped pens or drawing markers of different colors available when preparing the storyboard.

Backgrounds and Color

Written information, words, or numbers that are to be displayed in a frame must have a background of some kind, and this should also be indicated in the storyboard. Here again, color can play a major role in the viewer's comprehension of the module. For example, a series of frames on a specific piece of information can be linked by selecting the same color background. This is called a *background color theme,* and it can be quite useful in a module containing several separate series of information.

For instance, in a module consisting of forty-five frames that contain perhaps three fifteen-frame sections of information, the use of a different-colored background for each of the sections can help avoid viewer confusion as to where one

FIGURE 1–7 By making the arrow that indicates the movement of the decimal point red or another bright color that does not appear elsewhere in the frame, the viewer's attention is immediately focused on it.

$$8.7. = 87$$

set of information ends and a new set begins.

Question or problem sequences can also be separated visually from the mainstream by printing them against a different-colored background. In a module of sixteen frames, for example, the colors used for the background could reflect the different subdivisions of information in the module, as shown in Figure 1–8. In this figure, frames 1 through 6, expressing a segment of information, are given a blue background. Frames 7 and 8 consist of a question and an answer, respectively, and are given a yellow background. Frames 9 through 14 are a continuation of the information given in the first six frames and therefore have a blue background again. However, frames 15 and 16, as a final question and answer, have been given a red background.

The preceding examples of the use of background color have all been confined to words or numbers or other type that is superimposed on a plain, solid color. However, in frames containing both type and pictorial information (such as drawings and photographs), a partial color background can be used.

When print is superimposed on a drawing or a photograph, there is of course no need for a background. However, in a frame that must show both print and picture separately, a background is still needed (see Figures 1–9 and 1–10).

The more complete the script is in both its narrative and its visual segments, the easier it will be to translate it into a clear, useful, and professional-looking presentation. Even if you are going to write the script and prepare the illustrations for the frames yourself, a well-planned storyboard will not only save time and materials but avoid confusion.

FIGURE 1-9 A full-frame photograph with superimposed type.

FIGURE 1-10 Picture and type superimposed on a background sheet (usually of a solid color).

FIGURE 1-8 Pieces of information presented in a series of frames within the total concept of the module can be separated and enhanced by the selective use of background color themes.

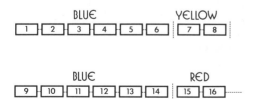

GLOSSARY

Active module An audio-visual module that asks questions of the viewer as part of the learning sequence or requires some other form of actual participation.

Audio visual A teaching system that combines pictorial or other visual information with an explanatory sound track or written script. Video (television), motion pictures, film strips, and slide sets with cassette tapes or records would all be considered audio-visual systems.

Background The part of the frame against which printed and/or pictorial materials are placed or superimposed.

Background color theme The process of linking a series of frames visually by using the same color background in order to differentiate them from other frame sequences in the same module.

Frame In audio-visual materials, one slide or one segment of a filmstrip.

Graphic All visual information such as pictures, type, and colors.

Layout A complete diagram of all of the type, background, and/or pictorial content of a frame. All of the visual information.

Learning objective The instructional goal of the module. This can be a new physical skill or mental skill or a combination of both.

Module A complete audio-visual system including visual, recorded, and/or written information.

Narrative script A written script containing a frame-by-frame account of all the spoken or recorded audio portions of a proposed module.

Passive module An audio-visual presentation that does not ask questions of the viewer and requires no participation other than to comprehend and remember the information.

Pause A logical break in the module frame sequence in order to insert questions.

Roughs A brief sketch or outline of the graphic and/or pictorial content of a frame.

Script pattern The logical interrelation between the audio, or written, and the visual content of a module.

Selective content In preparing the script, the process of eliminating nonessential information from the subject matter. Also referred to as *focus*.

Sequence The step-by-step structure of the module, leading to the learning objective.

Sound-slide system An audio-visual system that uses a set of 35-mm slides in conjunction with a recorded sound source.

Split screen A frame that is divided into two or more subdivisions when certain subject matter cannot be presented in a single frame or would be less effective if presented in two separate frames.

Storyboard A frame-by-frame graphic or pictorial description of the module content (see *roughs*).

Superimposed In graphic art, this term refers to a design process in which one graphic element, such as type, is placed over another graphic element, such as a picture or a background.

Title The stated learning objective or objectives of a module.

TV board A pad whose pages are printed with a series of boxes. A useful tool in the preparation of sketches of frame contents.

Visual keys Directing the viewer's attention to selected parts of the frame through the use of color or graphic indicators such as arrows, brackets, parentheses, and underlining.

Visual script A written script describing all the visual-pictorial information in a proposed module.

Written script A complete written description of all the audio and visual information in a proposed module.

2
THE TYPE

THE TYPE

Preparing the artwork and type that will be photographed and turned into the visual portion of a slide module is not difficult if you work systematically. Just as there are a series of steps to be taken in the proper working order to produce the complete, segmented script, so a proper working order should be set up for the production of the art.

Note that the procedures outlined in this chapter and in the following chapters are general in nature. They are intended as *outlines* whose principal merits are expediency, economy of materials, and simplicity of use. These procedures are meant to be adapted by the individual audio-visual designers to better fit their needs. These adaptations are also part of the creative process, and our primary goal here is to present a "vocabulary" of methods that will help the designer develop a professional-looking product.

The visual portions of the sound-slide module are called *frames* when they are in a completed form. The visual portions of the module are called *flats* before they have been photographed into frames. The process of turning a simple sketch on a file card or storyboard pad into a flat that is *camera ready* is called *designing a layout*.

Designing a proper layout is both a physical process and a series of decisions that would not have been made in the sketch, or rough—for example, the style of type, or the combination of type and graphic symbols (such as arrows), or even the *size* of the type for selected parts of the layout (such as in emphasizing certain words).

These decisions are an in-process part of the layout, and only an extensive knowledge of the design process and its limitations, as well as familiarity with the available graphic materials, can lead to the production of a camera-ready flat (see Figures 2–1A and 2–1B).

THE FLAT

By definition, any graphic material that is *camera ready*, whether it contains just type (words, numbers, or symbols) or type and pictorial images, is considered a *flat*.

A flat has no set size, but as we shall see, a *standardization* of flat size is necessary for proper module production.

FIGURE 2–1A A rough layout sketch indicating the written copy used in the frame as well as the position and type of accompanying pictorial image and background.

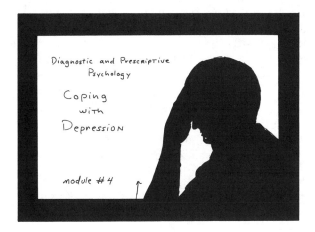

FIGURE 2–1B A finished version of the rough sketch, ready to be photographed into a slide (in this case, a title frame for the module).

The flat can consist of a single page of graphic material, but in graphic design for an audio-visual module, the flat is usually produced in *layers*. One layer will contain the background or any pictorial images while a separate layer, containing the type, is superimposed on the first. This process is the usual method employed because of its speed, economy, and adaptability.

Standardizing the Flat Size

The main decision when beginning to produce the visual content of a module is the *size* of the flats. Since these designs will be photographed at a later point with the aid of a copy camera and stand, the constant shifts of camera-to-copy distance can be eliminated if all the flats for a module are of the *same size*, thus saving a great deal of time and effort.

The flat must be large enough to work on comfortably but small enough to save materials and time. The actual dimensions in terms of length and width must also be in the proper *proportion* so that they will be compatible with the size of the film format.

The 35-mm film format for transparencies, or *slides* that is illustrated in

Figure 2-2 is rectangular. Its length-to-width ratio is 2 to 3. Therefore, if a flat is produced that *does not* have a 2:3 ratio, it will be difficult to fit the design into the film format without cutting some part of it off (see Figures 2-3A and 2-3B).

A good working-size format for flats is 6½ by 9¾ inches. This size is recommended because it fits the 2:3 ratio, is comfortable to work with, allows the use of 8-by-10-inch photographs for backgrounds if desired, and can be covered by a smaller, less-expensive 11-by-14-inch sheet of *clear acetate* for the type

FIGURE 2-2 A 35-mm slide mount. Notice that the rectangular opening has a length-to-width ratio of 2 to 3.

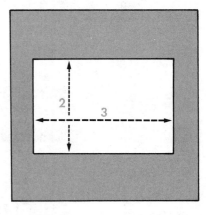

FIGURE 2-3A If original art is prepared having a 2:3 length-to-width ratio, when photographed it will fit into the 35-mm slide format perfectly.

FIGURE 2-3B If the original art does not have a 2:3 ratio, it will not fit exactly into the slide format and will require additional colored background to fill up the empty space in the image.

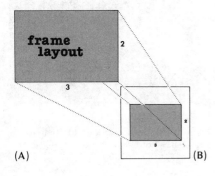

(A)

(B)

layer (see the section entitled "Type" in this chapter). Whether you decide to make 6½-by-9¾-inch flats or another size in proportion to the 2:3 ratio, you will need a format guide.

THE FORMAT GUIDE

The *format guide* is simply a cardboard sheet with the frame size opening cut out of it. This guide is very useful in determining the position and length of the type, words, background, pictorial material, and other elements of the frame so that they will not spill over the 2:3 ratio.

A format guide can be made quite easily from a thin sheet of gray or white cardboard. Do not use black or colored cardboard, as this will make it difficult to judge colors in the type and background later. Use a piece of cardboard that will allow at least a 1-inch border around the cutout area. The minimum size would therefore be 8½ by 11¾ inches.

The cardboard need not be thick. It can be a scrap piece such as would be packed with a box of craft paper, or it can be the backing of a small drawing pad. Try to find a cardboard scrap that is already square or rectangular, and then, by using a metal ruler or a T square, you can produce a very accurate rectangular cutout. A good-quality T square that is made of either metal or plastic and is at least 16 inches long is a useful tool both for this process and for the later preparation of the lettering and background. The T square illustrated in Figure 2-4 allows the user to measure, mark, or cut very accurate right angles or parallel lines with a minimum of effort.

FIGURE 2-4 T squares are manufactured of metal, and also of wood laminated in plastic with clear edges.

After you have cut out a piece of cardboard that measures 8½ by 11¾ inches, use the T square to measure and mark out the rectangular opening on your cardboard format guide. Begin by hooking the edge of the T square onto the edge of your cardboard and mark off two short lines at the beginning and end of the cutout edge, leaving room for the border area before the first of these lines and after the second (see Figure 2-5). Make the first pencil mark 1 inch in from the edge, then from that mark

FIGURE 2-5 Make two vertical marks indicating the length of one side of the format guide. To allow for a border area, make sure that the marks are at least 1 inch in from the edges of the cardboard sheet.

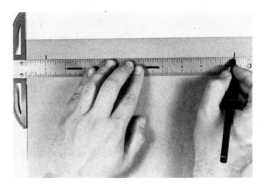

measure the length of one of the cutout edges (either 6½ or 9¾ inches) and make the second pencil mark. In placing the T square from the top edge of the cardboard, guess a distance of approximately 1 inch and make a good-sized pencil mark perpendicular to the T square shaft, at your measurements. Having done this, repeat the procedure approximately 1 inch up from the bottom edge of the cardboard (see Figure 2-6).

Now rotate the cardboard a quarter turn, place the T square on the edge, and align it with the two pencil marks on the upper part of the board. Measure in 1 inch from the edge and make a pencil mark perpendicular to the T square shaft. From this mark, measure the distance of the remaining length or width of your cutout, and make a second mark. You will then have made two marks that look like an upside down letter *T* (see Figure 2-7).

Having made these two marks, keep the T square in place and draw a straight line between the two marks (see Figure 2-8). After ruling this line in, drop your T square to the bottom of the cardboard, align the edge of the shaft with the two existing marks, and repeat the procedure just outlined. When you have finished, you will have two parallel lines, both the same length, on the top and bottom of the cardboard (see Figure 2-9).

Next, rotate the cardboard a quarter turn and align the T square with the two marks that are now on the top of the sheet. Connect these marks with a ruled line as was done earlier, and then repeat this procedure for the two marks on the bottom of the sheet (see Figure 2-10). You have now produced an accurately drawn rectangle that measures 6½ by 9¾ inches.

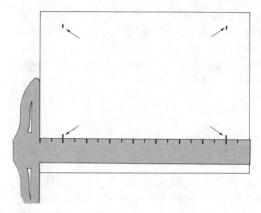

FIGURE 2-6 After measuring and making the first set of marks, drop the T square to the bottom of the sheet and repeat the process.

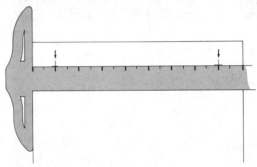

FIGURE 2-7 Rotate the cardboard sheet a quarter turn and align the T square with the upper set of marks. Measure and make marks perpendicular to the T square shaft, as was done earlier.

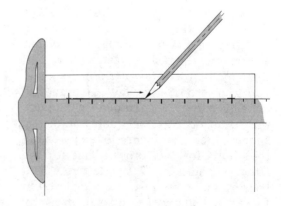

FIGURE 2-8 Having made the two marks, rule a pencil line between them.

FIGURE 2-9 Drop the T square to the bottom of the sheet, and repeat the measuring, marking, and ruling process.

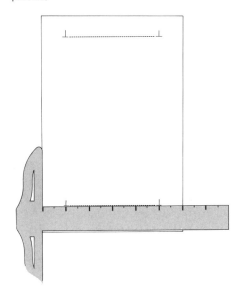

FIGURE 2-10 Rotate the cardboard another quarter turn, and rule a pencil line connecting the two open sides, completing the rectangle.

Cutting Out the Rectangle

When cutting cardboard, paper, and so on, the graphic designer will seldom use a scissors, even when following a ruled line. The reason is that slight shifts can occur in the cutting process and consequently ruin the desired profes-

sional look of the design. *Always* use an all-metal or metal-edge T square or ruler and a *stencil knife*, or *mat knife*, for this type of cutting. A sharp cutting blade can accidently cut or gouge the edge of less-hard materials, such as plastic or wood, and can therefore ruin rulers made of these substances.

The stencil knife, or mat knife, is a versatile cutting tool that usually consists of a metal handle and a replaceable steel cutting blade. These knives are manufactured in a number of sizes and styles, but any knife that has a good-sized handle and a sharp, pointed blade can be used for cutting cardboard or other graphic materials. Three kinds of cutting knives are illustrated in Figure 2-11, along with a single-edge razor blade. The single-edge razor blade can also be used as an inexpensive cutting tool. However, these blades are harder to grip with the fingers than are the other tools, and when applying pressure to cut through a material such as cardboard, they can easily wobble and miscut.

FIGURE 2-11 Cutting tools (*left to right*): (1) a mat knife blade and the handle it fits into, (2) an X-Acto hobby knife (the blades are replaceable), (3) a stencil knife with a blade that swivels, (4) a heavy-duty X-Acto hobby knife, and (5) a single-edge razor blade.

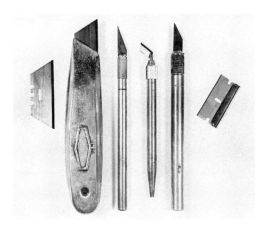

When the blade of a replaceable-blade knife becomes dull, a fresh one should be substituted immediately. There is no reliable way to resharpen dull blades because they are generally quite thin, and any attempt at giving them a sharp edge increases the risk that they will snap or break during use. Some kinds of cutting blades are manufactured in a plastic dispenser that has a built-in compartment for storing old blades. If you do not have this type of dispenser, wrap the old blade in a small piece of masking tape or cellophane tape and dispose of it immediately. This eliminates the risk of accidentally cutting yourself on a blade left lying about, or confusing an old dull blade for a fresh one.

When cutting out the center rectangle of your *format guide*, arrange the T square or ruler so that you are cutting with the inside rectangular area exposed and the body of the ruler covering the border (see Figure 2-12). Always arrange the materials to be cut so that the ruler shields the area to be

saved. In the case of your format guide, if the mat knife slips, it will only damage the interior area of the rectangle, which is waste cardboard and will be discarded anyway.

When making a ruled cut such as this on cardboard, paper acetate, or any graphic material, the ruler and cut direction should be *vertical* to you, and the movement of the knife when making the cut should be from the top of the sheet *toward* you, as indicated in Figure 2-12. Holding the ruler and making a cut in a horizontal position (from left to right or vice versa) is extremely difficult because the ruler is much more likely to slip or shift during the movement of the knife and ruin the cut. It is perfectly acceptable to cut through the cardboard with more than one stroke of the knife. To avoid a rough-edged cut, however, make sure that the ruler does not shift or move between strokes and that the actual movement of the knife is smooth and continuous.

Repeat the cutting process for all four sides of the rectangle by simply rotating the cardboard sheet a quarter turn after each side has been completed. After finishing all four sides, lift out the center rectangle and discard it. The remaining cardboard frame is your permanent, reusable format guide (see Figure 2-13).

FIGURE 2-12 When cutting out the center rectangle of the format guide, your hand and cutting knife should be positioned over the center rectangular area, with the body of the T square or ruler protecting the border edge. Always make the cutting strokes toward you, from the top of the sheet.

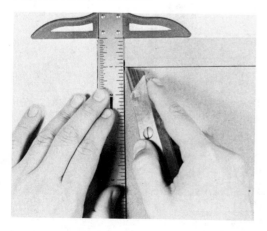

FIGURE 2-13 The finished format guide.

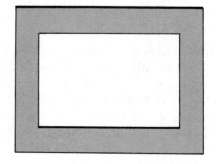

TYPE

Until recently, one of the most difficult parts of graphic design was in the production of hand lettering. The use of specialized lettering pens and guides is a skill that takes a lifetime to acquire. However, with the introduction of *pressure-sensitive type*, almost anyone can create perfect, professional-looking words, numbers, symbols, and even pictures with a minimum of eye and hand skills.

Pressure-sensitive type is essentially letters, numbers, or other symbols that are printed on a page of semitransparent plastic. Depending on the size of the type and the size of the page it is printed on, anywhere from four to ten of each of the letters of the alphabet in capital and lower-case letters are supplied. Various punctuation marks, and a set or two of numbers from one to nine (and zero) may also be included in a single sheet.

Included with the lettering sheet is a page of backing paper that has a smooth waxlike surface. The backing page protects the lettering page from scratches or from sticking to other surfaces it may come into contact with, as well as being the means of making the type adhere permanently to the graphic design (see the section entitled "Burnishing the Type").

Pressure-sensitive type is a decal that can be transferred from the master page to the graphic design being made by aligning each letter where desired and rubbing it down and off the master sheet with the aid of a tool called a *burnisher*.

The actual type on the lettering sheet is printed on the back of the page and is coated with a pressure-sensitive waxlike adhesive. The lettering page is not sticky to the touch on either the front or the back, and the surface to which you are transferring the lettering will also remain dry and clean.

The lettering page is used face up, so that the letters can be read normally, and the wax paper backing is removed and set aside for later use. Because the lettering page is semitransparent, the alignment of individual letters into words, as well as the placement of the lettering along a guideline to keep it straight, is relatively easy. A typical sheet of pressure-sensitive type is illustrated in Figure 2–14.

The transfer process for the type, from lettering page to work surface, is accomplished by rubbing and applying pressure to the front of the lettering page, *over* the letter to be transferred, with a *burnisher*. Any smooth, round pointed tool, such as a pencil, or a ball point pen, can accomplish this, but

FIGURE 2–14 A page of pressure-sensitive type (Courtesy *Chartpak Graphic Products*).

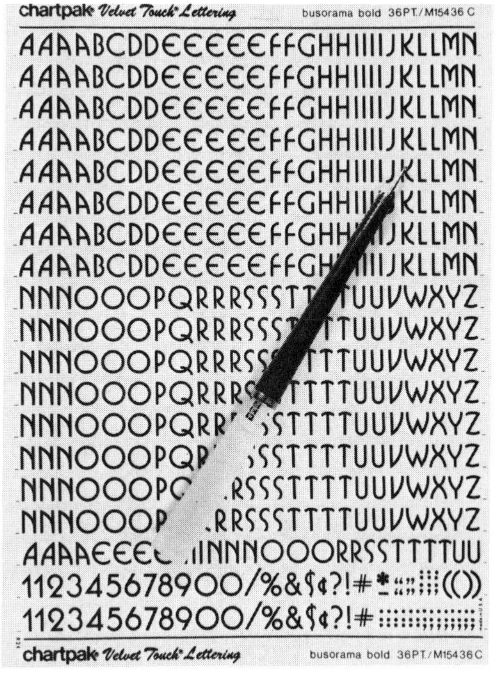

these do not work as well as the tools specifically designed for the process. Four kinds of burnishers are illustrated in Figure 2–15.

The first burnisher in Figure 2–15 has a small polished steel ball at its tip. It is held like a pencil and has a spring inside the shaft, which allows the user to adjust the amount of pressure applied during the transfer process. The small tip ball is most useful for the transfer of small intricate type. On the top end is a flat, flexible white plate, sometimes referred to as a *bone*. This is used in the final burnishing of the transferred lettering to bond it permanently to the page surface (this separate process will be described later in this chapter).

The second burnisher illustrated in Figure 2–15 has a large polished steel ball and is otherwise identical to the first burnisher. The larger ball covers a larger

FIGURE 2–15 Four kinds of type burnishers (*left to right*): (1) small, fixed ball; (2) large, fixed ball; (3) ball-bearing type (note: burnishers 1, 2, and 3 are Chartpak brand); and (4) shaped wood burnisher.

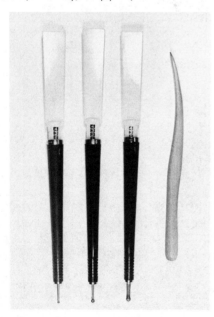

area and is therefore quicker and better at transferring larger type sizes.

The third burnisher illustrated is a ball-bearing-tipped one. The steel ball in the tip is about the same size as that of the second burnisher, but the ball is free moving and is partially enclosed in a metal jacket. The advantage of this type of burnisher is in the reduction of tip friction during use, especially when transferring large type or numerous letters or figures. It causes much less wear and tear to the lettering sheet and helps to minimize hand fatigue. Like the first and second burnishers, the ball-bearing burnisher has a spring-loaded pressure adjustment for its tip. The tip pressure of all three burnishers discussed so far can be adjusted by screwing in the *bone* at the far end a few turns. Screwing the threaded bone section in will increase the burnishing pressure of the tip; unscrewing the bone a few turns will decrease the pressure.

A Maintenance Note on the Ball-Bearing Tip Burnisher. The ball-bearing tip burnisher is highly recommended for its ease of operation. After continued use, however, minute amounts of wax adhesive (which is present in small amounts on the front of the lettering sheet) can accumulate on the tip ball, causing it to work sluggishly. This problem is characterized by a slight feeling of drag when moving the tip back and forth over the lettering sheet during the transfer process.

To remove this wax adhesive build-up from both the tip ball and the socket, hold the tip of the burnisher in the flame of a cigarette lighter for a second or two to melt the buildup, and then quickly run the tip over the surface of a scrap piece of paper towel or a soft cloth. *Do not* use a match to melt the buildup because it will add carbon particles to the wax and will only compound the problem. After cleaning the tip and allowing it to cool, lubricate the tip ball by very gently rubbing it along the side of your nose a few times. This will coat the tip ball with a thin film of oil from your skin and allow it to rotate with much less friction in the tip mount. *Do not* use machine oil on the tip because it will collect dust and other foreign particles very quickly and will foul the tip ball rotation much sooner.

The fourth burnisher illustrated in Figure 2-15 is a simple piece of shaped polished wood. It is the least expensive and has the shortest life span. The reason for its wearing out so quickly is that a wood surface will lose its polish through friction much sooner than will a polished metal surface. The wood burnisher, however, is still preferable to other "homemade" burnishers such as pencils and pens. Although some pressure-sensitive type manufacturer's instructions may say otherwise, it is not recommended that you attempt to use pencils or ball point pens to achieve type transfer.

The amount of pressure needed to achieve a proper transfer varies with the name brand of the type, and some brands are slightly more difficult to transfer than others. Even the easiest-transferring type is poorly transferred by a pencil or pen. The pressure on so fine a point scars the lettering page surface badly and frequently leaves indentations, or "grooves," in the transferred letter and surrounding page surface, which can show up later when the finished design is photographed.

THE TYPE-TRANSFER PROCESS

Pressure-sensitive lettering can be transferred to any smooth, clean, nongreasy surface such as paper, cardboard, or clear plastic acetate sheets for audio-visual frame layouts. The transfer process itself is quite fast and simple. However, several important rules must be observed. The words or symbols must be positioned properly, and the individual letters of the words must be on a level line and properly spaced. Therefore, the first thing needed is a *guideline* of some sort.

For purposes of demonstration, draw a short, light pencil line with the aid of a ruler on a piece of scrap paper (see Figure 2-16). Position the type page over the paper surface and place the bottom of the letter you wish to transfer on the penciled line (see Figure 2-17). Place

FIGURE 2-16 Draw a short guideline, in pencil, on a sheet of scrap paper.

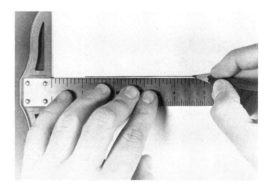

FIGURE 2-17 Position the type carrier sheet so that the letter you wish to burnish down will rest on the guideline.

your free hand so that your fingers rest *lightly* on the lettering page surface with just enough pressure to hold the page in place. Next, using the burnisher, rub in a back-and-forth motion *over the entire letter*. This rubbing action should extend slightly beyond the letter area as well (see Figures 2-18A and 2-18B).

As the burnisher is being rubbed back and forth, the letter will begin to *lighten* slightly, and this means that it is being transferred to the page surface. When the entire letter finally turns lighter, it has been transferred and you may stop burnishing. Then *gently* peel back the lettering page off the paper surface by grasping one corner and pulling slowly across, as shown in Figures 2-19 and 2-20. *Never* attempt to

FIGURE 2-18A Burnish the letter down smoothly, from one edge across to the other. Use a back-and-forth motion consisting of short strokes. It should not be necessary to press hard.

FIGURE 2-18B Burnish an area slightly larger than the letter. This will ensure that the extreme edges of the letter will transfer properly when the carrier sheet is removed.

FIGURE 2-19 Note that the shade of the burnished letter is lighter than that of the surrounding letters on the carrier sheet.

FIGURE 2-20 After each letter has been burnished down, the carrier sheet is gently peeled back from the paper surface by grasping one corner and pulling slowly.

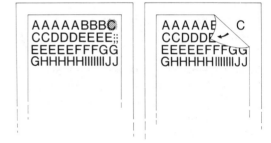

pull the lettering page straight up or pull it harshly, as this will damage the transferred letter.

At this stage, the transferred letter is removable if you have made a mistake. To remove a letter from the page surface, you can either "erase" it with a clean soft pencil eraser or lift it off the surface with a small piece of cellophane tape or masking tape. The letter will not erase as a pencil mark would; instead, it will break up into small bits that can gently be brushed from the surface of the page. If you use a pencil eraser, do not rub too hard, as this will fray the paper surface before you remove all of the letter. Make sure that the eraser is completely clean before you start, otherwise the paper surface will become soiled with whatever is on the eraser.

If you use tape to lift the letter, use a very small piece and *do not* press it over the entire letter (unless you are removing the letter from an acetate sheet, as will be explained later). Instead, use a small part of the tape to pick up small portions of the letter in a "tapping" motion. This action will break up the letter as it is being removed and will do much less damage to the surrounding paper surface (see Figures 2-21 and 2-22).

If, after removing a letter by using either an eraser or tape, the surface of the paper show signs of fraying or becoming too rough, place the backing paper from the lettering sheet over the spot and rub the sheet with the *bone* end of your burnisher a few times (see Figure 2-23). This will help flatten the rough surface and make it less noticeable. This rubdown process should be done *before* transferring a new letter to the paper surface.

FIGURE 2-21 A transferred letter can be removed by gently rubbing it off the page surface with an eraser. Use a back-and-forth motion to break up the letter and remove the small pieces.

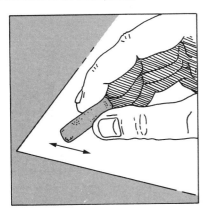

FIGURE 2-22 A small piece of masking tape can also be used to remove a transferred letter. Place the tape over the letter and press *very gently* (a light tap with the finger tip) and then pull the tape gently away. Repeat this tapping process until the letter is removed. *Remember: The less contact the tape has with the area surrounding the letter, the less chance of damaging the paper surface.*

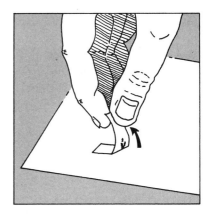

FIGURE 2-23 If the paper surface has been damaged, the rough spot can be smoothed by placing the type backing sheet over the page and rubbing with the bone end of the type burnisher.

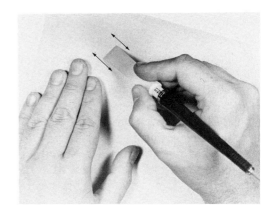

Note that if a pencil, eraser, or tape is unavailable, the lettering can be removed by using a *rubber cement pickup*. This is a small, spongelike piece of rubber that is normally used to remove excess rubber cement from surfaces. However, it will remove lettering very well by gentle rubbing and usually does not damage the paper surface. As with the other materials already mentioned, the rubber cement pickup should be very clean and should have no materials on it that would smudge or soil the paper surface.

When using pressure-sensitive lettering, try to avoid mistakes as much as possible by examining each of your words or symbols *before* transferring the letters down. Removing mistakes is a bothersome process, and since this lettering is not reusable, a removed letter or word is also an additional expense.

SPACING THE LETTERING

When applying transfer type to a surface to make words or sentences, three principal considerations should be kept in mind. We have already discussed the first of these, aligning the individual letters along a guideline. The other two are *type spacing* and *type verticality*.

Type Spacing

Type spacing refers to the distance between the letters that compose a word. In industrial typesetting, such as that used in books and other printed matter, type spacing is an automatic part of the printing process. But because the transfer lettering page is positioned by hand for each letter and word, the process of even-letter spacing is an eye skill that has to be learned.

There is no set formula for transfer-type eye spacing. It is the kind of skill that has to be acquired through practical experience. Once you have lettered a few words, and the words you then produce look clean and even and read clearly, you will have mastered type spacing. There are, however, a few terms and practices that can help you acquire this new hand-and-eye skill.

Most persons who use transfer type for the first time have a tendency to place the letters either too close together or too far apart. Additionally, some letters, because of their shape, tend to present more of a spacing problem than others.

*Crowded Type
and Overspaced Type*

Crowded type, as the name implies, occurs when letters are placed too closely together. This is not desirable for two reasons. First, the word is much more difficult to read, and the possibility of the reader's misinterpreting the word is greatly increased. Second, because this

An example of normal spacing
An example of crowded type

FIGURE 2-24 When letters are placed too closely together, the readability of the words suffers.

lettering is for a slide module, the graphic layout and transfer-type words will later be photographed into slides. This means that the letters and words will be reduced, or shrunk, by the camera lens, and already crowded type may *fuse*, or run together, making it even more difficult to read (see Figures 2-24 and 2-25).

FIGURE 2-25 When a word with crowded type is photographically reduced in size, the letters can fuse together, making it even more difficult to read.

Crowded

Crowded

Crowded

The opposite of crowded type is *overspaced type.* Overspaced type is better than crowded type because, although it may look less professional, it is at least readable. An example of overspaced type is shown in Figure 2-26. No one, not

Overspaced Type

FIGURE 2-26 An example of letters spaced too far apart. Overspaced type is difficult to read because the space between the letters is almost the same as the space between words, causing visual confusion.

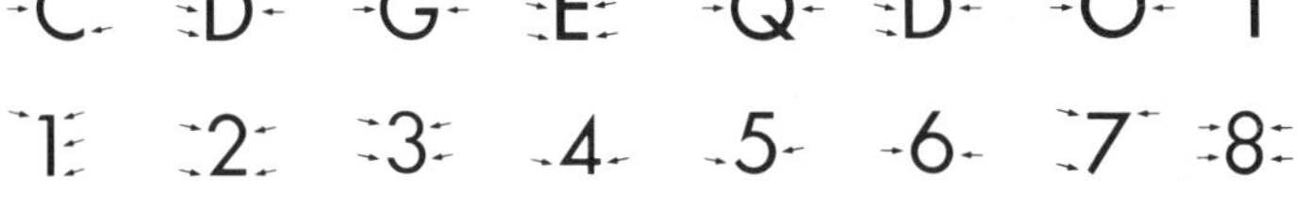

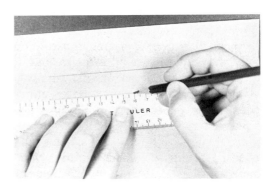

FIGURE 2-28 Rule several lines on a sheet of tracing paper.

even a professional graphic artist, can measure and produce perfectly spaced lettering by eye alone. However, with a little practice and determination, almost anyone can produce acceptable-looking words and sentences.

Problem Letters

Round letters seem to present the greatest spacing problems. The letters *C, G, O,* and *Q* and sometimes *V* are difficult to space in relation to letters before and after them, especially if these are capital letters. If you experience difficulty in spacing these letters, practice transferring down words that contain one or more of these characters.

Develop a point of constant distance between each letter as you position and burnish them down. This point of constant distance occurs at the nearest point between two letters, and it should be kept the same between all the letters of the word (see Figure 2-27).

FIGURE 2-27 All capital and lower-case letters and all numbers have a plane, or one or more points on the left and right side that will be nearest to the letter placed before and after them. These *points of nearest contact* should be kept equidistant between the letters making up each word.

FIGURE 2-29 Place the tracing paper *over* the type carrier sheet and align one of the ruled lines under the first letter you wish to trace. Be sure to keep the wax backing sheet *under* the type carrier sheet.

If you feel the need to practice but do not want to waste your transfer type, you can set up a simple practice page on a sheet of tracing paper. Take a sheet of tracing paper and rule several light pencil lines across it, as shown in Figure 2-28. Then place the tracing paper *over* the lettering sheet. Keep the wax paper backing *under* the lettering sheet. Move the tracing paper so that one of the pencil lines is at the bottom of the first letter you want (see Figure 2-29). Now,

-C- -D- -G- -E- -Q- -D- -O- -T-

-1- -2- -3- -4- -5- -6- -7- -8-

instead of burnishing the letter to transfer it, use a pencil to trace its outline through the tracing paper sheet. You may shade the letter in, after tracing it, if you feel that this improves its visibility. After completing the first letter, move the tracing paper to align the next desired letter to your base line. In this manner, you can practice spacing and creating groups of words without damaging the lettering sheet or wasting the transfer type on it (see Figures 2-30 and 2-31).

FIGURE 2-30 You should outline the letter first, and then you can shade it in a solid tone. If you make an error, begin the process again on the next ruled line.

FIGURE 2-31 By tracing words with this process, you can practice letter and word spacing without using up any actual type.

Type Verticality

Type verticality is the third and final principal consideration during the lettering process. While trying to keep the type straight along the guideline and spacing each letter of the word being formed, the lettering page will sometimes tilt slightly, producing letters that lean slightly to the right or left (see Figure 2-32). All too frequently, you will not notice this until the word is finished, which then requires the extra time to go back, remove the slanted letter, and transfer down the new one.

Type character verticality is as important as proper letter spacing.

FIGURE 2-32 Although the letters *h* and *t* in the word *character* and the letter *i* in the word *important* are only slightly slanted from the vertical, it is enough to make the word "feel" wrong. This can cause the viewer to pause to reread the word, throwing the module progression of words and images off.

When aligning a letter you want to transfer along the guideline, you can prevent this slanting effect if you *also* line up the bottoms of two or three other letters in that row on either side of the desired letter that you are transferring (see Figure 2-33). This will ensure that the letter you transfer down is in the proper orientation to the other let-

FIGURE 2-33 When aligning a letter to be burnished down (in this case, the *h*), use the other letters on that line of the carrier sheet, to the left or right, to establish proper verticality. In the upper example, note that the row of letters begins to lift up from the base line to the right of the *h*. This will cause the *h* to lean to the left. All the letters of the row should rest on the base line. This process also makes positioning round-bottomed letters such as *o* and *e* much easier.

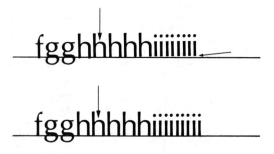

ters in the word. Do not hurry during the lettering process. There is a natural tendency to rush through the last two or three letters of each word, and it is here that you will be most likely to make a mistake. The production of good graphic design takes both careful thought and patience.

Burnishing the Type

As mentioned earlier, after transferring down a letter with the ball end of your burnisher, it is removable if a mistake has been made. However, after you have finished transferring down the words you want and have checked them for accuracy, a *final burnishing* is necessary. This is to ensure that a good adhesive bond has been established between each letter and the page surface, and that the lettering does not shift, peel, or flake off during later handling. The final burnishing is done with the *bone* end of your burnisher and the wax paper backing that comes with each lettering sheet.

The first step is to place the wax paper over the transferred words on the page surface. Then, using the flat, top edge of the bone, rub back and forth a few times over each letter (see Figure 2-34). Do not press too hard, as this may cause the letter to crack or shift. The purpose of this final burnishing is to press out minute air bubbles that may be trapped under the letter decal material. After burnishing down all the letters and words, remove the wax paper and *gently* erase the pencil guideline with a soft, clean pencil eraser (see Figure 2-35). Use the edge of the eraser to remove the guideline between each of the letters, and try to keep the eraser from going over the actual letters as much as possible. Sometimes the wax adhesive from the lettering sheet is quite

FIGURE 2-34 After you have completed transferring the type, place the wax backing sheet (which is supplied with the type carrier sheet) over the lettering and burnish a final time with the bone end of the burnisher to ensure firm adhesion. Use a back-and-forth motion. Do not press hard because this may crease or dent the paper surface beneath.

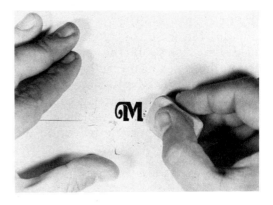

FIGURE 2-35 The pencil guideline can be removed by gently using a soft eraser.

heavy over the guideline, and therefore it takes longer to erase. If this occurs, be patient and continue erasing each area between the letters with a light back-and-forth movement. *Do not* grind the eraser against the surface or rub very hard, as this may chip the edges of the transferred letters.

Cracks and Chips

During the final burnishing, a letter will occasionally develop a crack or chip that cannot be seen until after the burnishing is finished and the wax sheet removed (see Figure 2–36). Although lettering can be removed after the final burnishing, it is much more resistant to the removal process described earlier and greater care must be taken not to damage the surrounding paper surface. If the crack is a minor one and does not affect the readability of the letter or the word containing the letter, it can sometimes be *touched up*. This is done with a fine felt-tipped marker that is the same color as the type, or it can be done with a triple-zero watercolor brush or extra-fine pen and India ink (see Figures 2–37 and 2–38). The crack can be filled in with ink by a light dotting motion of the marker or pen tip and then allowed to dry (see Figure 2–39).

In the case of *chips*, or small pieces breaking off the edge of the letter, the touching-up method does not work as well. The best course of action with a badly chipped letter is to remove it and transfer down a replacement. If removing the chipped letter is too dif-

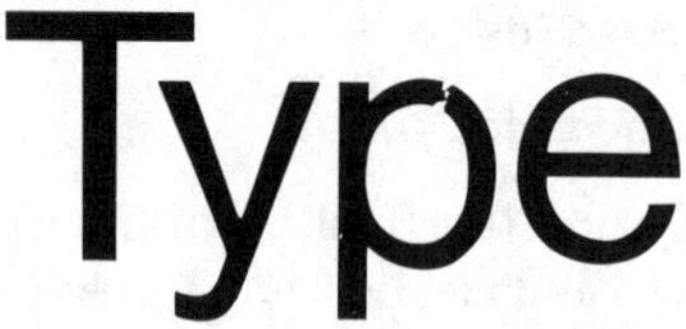

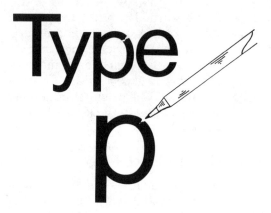

FIGURE 2–38 Using a fine-pointed, felt-tipped marker, fill in the crack with a series of small dots.

FIGURE 2–39 With practice, the correction will not be noticeable.

FIGURE 2–36 Three major flaws can show up in transfer type, especially in large, thick letters: *chips*, such as those that appear in the letter *t*; *cracks*, such as those that appear in the letters *y and e*; and *pinholes*, such as those that appear in the letters *p* and *e*.

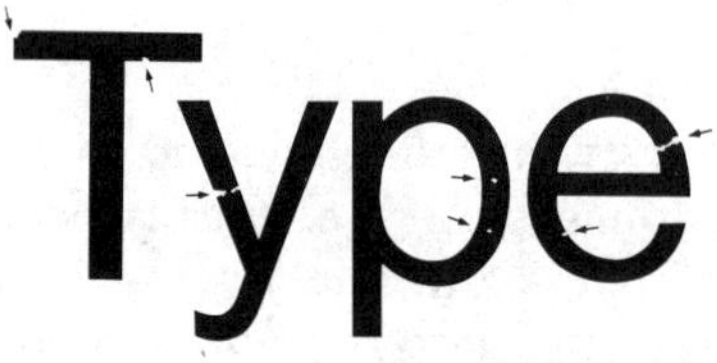

FIGURE 2–37 Even an extensive crack, such as the one in the letter *p*, can be repaired.

ficult or in too intricate an area, try transferring a new letter *over* the chipped one. This will require very accurate alignment of the two letters and a delicate touch because the transfer letters do not adhere that well to each other.

With patience, however, a new letter can be overlaid on a damaged one. The replacement letter should also have a final burnish.

Type Sizes

Transferred type is manufactured in numerous sizes and styles. The size range is determined by a unit of measure called a *point*. The higher the point number of a specific type, the larger the letters will be.

Point Size

The point-size range offered by different type manufacturers varies somewhat. Generally, however, the smallest size would be 8 points (a standard typewriter type is approximately 12 points), and the largest size would run up into the hundreds of points. Some point-size samples are shown in Figure 2-40.

Type sizes that measure 60 points or more are usually offered with separate sheets for the capital and lower-case letters because fewer letters can be fitted to a page. There may also be a separate sheet for numbers if they are needed. Bear this in mind if you should decide to use large type in your layouts, as the additional sheets will be more expensive.

A general size range for an audio-visual frame design would be from 24 points to 60 points. This range incorporates four sizes: 24-point, 36-point, 48-point, and 60-point. Type sizes outside this range could also be used but would require far more camera adjustments later, during the photography process.

If it is necessary to have several sentences appear in a frame (with no illustrative material), the information

can be printed with a typewriter and photographed later on special film (see Chapter 7).

A good general rule for type size in graphic design for audio-visual frames would be: *Keep the number of words to a minimum, keep sentences short, and use larger type to ensure clarity.* To add special emphasis, selected words can be printed in all capitals or in capitals of a larger point size than that used in the rest of the design, or they can be printed in a different color if the additional expense is not a factor (see Figure 2-41).

Keep sentences short, for clarity.

Keep sentences SHORT, for CLARITY.

FIGURE 2-41 Using all capital letters in a word adds special emphasis.

MANUFACTURERS' BRAND NAMES

A number of manufacturers produce transfer type, as well as a broad range of other special graphic tools and materials. These manufacturers include Letraset, Chartpak, Tactype, Artype, Prestype, and Paratipe. Most of these manufacturers issue catalogs or illustrated brochures that can be obtained free of charge or can be purchased from the manufacturer or a local art supply store for a nominal fee.

A good idea is to begin a collection of catalogs not only to familiarize yourself with the various styles, sizes, and colors of type produced by each manufacturer but also to generate ideas for your own graphic designs. The number of styles of types produced by some manufacturers is staggering, and therefore the best course of action is to rely

FIGURE 2-40 Four point-size samples in upper and lower case.

A a   60PT.

A a   48PT.

A a   36PT.

A a   24PT.

on your own taste and personal preference as to which style of type is clear and readable and fits the subject and graphic needs of the module you are preparing.

Styles of Type

The *style* of type refers not only to the way in which the letters are formed but also to whether they are tall and elongated or short and wide, whether they are thick or heavy, whether they slant to the left or to the right, and whether their design is modern or antique.

Type styles can be very plain or very decorative, and this information is usually contained in the formal name of the type. For example, one type-style name is *Helvetica*, but within this style category there is Helvetica extra light, Helvetica light, Helvetica medium, Hel-

vetica bold, Helvetica light italic, (which is inclined at an angle), Helvetica medium italic, Helvetica bold italic, and Helvetica outline (in which just the outline of the letter is given).

The name *Helvetica* refers to the way in which the letters are formed in this particular alphabet. The terms *light*, *medium*, and *bold* refer to the thickness of the letters. The term *italic* means that the letters are slanted. The term *outline* means that the letters are white, or clear, with just a thin line detailing their shape, rather than being solid black (see Figure 2-42).

When ordering type from a catalog, first give the exact name, then the desired point size, and then the manufacturer's code number if necessary. Most large art or graphic supply stores carry a selection of transfer type offered by one or more manufacturers.

FIGURE 2-42 Many letter styles are available in a number of variations.

Style Reference Chart

PAGE NO	STYLE NO	PT SIZES	
88	30	8-96	Futura Medium
88	14	8-180	Futura Demi Bold
90	15	8-180	Futura Bold
91	280	12-180	Futura Extra Bold
92	287	12-180	Futura Extra Bold Condensed
92	323	12-72	Futura Light
93	324	12-72	Futura Bold Italic
93	243	36-72	FUTURA INLINE
93	363	18-72	Gill Sans Light
94	364	18-72	Gill Sans Light Italic
94	358	14-72	Gill Sans
94	348	14-72	Gill Sans Italic

PAGE NO	STYLE NO	PT SIZES	
98	327	18-96	Helvetica Extra Light
98	328	14-96	Helvetica Light Italic
99	52	10-180	Helvetica
100	101	14-180	Helvetica Light
100	210	10-96	Helvetica Italic
101	100	8-180	Helvetica Medium
102	198	8-96	Helvetica Medium Italic
102	122	24-180	Helvetica Medium Outline
103	107	14-180	Helvetica Bold
104	214	8-180	Helvetica Bold Extended
104	207	14-96	Helvetica Bold Italic
105	288	12-180	Helvetica Extrabold Condensed

Many brands and styles of transfer type are available in colors. The basic color is black, but some popular type styles are available in red, yellow, blue, green, and white. These colored types are very useful when special emphasis on a word is needed or when the lettering is to be superimposed on a very dark background and black would be less visible than a bright color. Brightly colored type can also increase the viewer's interest by calling attention to complex subjects, thus aiding the general learning experience of the module.

After selecting a type style for the wording in the module you are preparing, you should use the same type style for all the frames. It is quite acceptable to mix lettering of different point sizes, even in the same individual frame. However, refrain from mixing type styles as much as possible, as this will only add one more possible source of confusion when the module is viewed later.

In addition to all the various sizes, colors, and styles of transfer type available, many manufacturers produce a wide variety of symbols and pictures in this transfer medium. You may find these useful when preparing the layout of your module.

Here is just a partial list of the pictorial symbols available as transfer decals:

Decorative borders and corners
Electronic data-processing symbols
Universal product code (upc) symbols
Military plotting symbols
Highway signs and symbols
Music symbols, figures, and equipment
Blank compasses and directional arrows
Drawings of seated and standing people
Architectural symbols (trees, shrubs, groups of people, etc.)
Architectural scales
Transportation symbols (buses, trucks, cars, trains, aircraft)
Mathematical symbols
Arrows and directional indicators
Circles, squares, and dots of various sizes
Decorative initials
Brackets and parentheses
Triangles, ovals, and other geometric forms in either solid or outline form
Male and female faces and heads
Hands (pointing, holding objects, etc.)
Astrological symbols
Outline maps of the various continents
Symbols of the seasons (Christmas trees, snowmen, a man raking leaves, etc.)
Pets (dogs, cats, horses, birds, etc.)
Food symbols (place settings, wine bottles, etc.)
Chessboards with separate sheets of symbols for chess notation

The images included in this list are actual line drawings that are reproduced on a lettering type page. They are positioned and burnished down in the same manner as that used in transfer lettering. The illustration range offered by some manufacturers is quite large; however, the above list was compiled from several catalogs. Most of the pictorial images are small, and several ranges of different kinds are usually offered on a single sheet. They are most appropriate in designs where simple, nontechnical drawings are needed, or where a standard, repeatable symbol is being used (see Figures 2–43 and 2–44).

These transfer illustrations can of course save a great deal of time if they can be used instead of preparing the drawings by hand, or if the person designing a module whose subject calls for extensive illustrations has limited drawing skills.

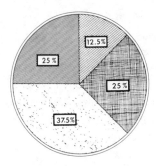

FIGURE 2-43 Sheets of line textures, as well as rectangular boxes and other geometric shapes in different sizes, are available in transfer type or self-adhesive form.

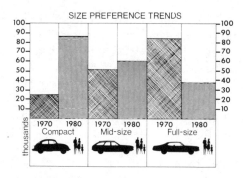

FIGURE 2-44 Many kinds of pictorial images and symbols, in outline or solid form, are available.

Transfer-Type Storage and Shelf Life

Transfer type, as well as most graphic materials, should be stored in a cool, dry place away from direct sunlight. The term *shelf life* refers to the length of time, from the date of its manufacture, that a product remains at optimum usefulness. Transfer-type products have shelf lives that vary, depending on the chemical composition of the materials used by different manufacturers.

There is no reliable way to determine the age of graphic materials when they are purchased. However, some symptoms of deterioration will be apparent when the materials are used. If the transfer type you are using requires a great deal of pressure in the burnishing process and the resulting transferred letter does not hold properly to the paper surface, it could be that the type is old and its adhesive has deteriorated. Try transferring a letter from the problem sheet to a different kind of paper surface. If the problem still occurs, take the sheet back to where it was purchased and ask for a replacement.

Another symptom of deterioration occurs when transferred letters crack, chip, flake, or shatter during the burnishing process. Sometimes only the letters or other characters near the edge of the sheet will be affected, or any delicate lines that may be part of the letters. If letters peel or fall off the main sheet when it is flexed or bent during normal handling, this is also an indication of old or defective materials.

A FINAL NOTE

Because of rapidly changing economic conditions, it is impossible to give any price ranges for the graphic materials described here. However, by purchasing only what you need when it is needed, and working carefully with the proper tools, expenditures can be kept to a reasonable level. Wherever less-expensive or substitute materials can be used in any of the processes described in this text, they are described in detail. But when purchasing graphic materials or tools, it is usually good practice to consider quality rather than price. Cheap, shoddy, or "make do" materials or tools will invariably produce a final product that reflects them.

GLOSSARY

Acetate A clear, tough flexible plastic sheet that is used as a base for transfer type in the production of layouts for slide modules. A frosted semiopaque acetate is also available.

Burnisher A special tool designed for the application of pressure-sensitive type. The burnisher usually consists of a pencillike shaft with a spring-loaded steel ball at one end (for type application) and a flat, polished, flexible plate called a *bone* at the other end (for a final burnish of transferred type) to ensure that the type is securely in place.

Camera-ready copy A finished graphic design that is ready to be photographed into a slide frame.

Crowded type Words or letters that are spaced too close together to either read or reproduce photographically.

Flat The complete and finished graphic layout of a sound-slide frame before it is photographed (see *camera-ready copy*).

Format guide A cardboard mat or frame that is cut out to have an opening whose dimensions are in a ratio that reflects the ratio of the film frame size that will eventually be used to produce the final slide version of the graphic design. For 35-mm slides, the length-to-width ratio of the film frame is 2 to 3. The format guide, which also has a length-to-width ratio of 2 to 3, is used in determining the placement of type, words, backgrounds, and pictorial material and in copy balancing and copy fitting.

Frame A complete and finished slide or visual unit of a sound-slide module.

Graphic A term used to describe the art materials, the type, the process of making the layout, the photographing or presenting of a two-dimensional design or image that involves the elements of type, color, and/or pictorial materials.

Layout The process of making a finished graphic design from a script and/or preliminary sketches.

Point size A measurement system used for pressure-sensitive and other kinds of type. The higher the type point-size number, the larger the letter or character.

Pressure-sensitive type Also known as *decal type* and *transfer type*. This material consists of letters, numbers, and punctuation marks that are printed on the back of a tough plastic page and coated with a pressure-activated waxlike adhesive. The characters are transferred to the working surface by rubbing over them on the main sheet with a specialized tool called a *burnisher*. Pressure-sensitive type is available in many sizes, and colors, as well as many symbols and pictures.

Proportion In graphic design, the relationship (sometimes mathematically determined) between the elements being combined. For example, the size relationship between type size, what the type must spell out, and the size area the type must be fitted into (see *ratio*).

Ratio The size relationship between the length and width of a given area. For example, a 2-by-3 inch rectangle has two sides that are an inch longer than the other two sides. Using 1 inch as a common denominator of measurement for both side lengths, the ratio would be 2 inches to 3 inches, or 2:3.

Rubber cement pickup A small, thin square of rubber with a spongelike texture that is used to remove excess rubber cement from various surfaces. The pickup can also be used to remove pressure-sensitive type by gently rubbing it over the letter or character to be lifted.

Shelf life The period of time that graphic materials such as pressure-sensitive type, tape, and paper can be stored without loss or impairment of their usefulness. The length of storage shelf life varies with both the kind of product and the manufacturer. Many photographic products, such as film, paper, and chemicals, will have the manufacturer's storage and shelf-life data included in their instructions. With most graphic arts materials, the user determines shelf life through experience over a period of time.

Slides Positive color images that are produced on a clear film base and are viewed with a light source behind them and some type of optical system to magnify and enlarge the image. Slide films, depending on the type of film, can be used in both daylight and artificial light. After development, the film frames either can be separated and mounted in small cardboard frames (for use in a slide viewer or projector) or can be left in a continuous strip and projected and viewed with a filmstrip projector. Unless otherwise indicated, the term *slides* in this text refers to cardboard-mounted 35-mm color film.

Stencil knife, or mat knife A graphic cutting tool usually consisting of a metal, wood, or plastic handle and replaceable and disposable steel cutting blades. Also referred to as a *razor knife* or *X-Acto knife*.

Tracing paper A thin, semitransparent, smooth-surfaced paper used to delineate the outlines of graphic materials placed beneath it.

Transparencies See *slides*.

T square A device used to measure and mark right angles and parallel lines. T squares consist of a ruler or straight shaft with a crosspiece on one end that is set to form a right angle. T-squares are made of metal, wood, or plastic. A metal T square should be used if graphic materials are to be cut, because wood or plastic edges are fragile and subject to damage by cutting blades.

Type spacing The distance between individual letters and words that are composed of pressure-sensitive type (see *crowded type*).

Type verticality An important consideration when applying pressure-sensitive lettering along a guideline is to ensure that the letters are completely perpendicular to the base line. Individual letters should not slant to one side or the other.

3
THE OVERLAY

THE OVERLAY

The placement and position of the type, the pictorial images, or the graphs, charts, and diagrams that may be needed in an individual frame are strongly influenced by the subject of the module, as well as the pace of the information flow that is building from frame to frame toward the learning objective.

When preparing the visual portion of a second-slide module, you should collect all the pictorial materials (photographs, graphs, charts, diagrams, etc.) that do not have to be drawn or prepared specially from their original sources and label them (on the back) as to the frame in which they will eventually be placed. This is done in conjunction with the narrative-visual script (see Chapter 1).

This practice is also very useful if certain pictorial materials are to appear in more than one frame. Note that since virtually all type is placed on a clear plastic sheet called an *acetate overlay*, the background pictorial materials do not have to be redrawn or otherwise duplicated if they are required to appear again in another frame. This is especially convenient in the case of complex, hand-drawn charts and maps, as well as any pictorial material that must be preserved in its original state (see Figures 3-1A, 3-1B, and 3-1C).

The acetate overlay in frame design is useful in a number of ways. The overlay permits the placement of type in any desired manner without the necessity of drawing guidelines on the pictorial or background materials. Information can also be added to (or deleted from) the overlay, and it can then be used again in another frame. For example, in a series of frames demonstrating the steps necessary to complete a mathematical process, the original set of numbers and characters

FIGURE 3-1A Any drawing or graphic that is to be utilized in more than one frame can be adapted and preserved at the same time through the use of a clear acetate overlay sheet.

(A)

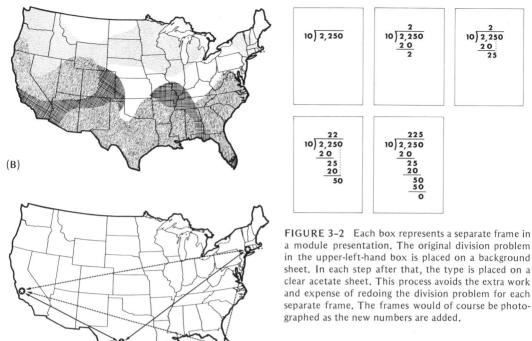

(B)

(C)

FIGURE 3–2 Each box represents a separate frame in a module presentation. The original division problem in the upper-left-hand box is placed on a background sheet. In each step after that, the type is placed on a clear acetate sheet. This process avoids the extra work and expense of redoing the division problem for each separate frame. The frames would of course be photographed as the new numbers are added.

FIGURE 3–1B, C Here are just two possible variations of the same graphic seen in Figure 3–1A. The shaded and rendered areas on one, and the arrows and lines on the other, are all placed on acetate overlay sheets. This allows the original drawing to be preserved untouched, for reuse again in another frame.

applied to an overlay is kept throughout the series. The additional numbers or characters are added to each frame *as it is being photographed*, thus saving a great deal of time and expense (see Figure 3–2).

The overlay not only permits the use of different written information with the same background but also allows for freehand drawing and outlining over background pictorial materials with the aid of *acetate inks*. These special inks are available in different colors and are compatible with the plastic acetate surface (see Chapter 4).

TYPE AND THE ACETATE OVERLAY

Regardless of the amount, size, or nature of any pictorial material on which type is to be superimposed, the nature and format of the individual flat remains constant—except in rare instances, the flat contains *two* layers of visual information, the background and the overlay.

The *background* consists of any combination of flat color, patterns, pictorial material (photographs or drawings), or graphics (charts, maps, graphs, etc.). Over this base layer is placed the *acetate overlay*, which contains the pressure-sensitive type, numbers, and characters or figures. The background, of course, may also contain type, but the usual and recommended practice is that any printed information that is to be added to existing background material be applied to the overlay (for reasons already stated).

The application of pressure-sensitive type to acetate is, in many respects, easier than to a paper surface. Mistakes are much easier to remove from acetate than from paper, and no drawn guideline is necessary for the proper placement of the type.

The first step is to align and tape down a sheet of clear acetate to a drawing board, drafting desk, or other working surface. (Normally, the acetate is placed over the background, but for purposes of demonstration, this will be described later.) It is important to align the acetate sheet (and the background) by using a T square to ensure that the type is exactly parallel to both the background layer and, later, to the frame dimensions of the slide into which it will be photographed. Therefore, the working surface that is being used, such as a drafting table or a drawing board, should have exactly parallel edges.

Homemade working surfaces such as a piece of cut masonite or the heavy cardboard backing of a drawing pad *should be avoided*, as these may not have accurate edges and may therefore affect the accuracy of your T square measurements. The size of the acetate sheet used for most overlays is 11 by 14 inches. This material is available from graphic and art supply stores in pad form as well as loose sheets. Large- and smaller-size pads are also available, as well as acetate in rolled sheets of varying lengths, but these are seldom used in the preparation of overlays.

Acetate is as clear as glass and is both flexible and tough. It will readily accept almost all brands of pressure-sensitive type, as well as other graphic materials such as markers, acetate inks, and charting tapes. To tape down the acetate to the working surface, first place your T square horizontally on the working surface and align the lip of the crosspiece firmly on the edge of the desk or drawing board (see Figures 3–3A, 3–3B, and 3–4). The T square can be

(A)

FIGURE 3–3A, B Whether working at a small drawing board or a drafting desk, a smooth working surface and a reliable T square or parallel guide are essential.

(B)

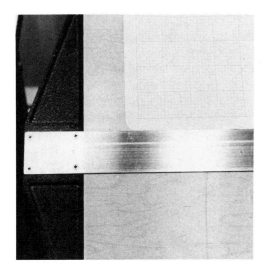

FIGURE 3-4 The crosspiece, or head, of the T square butts against the edge of the drawing board or drafting desk.

slid up and down the working surface to accommodate the acetate and background placement, but always make sure that the crosspiece is firmly against the edge of the working surface (see Figure 3-5). Even a small misalignment will become apparent later when the overlay and background are combined for photographing.

FIGURE 3-5 If the T square crosspiece is not butted firmly against the drawing surface edge, all the type in the layout will be misaligned. Even a slight misalignment, as shown on the left, will ruin a layout. The correct position is shown on the right.

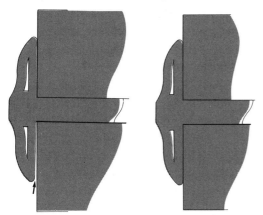

Having placed the T square across the working surface, hold it in place and slide a sheet of acetate on the working surface so that its *bottom* edge contacts the T square shaft. Then tape down the *top* of the acetate sheet with two small pieces of masking tape or cellophane tape. Here again, make sure that the acetate sheet does not shift during the taping process (see Figures 3-6 and 3-7).

Pressure-sensitive type or characters can be applied by using almost the same alignment and burnishing process as that described in Chapter 2. The only difference is the absense of a drawn guideline. The guideline or base for the alignment of the words or sentences is provided by

FIGURE 3-6 Gently press the bottom of the acetate sheet against the T square shaft edge.

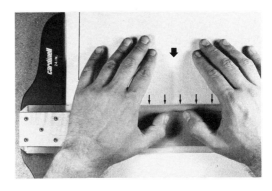

FIGURE 3-7 Holding the acetate in place, apply two small strips of tape overlapping the top edge of the acetate to hold it down to the drawing surface.

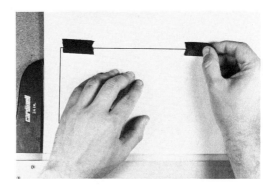

a paper *slipsheet* placed *under* the acetate overlay sheet, between it and the desk surface, or between it and the background sheet (if present).

The slipsheet is simply a clean, rectangular sheet of paper. Typewriter paper is acceptable for this procedure. To form a base line for a line of type, lift the bottom (untaped) edge of the acetate sheet and raise it upward a few inches. The tape holding the top edge of the sheet to the desk or working surface will act as a set of hinges and keep the acetate sheet from shifting out of its parallel alignment with the T square (see Figure 3–8).

Place the slipsheet under the overlay sheet and slide it upward until the top edge of the slipsheet is approximately where you wish the first line of type to appear on the overlay (see Figure 3–9). At this point allow the overlay to drop back and *gently* smooth out any bulges that may have appeared (see Figure

FIGURE 3–8 Lift the acetate sheet up from the working surface, on its tape hinges.

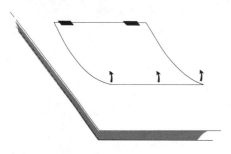

FIGURE 3–9 Place the slipsheet under the acetate sheet.

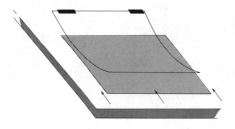

3–10). Because the slipsheet edge must also be exactly parallel to the overlay, place the T square over the overlay sheet and align the top edge of the T square with the top edge of the slipsheet appearing through the overlay.

To align the slipsheet with the T square edge, gently grasp the slipsheet where it extends below the lower edge of the acetate overlay and shift it so that the top edge aligns perfectly with the edge of the T square shaft. This procedure is illustrated in Figure 3–11.

After aligning the slipsheet, the T square can be removed, and the type can be applied to the overlay, aligning the bottom edge of the letters along the edge

FIGURE 3–10 Place the acetate sheet down, and gently smooth out any wrinkles or bulges.

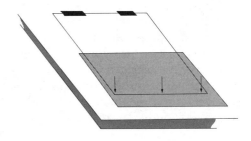

FIGURE 3–11 Place the T square over the acetate sheet and align the slipsheet edge with the upper edge of the T square shaft.

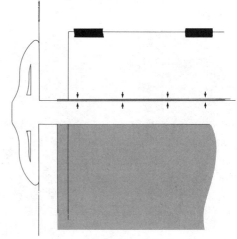

of the slipsheet beneath the overlay (see Figure 3–12). After this line of type is completed and given a final burnish, the slipsheet can be pulled down or moved to a new desired position and realigned with the T square edge, and a new line of type can be started (see Figures 3–13 and 3–14). Should the slipsheet shift during the type application, it can be held temporarily in place by two small pieces of tape at the upper corners, under the overlay sheet. These tape

pieces can be removed when the slipsheet is moved to a new position (see Figure 3–15).

Type application to the overlay surface is smooth and easily accomplished. Mistakes can easily be corrected by placing a small piece of masking tape or cellophane tape over the letter or word, pressing down *gently*, and peeling the tape and letter off the surface. If the letter being removed breaks into pieces, leaving small fragments still on the sur-

FIGURE 3-12 To apply a line of type, align the letters on the type carrier sheet along the slipsheet edge and burnish each down. The T square is removed for this operation.

FIGURE 3-13 After the desired letters and words are burnished down for the first line, the slipsheet is pulled down to the position for a new line of type. After pulling the slipsheet down, always realign its edge with the T square shaft before applying the new line of type.

FIGURE 3-14 After aligning the slipsheet in its new position, the next line of type may be applied.

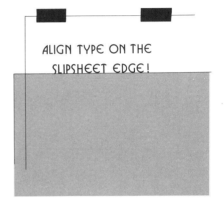

FIGURE 3-15 To ensure that the slipsheet does not shift position accidentally during the type application process, the edges may be held down temporarily with small pieces of tape.

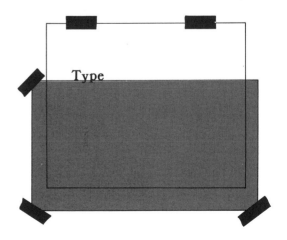

face, simply repeat this procedure until the area is completely clean. The acetate surface is both tough and resistant to damage, and the tape removal process can be used as often as necessary. New words or letters can be transferred to the cleaned area immediately (see Figures 3–16 and 3–17).

The slipsheet can also provide guidelines for type that is not meant to be placed in a straight line. With the aid of a compass, a protractor, French curves, and a stencil knife or single-edge razor blade, the upper edge of the slipsheet can be cut to a variety of shapes, all of which can be used as type guidelines (see Figures 3–18A and 3–18B).

FIGURE 3–16 To remove transfer type from the acetate overlay sheet, press a small piece of tape over the entire letter.

FIGURE 3–17 Peel the tape back slowly to remove the letter. If the letter fragments, repeat the procedure to remove any remnants adhering to the acetate. New letters may be transferred down to the cleaned area on the acetate immediately.

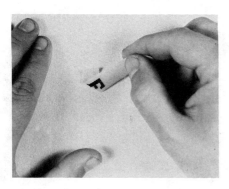

FIGURE 3–18A, B Some examples of shaped slip-sheets and the way these shapes affect the application of lines of type.

(A)

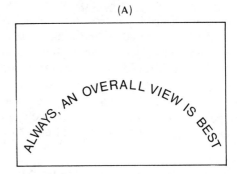

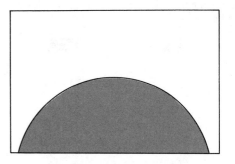

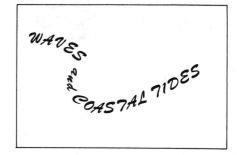

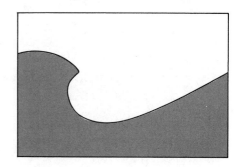

FIGURE 3-18 (continued)

(B)

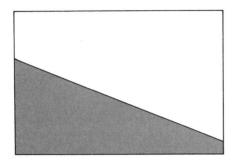

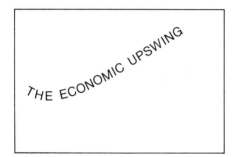

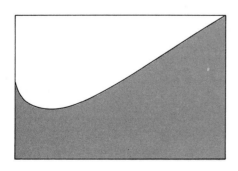

LINE SPACING, COLUMNS, AND WORD CENTERING

As with all forms of graphic design, clear, well-spaced words and characters are just part of the process of producing a well-balanced layout. Attention and care must be given equally to all the elements that make up a design, especially in the areas of line spacing, columns and word centering.

Line Spacing

Line spacing is an important aspect of the professional look and readability that is necessary for a successful module. Sentences or information arranged into lines within the frame must be properly spaced in order to aid the viewer's comprehension of the data being offered. Like letter and word spacing, line spacing becomes an automatic part of the frame design process, and should (like all the spacing requirements in graphic design) be noticeable only when it is not done properly. Fluctuating distances between type lines can be very disturbing visually. Even small discrepancies are easily discernible to the average person who is used to reading materials where the line spacing is always perfect (see Figure 3-19).

FIGURE 3-19 Here is a statement consisting of several lines of type with nonequal distances between the lines. Notice how this small distance fluctuation adversely affects the readability of the statement.

The spaces between the base lines along which type is placed should always be kept at the same distance.

Having applied a line of type along the paper slipsheet edge on the acetate overlay, the next step is to determine how far the second line should be placed below the first line of type. There is more to consider here than simply a mechanical spacing process that would be applied to letter and word spacing.

The information content of the frame profoundly affects the placement of the type lines. For example, assume that the following written information must appear in a frame:

Final Review of Processing Steps

1. Add developer, at the proper working temperature. 2. Agitate the film every *30* seconds. 3. Drain and rinse with clear water. 4. Add hypo for required time; remember to agitate. 5. Wash for 15 to 30 minutes.

The information will be much more readable if the five elements of the statement are separated by additional line spaces:

Final Review of Processing Steps

1. Add developer, at the proper working temperature.
2. Agitate the film every *30* seconds.
3. Drain and rinse with clear water.
4. Add hypo for required time; remember to agitate.
5. Wash for 15 to 30 minutes.

In listing the statement elements in this manner, with the spacing between each element emphasizing it as a separate and distinct step, the ovarall clarity of the frame is greatly improved from a comprehension viewpoint, as well as a graphic one. The same process is true of *two or more* line statements, but an additional spacing factor is added here. For example, the following two statements are to be grouped to emphasize each equally.

Line spacing is always an important factor in the design of proper layouts. Line spacing is as important as word spacing.

The first step is to separate the statements and to determine how many words will be on each line of the first and longest statement. An important rule to remember is that *the first line of a two-line statement is always the longest.* It would look both unbalanced and improper if the first statement were printed like this:

Line spacing is always an important factor in the design of proper layouts.

Words and sentences, when placed on a page or in a graphic design, set up rhythms and interact with both the pictorial information in the frame and the other lines of type.

A proper layout for the first statement would be:

Line spacing is always an important factor in the design of proper layouts.

The second statement can be added below at two or three times the space distance that exists between the lines of the first statement. The distance between the two statements is flexible and can be adjusted to fit within the frame area with accompanying pictorial materials or other written information.

Note that *within* a given statement of more than one line, the spacing between the lines should be *equal*, but by *increasing* the distance between statements, they will be easier to read. And although being separated is an indication that they are to be considered individually, the information in the statement is linked by the fact that they appear in the same frame.

Multiple statements within a single frame can be separated by color as well as distance. Bands of color can be placed as a background to add emphasis to the statements (see Figure 3-20). However, the use of colored bands as a background works best in frames that contain *only written information*. The style of type that is chosen for a graphic design also influences the way the lines are spaced.

Some of the lower-case letters of any type alphabet contain parts that extend below the base line on which they are placed. These letters are *g, j, p, q,* and *y,* which have *descenders* and therefore influence where the next lower line of type will be placed. It is important that each line of type be placed so that any descending letters from the line above do not interfere with it (see Figure 3-21).

Most brands of pressure-sensitive type have their alphabets spaced on the carrier sheet so that the graphic artist can use the space between the lines of type as a distance guide. When working

FIGURE 3-20 Multiple statements within a frame can be differentiated by using either a different type color for each or (as demonstrated here) a different-colored background band behind each statement.

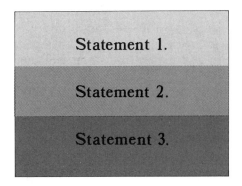

The spaces between lines of type should be kept wide enough to ensure against letter contact.

FIGURE 3-21 These lines of type have been placed too close together, and they interfere visually with each other.

on an acetate overlay, the graphic artist can use any line of type on the carrier sheet to establish where the next lower line will be placed. This spacing process is quite simple and works with most alphabet styles.

First, apply a line of type to the overlay where desired, and give the finished line a final burnish through the backing sheet (see Figure 3-22).

Next, place the carrier sheet over the just-completed line of type so that any row of letters *in the upper-case alphabet* falls on the base line (slipsheet upper edge) along which the burnished line of type is placed (see Figure 3-23). Then, being careful not to shift the carrier sheet resting on the overlay, reach down to the bottom of the overlay and pull the slipsheet under it *down* until the upper edge of the slipsheet falls to the bottom and aligns with the next

FIGURE 3-22 Transfer down a complete line of type along the slipsheet edge, on the acetate overlay.

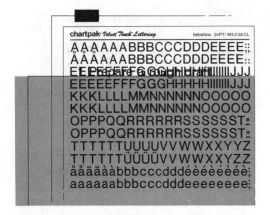

FIGURE 3-23 Place the type carrier sheet over the completed line of words (shown in Figure 3-22). Align any row of letters in the upper-case alphabet on the carrier sheet, with the line of type on the acetate overlay sheets (Courtesy of *Chartpak*).

FIGURE 3-25 The result of the movement of the slipsheet (described in Figure 3-24) is to move the sheet edge down, one row of type. Next, remove the carrier sheet and check the parallel alignment of the slipsheet edge in its new position with the T square before applying a new row of type.

lower row of letters on the carrier sheet (see Figures 3-24 and 3-25).

After pulling the slipsheet and aligning the top edge with the entire row of type on the carrier sheet, the carrier sheet can be removed and placed aside.

FIGURE 3-24 Be careful not to move the carrier sheet resting on the acetate overlay (shown in Figure 3-23), grasp the bottom on the slipsheet, and pull it gently down until the top of the slipsheet edge moves down to the bottom of the next row of type on the carrier sheet (Courtesy of *Chartpak*).

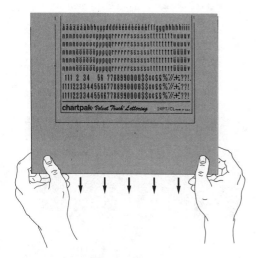

A base line has now been established for the next line of type. However, before burnishing down any new characters, *double-check* the slipsheet edge with the T square to make sure that it is exactly parallel. Make any small adjustments before burnishing down the next row of words.

This process can be repeated as often as necessary and will produce exactly parallel lines of type without interference from any lower-case descending letters.

Columns

Just as the slipsheet under the acetate overlay supplies a base line for words and sentences, a vertical guideline is also frequently needed. This guideline is important when applying columns of words or numbers (see Figure 3-26). To be clear and legible, the words in a column must be placed so that the first letter of each entry is exactly in alignment with all the others in that column.

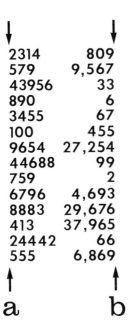

a	b
2314	809
579	9,567
43956	33
890	6
3455	67
100	455
9654	27,254
44688	99
759	2
6796	4,693
8883	29,676
413	37,965
24442	66
555	6,869

FIGURE 3-26 The series of numerical entries of a column, whether aligned vertically by the first number of each entry (as seen in column *a*) or arranged vertically for addition (as seen in column *b*) must be placed with great accuracy. A vertical slipsheet is a necessity in both cases.

As in horizontal line spacing, the vertical guideline for columns should be movable and adjustable. Therefore, a second slipsheet is called for. Since the vertical guideline for a column will remain the same, no matter how many entries are to be inserted, this slipsheet should be placed *beneath* the horizontal guideline slipsheet because the horizontal slipsheet is moved much more often.

This system is characterized by three active layers of graphic materials. First is the *vertical* slipsheet, over which is placed the *horizontal* slipsheet, over which is placed the *acetate overlay* on which the type will eventually be placed.

For this process, the initial placement of the acetate on the drafting desk or work surface is the same as that described earlier. Align the T square on the work surface. Butt the lower edge of an acetate sheet against the T square shaft, and tape down the upper edge of the acetate with masking or cellophane tape (see Figure 3-27).

The first slipsheet to be placed is the vertical one, and this can be accomplished in either of two ways. If the desk or work surface you are using has accurate parallel edges, the T square can be placed on the top edge of the work surface, and the slipsheet can be aligned with the vertically placed shaft (see Figure 3-28). Since the vertical slipsheet is moved less often than the horizontal sheet, the vertical sheet should be held down with tape after it has been aligned with the T square shaft.

If the slipsheet placement process described above is impractical because of the type of work surface or desk being used, or if the T square shaft is not long enough to reach over the area where the acetate is taped down, another method can be used. For this method, a *transparent triangle* is needed in addition to the T square. This triangle, a readily obtainable graphic measuring and drawing

FIGURE 3-27 The first step in establishing a vertical slipsheet for column entries consists of taping a sheet of acetate to the desk top or working surface with the aid of a T square (as described earlier).

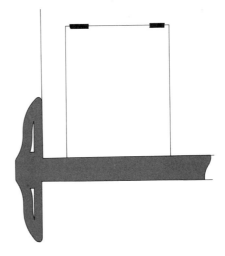

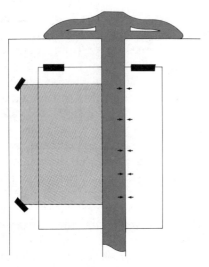

FIGURE 3-28 If the desk or working surface you are using has parallel edges on the top and sides, the T square can be positioned vertically. The slipsheet can then be placed beneath the acetate sheet and aligned with the T square shaft edge.

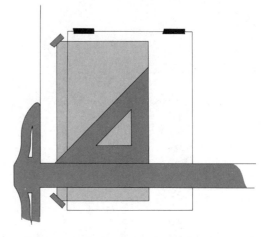

FIGURE 3-29 With the aid of a transparent triangle guide, the vertical slipsheet can also be positioned with the T square in a horizontal position. Place the triangle against the aligned T square shaft as shown, and position the slipsheet under the acetate overlay so that the vertical edge of the slipsheet matches the vertical edge of the triangle. Tape the corners of the slipsheet down to the desk surface after the alignment procedure.

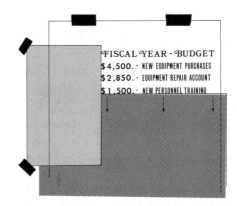

FIGURE 3-30 After the placement of the vertical slipsheet, a horizontal slipsheet may also be added to guide the placement of horizontal lines of type. When moving the horizontal slipsheet down for each new entry line, the vertical slipsheet is not moved.

tool, is available in transparent plastic (recommended for this process). The triangle used must have a 90-degree right-angle edge.

After butting the lower edge of the acetate sheet against the horizontal edge of the T square and taping the upper edge of the acetate to the working surface (as described earlier), the T square is left in place. The triangle is placed against and along the T square shaft to form a right-angle guide for the placement of the vertical slipsheet. The slipsheet under the acetate sheet and the two measuring tools can then be easily aligned and taped down (see Figure 3-29).

After the placement of the vertical slipsheet, the horizontal slipsheet can be aligned and, if necessary, taped down. This forms a perfect guide for the placement of column entries.

The first letter or symbol on each column line is placed so that it contacts the edge of the vertical slipsheet guide. (see Figure 3-30).

Word Centering

Centering one or more words above a column or as a title for pictorial material appearing in a frame may at first seem to be a minor technical process. However, since this same process is a major factor in the copy fitting of the entire frame, it must be carefully considered. Regardless of the type style of the alphabet being used in any graphic design, each letter occupies a certain fixed space. When the spaces of the letters (and the spaces between them) are combined, they create a fixed word length. This word length can then be divided, either by exact measurement or eye judgment, and the center point of the word can then be aligned with the center point of the column or pictorial material.

The first step is to establish a base line for the word to be centered. If the centered word is to be placed above a column or pictorial material, establish the base line with T square and slipsheet in the manner already described. Make sure that the base line is sufficiently above the first entry of the column or edge of the pictorial material so that any lower-case descending letters do not cause interference. If the centered word is to be placed below a column or pictorial material, establish the base line down, from the bottom word or edge. The distance from the base line to the lower edge should be the height of a *capital* letter plus approximately one-half that height (see Figure 3–31).

Having established a base line for the type, the second step is to determine, by measurement, the midpoint of the space into which the heading word or words will be placed. This is best done on the acetate overlay, even if the edges of the background or materials are being measured beneath it.

Any accurate ruler may be used, but its markings should at least be in $\frac{1}{8}$-inch increments. Align the ruler edge along the slipsheet base line established earlier, with the left end of the ruler aligned with the first word or left edge of the column, or the vertical edge of the slipsheet (see Figures 3–32A and

3–32B). The left end of the ruler can be aligned with the left vertical edge of the column by eye judgment—the distance between the base line for the heading and the column itself is so small that the possibility of inaccuracy is minimal.

Naturally, when measuring the

FIGURE 3–31 When placing words below a picture or column, establish the slipsheet edge, down from the bottom edge of the picture or column a distance equal to the height of a capital letter (of the type you are using) *plus* half again that height.

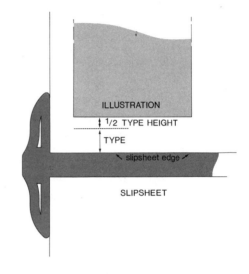

FIGURE 3–32A To establish the midpoint of a column, each of whose entries are the same width, simply place a ruler at the top or bottom of the column and measure its width and divide this number in half. The midpoint of the column may be marked on the acetate with a felt-tipped marker that has non-permanent ink. Use this same procedure when measuring a photograph or other illustration.

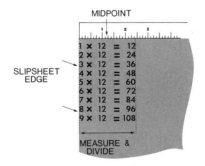

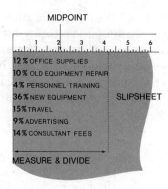

MIDPOINT

12% OFFICE SUPPLIES
10% OLD EQUIPMENT REPAIR
4% PERSONNEL TRAINING
36% NEW EQUIPMENT   SLIPSHEET
15% TRAVEL
9% ADVERTISING
14% CONSULTANT FEES

MEASURE & DIVIDE

FIGURE 3–32B To establish the midpoint of a column, each of whose entries are of different widths, place the ruler at the top or bottom of the column and measure the width of the longest entry. Divide this width in half and mark the midpoint of the column on the slipsheet edge on the acetate with a felt-tipped marker containing nonpermanent ink.

width of a column composed of transfer type, the measurement must be made on the acetate sheet. However, as mentioned earlier, when measuring the width of pictorial material that is part of a background, the measurement should also be made on the acetate overlay because the midpoint must be marked, and this mark must be *removable.*

Having measured the width of the column or pictorial material and divided that width in half, the best way to mark the midpoints is with the use of a fine-pointed felt-tipped, or nylon-tipped, marker such as a Flair brand or Pilot brand. The color of the marker is unimportant as long as it is clearly visible and the marker being used has *nonpermanent* ink. Nonpermanent marker ink can be wiped off the acetate with your finger or a damp cotton swab (such as a Q Tip) after the word-centering procedure has been completed. *Do not* use a ball point pen to indicate the midpoint, as the pressure of the point will leave a dingy mark on the acetate surface, which can show up in the photographed frame at a later point.

When indicating the midpoint, it may be necessary to touch the marker tip to the acetate several times to make sure that the mark is large enough to be easily visible. Allow the marker ink to dry several minutes before going on to the next step and applying the transfer type.

The next procedure is to determine the length of the work or heading that is to be placed above or below the column or pictorial material.

Take the carrier sheet of the transfer type you have selected and place it on a clear, well-lit area of the desk or work surface. Be sure to leave the blue wax paper backing sheet in place, under the carrier sheet.

Place a small piece of tracing paper over the carrier sheet. On this small piece of tracing paper, place a ruled line in pencil, much longer than is needed for the heading work of the column. The ruled pencil line can be placed approximately in the center of the sheet and should extend off the left edge of the sheet (see Figure 3–33).

Then, using a fine-pointed, soft

FIGURE 3–33 Place a small piece of tracing paper, with a ruled pencil line running off the left edge, over the type carrier sheet (Courtesy of *Chartpak*).

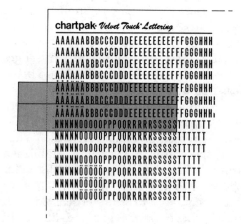

lead pencil, trace out the word or words of the desired heading.

The tracing paper sheet can be moved and positioned for each letter. The letters being traced can be merely outlined. They need not be shaded in with the pencil.

This tracing process is important because it establishes the exact word length that will be fitted to the column. Therefore, take as much care and be as exact in the tracing process as you would if you were actually transferring type to the acetate surface.

If you are tracing a title or heading that has two or more words, make sure that the distance between the words is the same as would be required in the actual transfer heading (see Figures 3-34A, and 3-34B).

FIGURE 3-34A The letters of the traced work should be spaced the same as they would be if the type were being transferred from the carrier sheet.

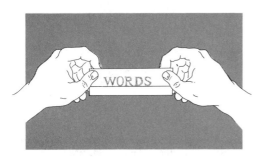

FIGURE 3-34B When more than one is traced down, the spacing between the words should be the same as it is intended to be in the final transfer-type version.

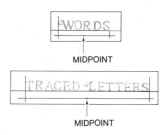

FIGURE 3-35 Having completed the word-tracing process, draw two straight-line brackets at the beginning and end of the word or words. These brackets should be butted against the first and last letters and extended down $3/4$ of an inch or so. The distance between the brackets is then divided in half, and the midpoint of the word or words is marked on the slip of tracing paper.

Having completed the word tracing, draw two straight-line "brackets" at the beginning and end of the word or entire statement. These lines, which are butted against the first and last letters, should extend down from the base line $3/4$ of an inch or so, and for reasons of accuracy they should be drawn with a ruler, T square, or straightedge (see Figure 3-35). The distance between the brackets can then be measured, and when divided in half, will indicate the exact center of the word or phrase.

Note that in a phrase consisting of two or more words, the spaces *between* the words are counted in the total length. The brackets marking the first and last letter edges, and the measured midpoint, should be clearly marked on the tracing paper sheet in pencil.

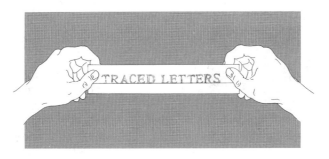

The tracing paper can now be placed over the acetate overlay sheet and aligned so that the traced letters fall on the slip-sheet edge, and the midpoint mark on the tracing paper sheet is exactly over the column midpoint mark (indicated by the felt-tipped marker used earlier).

The acetate sheet can now be marked (again with a felt-tipped marker) to indicate the exact position of the column heading. This can be done in either of two ways. Holding the aligned tracing paper sheet in place, measure the distance from the two brackets to the left edge of the acetate. Then, having removed the tracing paper, the acetate can be marked with a felt-tipped pen.

A shortcut to this method, which can also be quite accurate if done carefully, is to hold the center of the tracing paper sheet in alignment and slip the marker tip under the slightly lifted left and right edges of the sheet to mark the

acetate beneath (see Figures 3-36 and 3-37).

Finally, when applying transfer type to the area indicated by these guide marks on the acetate, try to keep the same letter and word spacing that was used in the preparation of the tracing paper sheet. This will ensure that the actual transfer-type heading will be exactly centered in relation to the column or pictorial material (see Figures 3-38 and 3-39).

FIGURE 3-37 Another method of marking the dimensions of the column heading on the acetate overlay is to position the tracing paper sheet so that its marked midpoint aligns with the column midpoint marked on the acetate earlier. Then, holding the tracing paper in place, gently lift the right and left edges of the tracing paper and mark the acetate beneath with a felt-tipped marker at the beginning and end brackets of the word or words. Be sure that you do not move the tracing paper sheet during this procedure.

FIGURE 3-36 The tracing paper sheet is positioned on the acetate overlay with the traced words resting on the slipsheet edge. The midpoint of the traced word or words is aligned with the midpoint of the column or illustration (marked on the acetate earlier). A ruler is then positioned over the tracing paper sheet, and the distance between the brackets and the left edge of the acetate is measured and noted on a separate piece of paper. Be sure that you do not inadvertently move the tracing paper during the measuring process.

FIGURE 3-38 Even when a title or a column heading is wider than the column or columns it is over, the same midpoint measuring process can be applied.

Subscription Inquiry Rate

YEAR	INQUIRIES	ACTUAL
1970	1203	901
1971	1444	1309
1972	1367	1122
1973	3245	2900
1974	4055	3435
1975	4566	4187
1976	5142	4567
1977	5200	4400
1978	5867	5001
1979	6566	5367
1980	7578	6888

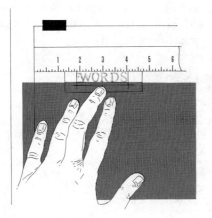

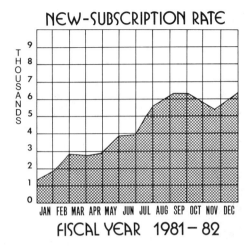

NEW-SUBSCRIPTION RATE

FISCAL YEAR 1981−82

FIGURE 3–39 Illustrations, pictures, graphs, and charts can also be fitted with centered titles or headings in the same manner as columns of numbers or words.

COPY FITTING AND BALANCING

Since the 11-by-14-inch acetate overlay is considerably larger than the 6½-by-9¾-inch standard frame size, it is necessary to establish guidelines for the type and pictorial materials as the frame design is being created. Here, the cardboard format guide described in Chapter 2 is an indispensable tool.

The goal is to make sure that all the elements of each frame design fit into the 2:3 length-to-width ratio, that is, the dimensions of the 35-mm slide format that these designs will be photographed to fit.

The cardboard format guide has an opening that represents the exact length-to-width relationships that are present in a 35-mm film slide. In fact, the format guide can be considered a giant slide and used as a form of preview indicating how a design will translate to the final film version, along with its more practical application as a copy-fitting device.

In the copy-fitting process, the format guide establishes vertical and horizontal guidelines into which all type, words, and pictorial material must be fitted if they are to appear in the slide.

When applying lines of transfer type to the acetate, the format guide is frequently fitted in place to ensure that the length of the sentence or information is within proper limits. Since the dimensions of the format guide represent the extreme edges of the slide, the type and pictorial materials should be placed so that they are insulated by at least ¼ to ½ inches, both vertically and horizontally, from the format edges. This central area of usable space is then approximately 6 by 9¼ inches (see Figure 3-40). The format guide is primarily intended as a general measurement guide for type or pictorial material that *must* be fitted into the slide in its entirety. However, pictorial material and parts of backgrounds need not be cut to fit the format guidelines. A part of them can be allowed to extend beyond the guide areas if not crucial to the viewer's understanding of the information in the frame.

FIGURE 3–40 Since the dimensions of the format guide represent the extreme edges of the slide frame, the type and pictorial materials should be fitted so that they are not closer than ¼ to ½ inch from the edges of the format guide. This central area of usable space is approximately 6 by 9¼ inches.

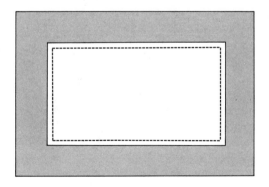

In some cases, it is in the best interests of the design and clarity of the frame to use this effect. By "dropping" illustrative materials so that part of them "falls off" the frame edge, more space is left for any type required (see Figures 3-41A and 3-41B). As will be demonstrated, the format guide is very useful

FIGURE 3-41A When using an illustration or picture as part of a frame design, consider whether it may be too large or whether it contains any superfluous visual information that could be cropped. This illustration uses up roughly half of the frame space and therefore crowds the words that must appear in the frame.

FIGURE 3-41B Here, the same illustration has been dropped down off the lower and right edges of the frame. Although the illustration still works visually, the frame is more successful because a larger, more readable type can be used to fill the extra space made available. Most of the hand appearing in the first version is not needed to understand the action being called for, and it can therefore be eliminated.

in positioning such elements as graphs, charts, diagrams, drawings, or photographs in the background, and aligning these elements with the type on the acetate overlay. The format guide can be fitted over the overlay or background or both as often as necessary while work progresses on the flat.

When the type overlay has been completed, the format guide can be placed over it and shifted so that the entire copy appearing in the frame is balanced in relation to the edges.

When designing the frame, copy balancing is as important as copy fitting. The difference between *copy fitting* and *copy balancing* is that copy fitting takes place as the type is being applied, word by word, on the acetate overlay; copy balancing takes place after *all* the type has been applied, and the total type copy on the overlay must be balanced in relation to the frame edges.

Here, the format guide again comes into use. For example, in a frame that has a simple statement or written example (without any background illustrations or pictures), the beginning and end of the statement should be equally distant from the right and left frame edges. The statement should also be positioned so that it is equally distant from the top and bottom of the frame (see Figures 3-42 through 3-45). The statement shown in these illustrations was finally balanced within the frame, not by moving the acetate, but by shifting the format guide and marking the balanced alignment on the acetate overlay.

The copy can be aligned within the format guide by eye judgment, or by using a ruler if absolute accuracy is required.

When the copy has been balanced to the desired position, fit the T square

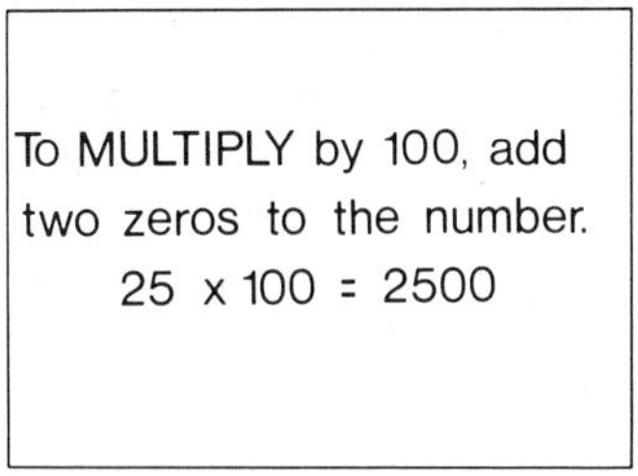

To MULTIPLY by 100, add
two zeros to the number.
25 x 100 = 2500

FIGURE 3-42 In this frame, the statement is too near the left edge of the frame.

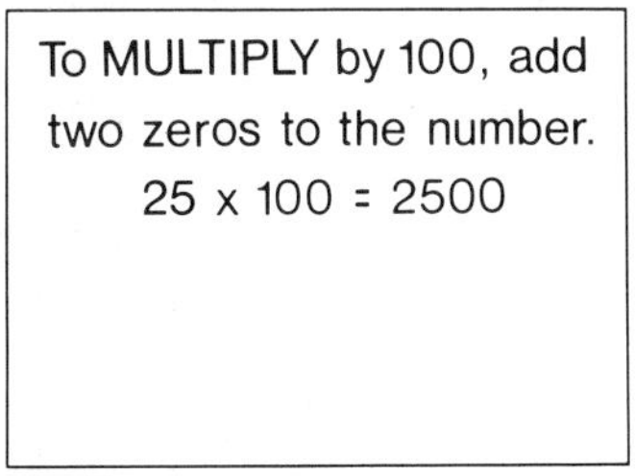

To MULTIPLY by 100, add
two zeros to the number.
25 x 100 = 2500

FIGURE 3-43 In this frame, the statement is too near the top edge of the frame. There is dead space at the bottom of the frame.

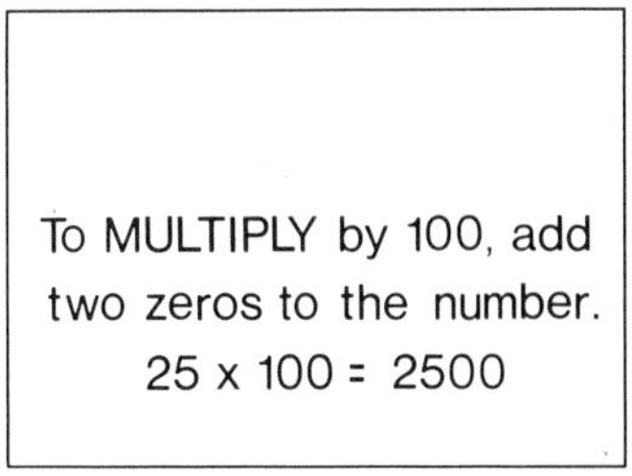

To MULTIPLY by 100, add
two zeros to the number.
25 x 100 = 2500

FIGURE 3-44 In this frame, the statement is too near the bottom edge of the frame. There is dead space at the top of the frame.

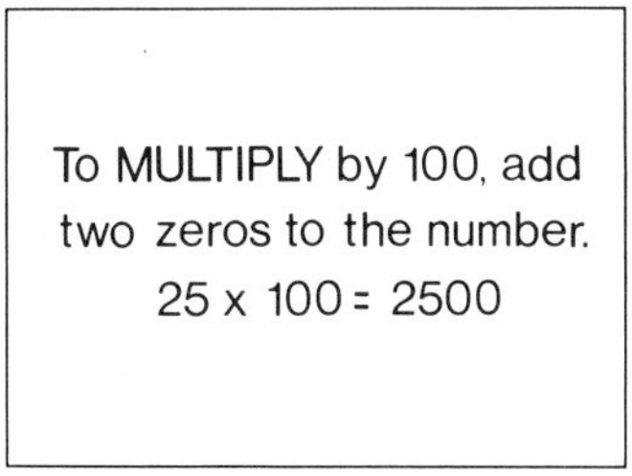

To MULTIPLY by 100, add
two zeros to the number.
25 x 100 = 2500

FIGURE 3-45 In this frame, the statement is equidistant from the four edges of the frame and is therefore properly placed.

below the format guide and butt the lower edge of the guide to the T square shaft to ensure that the format edges are exactly parallel to the copy lines of type. Then, holding the format guide in place, mark a small bracket at each of the four corners of the guide on the acetate overlay by using a nonpermanent felt-tipped marker. These brackets are left in place as an aid in preparing the background for the acetate overlay, as well as being guides for fitting the finished flat within the camera viewfinder during the photocopying process (see Figures 3–46 and 3–47).

The format guide can also be used to balance the copy on the overlay with both the edges of the frame and existing illustrative material in the background beneath it. (This process is described in Chapter 4, "The Background.")

FIGURE 3-46 Place the format guide over the type on the acetate overlay and move the guide until the type appears balanced with relation to the edges of the cutout. Use a ruler if necessary to ensure an accurate distance between the edges of the type and the format cutout edges. Then place the T square under the format guide and butt the guide against the T square shaft to ensure that the guide edges are parallel to the type lines. Mark the acetate at the corners of the format guide with a felt-tipped marker.

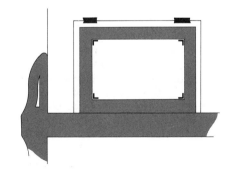

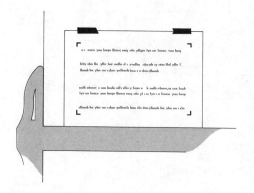

FIGURE 3-47 With the format guide removed, the felt-tipped marker brackets act as a guide for the placement of the background sheet or sheets. The marker brackets can be removed from the acetate sheet later with a damp piece of cotton or a swab.

SOME FINAL SUGGESTIONS

Always try to keep the number of words and lines of type appearing in a frame to a minimum. Wordiness is to be avoided at all costs because it constricts the information flow of any module.

When applying a line of type to the overlay, never break a word at the end of the line. If the word is too long to fit the statement within the format guidelines, shift it to the next line down.

In the design of the sequence of frames for a module, attempt to keep as many frames as possible in a *horizontal* rather than a *vertical* orientation. Shifting back and forth from horizontal to vertical formats during the frame sequence is confusing and can present technical problems should you wish to photograph vertical slides into a film strip at some future point (see Figure 3-48).

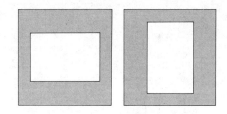

FIGURE 3-48 On the left is the horizontal slide orientation. On the right is the vertical slide orientation. Layouts should be designed to fit the horizontal orientation, which is used universally for sound slide modules.

GLOSSARY

Acetate overlay An 11-by-14-inch acetate sheet that is used to hold all transfer type for the frame.

Base line See *guideline.*

Brackets Ruled lines, in either pencil or pen, that are placed so that they butt against the first and last letters of a word or phrase. The bracket lines extend below the line of type, and the distance between them can be measured to determine the exact center of the word or phrase for positioning over a column of type, or pictorial matter at a later point.

Carrier sheet The plastic page on which the manufacturer prints the transfer-type alphabets.

Columns of type Transfer-type numbers and/or words arranged to form vertical rows.

Copy balancing The process of fitting the completed graphic design within the format guide so that it is equally distant from the edges of the guide.

Copy fitting The process of designing and making the frame layout so that it will fit into the 2:3 length-to-width ratio of the 35-mm slide (see *format guide*).

Cotton swab A thin plastic or cardboard shaft with a spun cotton pad or ball at both ends. Cotton swabs (such as Q Tip brand), although originally designed for medical or personal use, are also useful in many aspects of graphic design.

Descending letters The lower-case letters *g, j, p, q,* and *y,* whose descending parts extend below the base line (see *lower-case letters*).

Falloff A term applied to illustrations and pictorial material whose area partially extends beyond the edges of the slide mount cutout when they are photographed into slides. Sometimes referred to as "dropping" illustrative material.

Felt-tipped marker An ink-filled pen wth a fine-pointed hard felt or nylon tip. The type of marker generally used for audio-visual graphic design has nonpermanent (removable) ink.

Format central area The area of usable space, for graphic designs, as indicated by the boundaries of the format guide. The format central area is approximately ½ inch smaller on all sides than the actual format guide cutout.

Format guide A cardboard mat or frame that is cut out to have an opening whose dimensions are in a ratio that reflects the ratio of the film frame size that will eventually be used to produce the final slide version of the graphic design. For 35-mm slides, the length-to-width ratio of the film frame is 2 to 3. The format guide, which also has a length-to-width ratio of 2 to 3, is used in determining the placement of type, words, backgrounds, and pictorial material and in copy balancing and copy fitting.

Freehand drawing A drawing in any medium, done without any mechanical aids. A sketch, or rough guide drawing, for a layout, or one that will be transformed to a finished illustration at a later point.

Guideline A ruled line or edge of a slipsheet placed beneath the acetate overlay, used for the placement of lines of transfer type (see *slipsheet*).

Line spacing The distance between lines of transfer or other kinds of type.

Lower-case letters Any noncapitalized letter of the alphabet.

Masking tape A thin paper adhesive tape, usually manilla colored, available in a variety of widths. Used to hold graphic materials to each other where a nonpermanent bond is needed.

Multiple-line statements A transfer-type sentence whose length exceeds one line.

Pictorial material Photographs, maps, graphs, charts, or any artwork used in the production of a frame layout.

Ruled line A straight line made in pencil or ink with the aid of a ruler.

Slide orientation The positioning of the 35-mm film frame so that the longer edges of the rectangle are vertical or horizontal.

Slipsheet A sheet of thin paper, such as typewriter paper, that is placed and aligned beneath the acetate overlay. The upper edge of the slipsheet acts as a guideline or base line for transfer type being applied to the overlay.

Soft lead pencil There is actually no lead in a pencil; the term refers to the graphite core. A soft "lead" pencil is usually a 2B, 4B, or 6B. The 6B is the softest core pencil, 4B is a little harder, and 2B is harder still. All B designated pencils are considered "soft," and the one selected for use by the artist is dictated by personal choice or the specific needs of the artwork.

Straightedge A ruler or other drawing instrument with a perfectly straight edge.

Tracing type The process of outlining transfer type on the carrier sheet on a slip of tracing paper for the purpose of measuring the length of a word or phrase.

Transparent triangle A transparent plastic triangle used as a drawing aid and, in conjunction with a T square, for the alignment of graphic materials. The most useful type of transparent triangle, in slide format design, is one that has a *right angle* (90 degrees).

Upper-case letters Capital letters of the alphabet.

Word centering The process of placing a word or phrase in the exact center above or below a column, a sentence, or pictorial material.

Working surface A drafting desk or a parallel-edge drawing board.

4
THE BACKGROUND

THE BACKGROUND

The background layer of the frame layout is more than just a backdrop for the type-carrying acetate overlay.

The background is a valuable vehicle for both the enhancement and the clarification of type information on the overlay, but it is equally important as a display area for all the pictorial material, as well as maps, charts, graphs, and so on. Even when no pictorial material is to be included in the background of a frame, the selective use of color can not only greatly improve the readability of the type but emphasize special items and direct the viewer's attention to them. Pictorial materials are *floated* on a color background by a process that will be described shortly.

The only instances in which a color background would not be appropriate would be where pictorial materials are so large that, when photographed, they fill the entire camera frame. Although full-frame pictorial materials are perfectly acceptable in frame designs, these illustrations should have the same length-to-width ratio of 2 to 3 that was described earlier in relation to the format guide.

Pictorial materials that do not fit into the 2:3 ratio will have to be cropped in order to fit the slide film format. *Cropping* means that when an odd-sized piece of pictorial material is to be photographed to fit, full sized, into the 35-mm film format, the copy camera is moved nearer or farther away to accommodate the difference between the size of the illustration and the size of film format.

Although cropping is a camera manipulation (see Chapter 6, "The Camera"), materials that are slated for full-frame reproduction will need *partial backgrounds* if they are of odd sizes.

These partial backgrounds can be established with the aid of the format guide or by direct measurement. For example, assume that a 4-by-12-inch piece of illustrative material must be fitted into the slide frame format and be reproduced as large as possible. During the photography process, the 12-inch length of the illustration can be cropped to fit exactly edge to edge within the horizontal-oriented film format. However, the areas above and below the illustration will then be blank. Therefore, a background must be introduced into these areas.

The best approach to the installation of a background is to place the illustration on a larger sheet of colored paper, the size of which is determined by the total dimensions fitting the 2:3 ratio required by the film format.

In this example of a 4-by-12-inch illustration, if the 12-inch length is the horizontal dimension, then a vertical height of 8 inches is required (8 inches to 12 inches being a 2:3 ratio). Therefore, an additional 4 inches (2 inches above and 2 inches below) of background is needed to fit this odd-sized illustration into the film format (see Figures 4-1A and 4-1B).

FIGURE 4-1A A 4-by-12-inch illustration of a computer keyboard must be fitted into the 2:3 ratio frame size.

FIGURE 4-1B If, when fitting the illustration into the frame size, the left and right edges of the illustration are butted visually against the left and right edges of the frame, a space of approximately 2 inches above and below the illustration will remain to be filled by a background.

As additional insurance of a proper fit, add 1 inch of background border to the right and left edges of the illustration as well.

The total size of the background sheet then needed is 8 inches high by 14 inches long. During the photography of this frame at a later point, the camera can be adjusted to cover an 8-by-12 inch area (see Figures 4-2 and 4-3).

If frequently called upon to produce backgrounds for odd-sized or over-sized illustrative materials, a shortcut to the methods just described would consist of a using a very large background sheet, placing the illustrations on it, and doing all the sizing and fitting of the material

FIGURE 4-2 The spaces above and below the illustration must be filled with some sort of background or the illustration cannot be photographed properly.

FIGURE 4-3 Place odd-sized illustrations on a larger sheet of colored paper. During the photography process, the camera can be adjusted to fit the illustration into the slide format.

to the film format dimensions by eye, through the copy camera viewfinder. This method works well but requires practice and a thorough familiarity with the copy camera and copystand.

THE BACKGROUND SHEET

The material best suited to the production of the background is high-quality colored paper. Two kinds of paper can be recommended: Pantone brand by Letraset, Inc., and Color Aid paper. Tissue paper, colored oak tag paper, and construction paper are *not* recommended for backgrounds because they frequently lack uniformity of color and surface. Pantone and Color Aid papers are specially prepared for graphic arts use and are available from art and graphic suppliers. Pantone paper comes in 20-by-26-inch sheets and can be cut down and used for several backgrounds. Color Aid paper is available in 18-by-24-inch sheets and 6-by-9-inch sheets. Both product brands are of the high-surface quality required of materials that are to be photographed under magnification.

The usual method of cutting these materials is with a metal or metal-edged ruler and a single-edge razor blade, stencil knife, or X-Acto knife. Scissors are *not* recommended because of minute flaws created along the edges of cut paper by the "sawing" action of the scissor blades. Pantone and Color Aid papers are nonglossy and come in solid colors.

Solid-color backgrounds work best in module design because they confuse the eye least. However, patterned or printed papers can be used for backgrounds if the design is such that it does not interfere with the type of other pictorial material in the frame.

Do not use *textured* papers. Textured papers add the shadow of the texture to the pattern already present on the surface, and they create a difficult-to-read visual surface. Textured papers also lift or raise the acetate overlay and make the type lose its sharp edges when photographed, causing even more visual confusion.

Both Pantone and Color Aid are available in a large selection of colors, and Pantone also offers a catalog-type swatch book that can be purchased if colors need to be selected in advance.

Before selecting a color or a combination of colors for a background, the color of the type on the acetate overlay should be considered. Black or dark blue type will not photograph well against a dark-colored background. White will also be difficult to see against a light-yellow or equally pale-colored background. Choose background colors that *contrast* with the type color being used.

Contrasting colors are more likely to attract the viewer's attention, and the words are much easier to read. If you wish to direct special emphasis to a word or phrase appearing in a frame, use colors that produce simultaneous contrast. Colors that contrast well in the ordinary sense would include yellow and green, black and yellow or pale blue, and so on.

Simultaneous contrast is an optical phenomenon that occurs when certain bright colors are placed in close proximity. The eye cannot focus on both of these colors at the same time, and if they are both sufficiently bright, the colors will seem to flicker or shimmer. Simultaneous contrast color combinations are red and blue, orange and green, violet and yellow, and black and yellow.

Many other illustrative graphic devices can be employed in frame design, and these will be covered in the following sections.

Cutting and Assembling the Background Sheet

In the preceding chapter we saw that when pictures or other illustrative materials are placed on the colored background sheet, they are *floated* over that background. This process simply means that an illustration is cut to the desired size and affixed to the background sheet, where desired, with the use of tape (see Figures 4–4, 4–5, and 4–6).

The illustration must be taped down to prevent it from shifting accidentally out of place during handling and during the photography process. Illustrative materials can be held in place on the background sheet by using a double-sided masking tape, which is positioned between the back of the illustration and the surface of the colored paper sheet.

Double-sided tape is, as the name implies, coated with adhesive on both sides. This tape is produced by a number of manufacturers in rolls of different widths. The most useful width for general application is either ¾ or 1 inch. To prevent the tape from sticking to itself while in the roll form, a nonadhesive strip of paper is wound with the double-coated tape.

This strip of paper is sometimes difficult to separate from the double-coated tape, especially if you are using small pieces. The best procedure here is to separate the paper liner from the double-coated *on the roll* and peel back the liner as pieces of the double-coated tape are being cut and used (see Figures 4-7, 4-8A, and 4-8B). Keep a small 1-inch leader of both liner and tape lifted from the roll, as this will make it easier to start the tape when it is needed again.

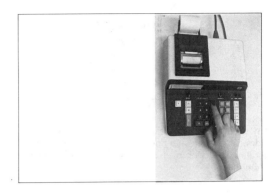

FIGURE 4-4 A half-frame illustration with a background sheet covering the left half of the frame.

FIGURE 4-5 A "dropped," or "bled," illustration, which leaves more room for type while still visually demonstrating a desired action.

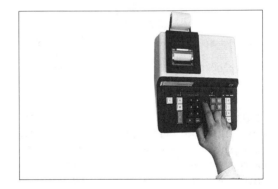

FIGURE 4-6 A cutout illustration that integrates the illustration with the colored background, eliminating the original background of the photograph.

FIGURE 4-7 Double-sided tape is sticky on both sides. The paper tape liner (upper flap) is peeled back to allow a section of double-sided tape to be removed from the roll.

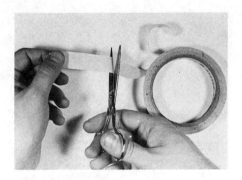

FIGURE 4-8A Cut pieces of double-sided tape directly from the roll, otherwise the tape will be difficult to handle.

FIGURE 4-8B Between uses, store the roll with an inch of leader and an inch of double-sided tape lifted from the roll to provide an easy start on the next job.

Double-sided tapes are somewhat difficult to handle because they stick to your fingers and graphic tools. Therefore, they should be cut to the desired size *before* application. The tape can be cut with scissors or even torn, and it should always be applied *to the back of the illustrative material first*. This is important because if the strip of tape applied to the back of the illustration is too

long, it can easily be trimmed before the illustration is adhered to the colored paper background sheet (see Figure 4-9). The excess part of a strip of tape can be trimmed with a scissors, or very carefully with a single-edge razor blade or stencil knife (see Figure 4-10). Remember that any tape protruding beyond the edges of the illustration may be picked up by the camera and ruin the quality of the final slide.

Application of the double-sided tape to the background sheet before positioning an illustration over it *should be avoided*. In this case, if any portion of the tape should protrude beyond the

FIGURE 4-9 Always place cut pieces of double-sided tape on the back of the illustration (rather than on the background sheet).

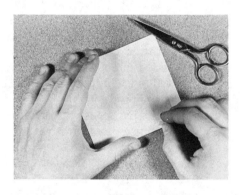

FIGURE 4-10 If a strip of double-sided tape is too long, it can easily be trimmed from the illustration edge by using scissors.

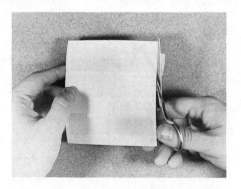

edges of the illustration, it will be impossible to remove without tearing or damaging the background colored sheet. For this reason, the illustration being taped down should be carefully aligned and measured before any pressure is applied to adhere it to the background sheet.

If repositioning an illustration is necessary, it will have to be peeled from the background sheet, and a new sheet of colored paper will usually be necessary. To properly align and fit illustrations to the background, the background sheet itself must first be cut properly.

The background sheet is rectangular for all standard module frames, and a good average size would be 10 by 12 inches. It should have sharp and accurately parallel edges. The most accurate cutting method involves the use of a T square.

Both Pantone and Color Aid papers are manufactured with properly cut edges, so the T square crosspiece can be butted against any edge for measurement or cutting. As mentioned earlier, the cutting of these materials should be accomplished with a single-edge razor blade, stencil knife, or X-Acto knife with a metal or metal-edged T square or ruler. Note that Pantone brand paper has a 1-inch-square grid printed on the back of each sheet, and this can be very useful in sizing and cutting out the background sheets.

The following cutting hints apply to all graphic materials: (1) always cut materials so that the stroke or hand movement is *toward* you—cutting horizontally or any other way increases the chance that the cutting blade will slip; and (2) change the cutting blade in your knife frequently—paper and acetate may seem to be soft materials, but they will dull cutting blades rapidly, thus causing frayed rather than cleanly cut edges (see Figure 4–11).

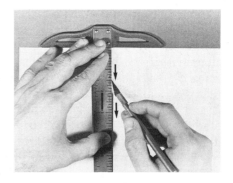

FIGURE 4–11 When cutting paper or other graphic materials with a T square and knife, always position the ruler or guide *vertically*, and make the cutting stroke from the top, toward you.

Illustrative materials that are to be taped down on the background sheet can be cut to the desired size in a similar manner. Whether cutting ordinary paper or photographs, a T square and cutting blade are a necessity. A small paper cutter such as that used in business offices or photographic labs, if it is available to you, can also be very useful in cutting small illustrations to the required size (see Figure 4–12).

The shape of illustrative materials is usually either rectangular or square, but these materials can also be specially cut to suit certain needs. This is particularly useful when photographs are part of

FIGURE 4–12 A hinged-blade type of paper cutter can be a useful tool for trimming backgrounds and illustrations.

your frame background and you wish to focus attention on a specific element appearing in one area of the image. Sometimes this can be accomplished by cropping the illustration in a tight rectangular or square shape (see Figures 4-13 and 4-14). Cropping the illustration or photograph provides an opportunity for focusing the viewer's attention by eliminating superfluous visual elements in the original image, *and* it can be very useful in supplying more blank space in the rest of the background for type information placed on the acetate overlay.

An illustration can also be further cropped by an outline-cutting process called *silhouetting*. Silhouette cutting of photographs is accomplished with the use of a fine-point razor knife, such as a stencil knife or an X-Acto knife. A swivel-type stencil knife is the best tool for cutting out images with intricate outlines because its blade will move in the same direction as the handle without having to shift the hand or illustration too frequently (see Figure 4-15). Regardless of the type of tool chosen for the cutting process, the objective is to separate the desired parts of the image from the rest of the photograph by cutting a *smooth* and *clean* outline around it (see Figure 4-16).

FIGURE 4-13 The main subject of this illustration is supposed to be someone talking on the telephone. As can easily be seen, a great deal more area and superfluous visual details are present in the illustration as well (such as the desk, books, office walls, and window).

FIGURE 4-14 By cutting off, or "cropping," excess visual details from the illustration, the viewer's attention can be drawn and focused on the main subject of the illustration. In addition, by reducing the total size of the illustration in this manner, much more area is provided for type in the final layout.

FIGURE 4-15 A stencil knife with a swivel-type blade.

FIGURE 4-16 By cutting out the outline of an illustration with a stencil knife, a visually effective silhouette can be produced.

Depending on the subject of the module, and the content demands of individual frame designs, this silhouetting process can provide the simplicity needed for illustrations while enhancing their visual interest in relation to the type content of the frame. (see Figures 4-17 and 4-18).

When cutting out parts of illustrations or photographs that are on heavy paper, it may be necessary to *touch up* the edges of these images. The white cut edges of the photograph or artwork may become noticeable, especially if the background sheet is of a darker color.

If you are using a black-and-white photograph for an illustration, use a soft lead pencil (4B or 6B) to color the edges of the cutout. The best way to accomplish this is to hold the picture up in one hand, and pointing the pencil point toward yourself, gently color the edges of the picture with the side of the pencil point. This method of coloring will enable you to see clearly without accidentally extending the color onto the surface of the illustration (see Figures 4-19, 4-20, and 4-21).

When using a colored photograph or illustration that is on heavy paper, use a colored pencil or inexpensive felt-

FIGURE 4-17 After the cutting process, the silhouetted illustration can be positioned and taped down to a background sheet.

FIGURE 4-19 The edges of a cutout photograph or other illustrative material are usually quite apparent. This is especially true when the illustration is to be mounted on a dark-colored background sheet.

FIGURE 4-18 The silhouetted illustration can provide needed visual simplicity while enhancing the information content and interest of the frame design.

CUTTING LONG-DISTANCE PHONE RATES...

for small businesses.

1. Determine an average monthly amount for business calls.

FIGURE 4-20 To color the edges of a cutout illustration, hold the illustration in one hand and gently rub the edges with the side of a pencil point while pointing the pencil itself toward you.

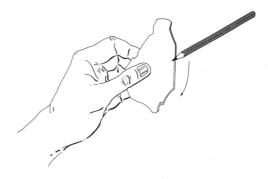

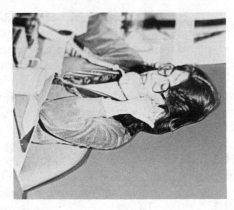

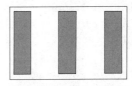

tipped marker to color the edges of the cutout. Exact color matching to the colors in the image is not always necessary, the objective here being to simply soften the visual attraction of the stark white edge.

Photographs and illustrations that are on thin paper will not usually have to be edge-colored prior to placement on the background sheet.

Having sized and cut out both the background sheet and the illustrations that are to be floated over it, the next step is to align and place the illustrations.

As mentioned earlier, the double-sided tape is placed on the back of the illustration first, and the excess tape trimmed away if necessary. The entire back of the illustration does not have to be coated with tape. For small rectangular or square illustrations, one or two strips of tape near the edge will be sufficient to hold it in place (see Figures 4-22 and 4-23). Larger illustrations will of course require more tape, especially if they are on very thin paper which has a tendency to curl up at the edges of the illustration. It is *not* advisable to use

rubber cement or glue for adhering illustrations to the background sheet. These will soak through the paper and will cause either stains or indented areas that will be difficult to remove. Likewise, cellophane tape should *not* be used to hold illustrations down. Even so-called invisible cellophane tape (which has a dull finish) will easily be picked up by the camera and ruin the professional look of the design.

When applying double-sided tape to the back of silhouette-cut illustrations, use small pieces of tape to follow the outline as close to the edge as possible (see Figures 4-24 and 4-25).

The alignment of square or rectangular illustrations on the background

FIGURE 4-24 When applying double-sided tape to the back of a silhouette-cut illustration, use small pieces to follow the outline edge.

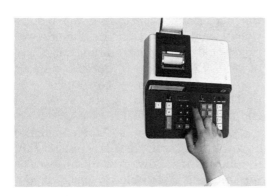

FIGURE 4-25 By following the edges of the silhouette-cut illustration with double-sided tape, the illustration will uniformly adhere to the background sheet when positioned.

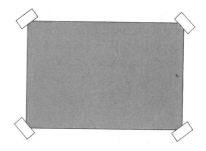

FIGURE 4-26 To keep the background sheet from accidentally shifting during the positioning and taping down of an illustration, place small pieces of masking tape over the corners of the background sheet and hold it securely down on the desk or working surface.

sheet is accomplished by using a T square. The T square crosspiece is butted against any edge of the background sheet, and the T square shaft becomes a guide for one of the edges of the illustration. To keep the background sheet from accidentally shifting during the positioning of the illustration, the sheet should be temporarily held in place on the desk or working surface with small pieces of masking tape at the corners (see Figure 4-26).

Having then placed the T square in the desired position, any edge of the illustration can be placed in contact with the T square shaft. This alignment should be done *only* with the edge of the illustration. The rest of the illustration should be held away from contact with the background sheet until you are sure it is aligned and positioned properly. Remember that illustrations can not be repositioned without risk of damage to them and the background sheet (see Figure 4-27).

FIGURE 4-27 When taping an illustration to the background sheet, butt the lower edge of the illustration against the shaft of the positioned T square. Keep the top and center of the illustration bent away from the background sheet until you are sure that the illustration is properly aligned.

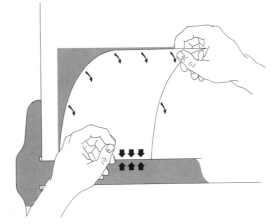

When alignment and positioning of the illustration have been accomplished, *gently* feed down the rest of the illustration so that the double-sided tape on the back can take hold. Begin by pressing along the front of the illustration, on the edge that is butted against the T square shaft. Do this process slowly, and *do not* apply a great amount of pressure (see Figures 4-28 and 4-29).

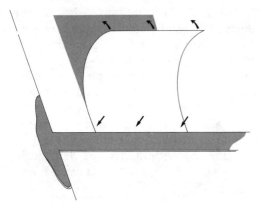

FIGURE 4-28 When the positioning of the illustration has been accomplished, *gently* feed down the rest of the illustration so that the double-sided tape can take hold to the background sheet.

FIGURE 4-29 After the illustration has been tacked down, remove the T square and place a clean sheet of thin paper (such as typewriter paper) over the illustration. Then press the illustration firmly down, from the center of the picture out toward the four corners.

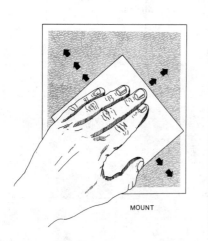

MOUNT

After lightly tacking down the illustration, remove the T square and place a clean sheet of thin paper (such as typewriter paper) over the illustration and gently press it down in all directions. This extra sheet of paper will reduce fingerprints and smudges on the surface of the illustration and the surrounding background sheet.

Some Application Hints

Do not use too much tape on the back of the illustration. Do not overlap pieces of tape, because this causes bumps and lifted edges in the illustration that can be picked up by the camera.

When mounting an illustration on the background sheet, feed the picture *slowly* and keep alert for buckles or ridges that may appear in the center area of the illustration. If buckles appear, *stop* the feed-down process and slowly peel the illustration back a little distance, and then begin again.

Never attempt to force buckles down, as they will form creases and ruin the illustration. Always work on the flat surface that is completely clear of any paper scraps beneath the taped-down background sheet.

FLAT AND DIMENSIONAL BACKGROUNDS

Depending on the type and the pictorial content of an individual frame, various design manipulations can be performed with the background sheet as well.

As mentioned earlier, type statements can be separated and emphasized in a frame by placing different colored areas behind each statement. This process can be accomplished in the same manner as the illustrations are being cut and mounted (see Figures 4-30 and

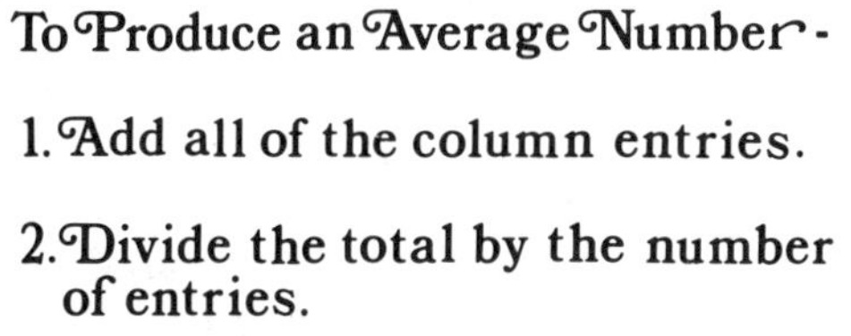

To Produce an Average Number‐

1. Add all of the column entries.

2. Divide the total by the number of entries.

FIGURE 4-30 In a frame that contains two or more written statements, the background can be manipulated to indicate separation and add visual emphasis.

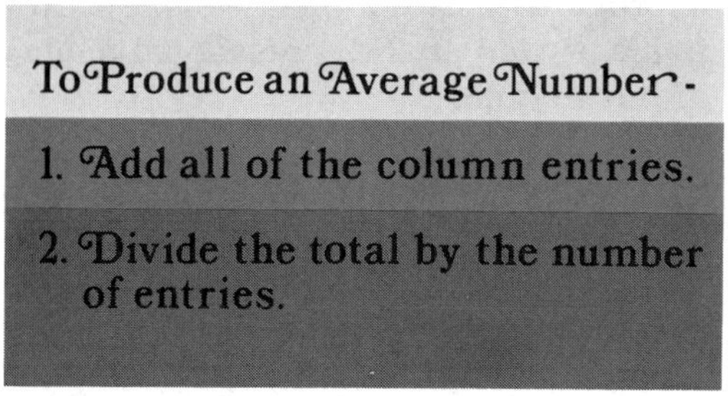

To Produce an Average Number‐

1. Add all of the column entries.

2. Divide the total by the number of entries.

FIGURE 4-31 Different-colored bands placed behind each statement will encourage the viewer to pay specific attention to each while still demonstrating that the information in the frame is interrelated.

4-31). The use of colored bands in the same frame encourages the viewer to pay specific attention to each statement while still demonstrating that the information is interrelated.

To make this kind of background, start with a full-size background sheet that is the color of one of the areas you wish to emphasize. Hold this 10-by-12 inch sheet down to the desk or working surface by placing small pieces of masking tape at the corners. Measure the width of the desired top band and mark it on the background sheet with two small pencil marks.

To determine the width of the upper band, it may be helpful to set the acetate overlay in place on the background sheet (see Figure 4-32). Measure from the top of the background sheet to a point between the statements you wish to separate, and then remove the acetate and place the pencil marks.

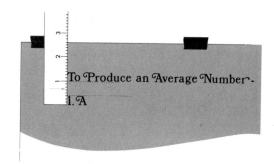

FIGURE 4-32 Begin the preparation of a multiple-band background by first positioning a full-size sheet of colored paper beneath the acetate. Then measure the distance from the top of the colored sheet to a point between the statements you wish to separate.

The next step is to measure the distance between the pencil marks and the *bottom* of the background sheet. This distance will be the size of the sheet bearing the second color.

Using a T square and a razor knife, measure and cut out this second sheet. Along the back upper edge of this new background, place a strip of double-sided tape. Align the new colored sheet on top of the original background, again with the T square, and press into place (see Figure 4-33). In this manner, more

FIGURE 4-33 *Subtract* the width (measured from the top of the background sheet to between the statements being separated) *from the total size* of another colored background sheet *that is the same size* as the first background sheet. Then cut off a strip from the top of the second colored background sheet and adhere it (with double-sided tape) to the original background sheet (see illustration 1). The resulting new background will be that shown in illustration 2.

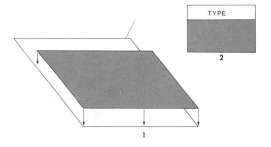

layers of background can be added to separate one statement from another or to separate the artwork from statements.

DIMENSIONAL BACKUP FORMS FOR TYPE

Although all the components of the graphic content of the frame are two-dimensional and flat, the illusion of depth or internal distance can be intro-duced into the background. These graphic effects can be particularly useful as backup forms to "raise" type above the background content, as well as a means of improving such graphic displays as maps and diagrams (see Figures 4–34 through 4–37).

Producing these dimensional forms is relatively simple, and they can greatly improve the clarity of the content in a frame as well as the professional quality of the module.

FIGURE 4–34 Shapes that appear in the background of the frame can be prepared to give the illusion of depth and can lift or float type over the background. This process can be utilized for instructional as well as decorative purposes.

FIGURE 4–36 By the use of dimensional depth, pie charts and other mathematically demonstrative graphics can be enhanced in terms of viewer under-standing and visual clarity.

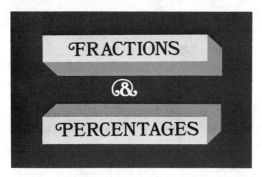

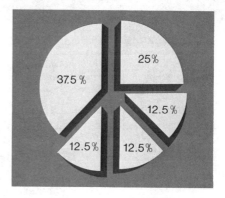

FIGURE 4–35 Here the use of a dark-colored *back edge* to the graphic forms appearing in the frame gives them the illusion of floating over each other on different levels. Note that the map, which has irregular edges, can be given a "thickness" just as geometric forms with smooth curves and straight edges, such as arrows.

FIGURE 4–37 Shapes with dimensional depth can also be combined with background sheets other than solid-color sheets. In this case, the geometric forms were placed on a self-adhesive printed texture sheet, which serves as the background against which they seem to float.

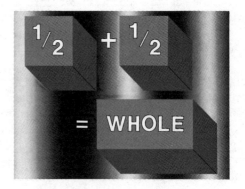

When placing type on dimensional forms, it is best to prepare a pencil rough layout of the frame content in advance. Using this rough layout as a guide, an acetate overlay bearing the type content of the frame can be prepared. Then, using the dimensions of the forms in the rough layout, the forms can be drawn on the various color sheets desired and cut out (see Figures 4-38 and 4-39). The pencil rough layout should be drawn on a 10-by-12-inch sheet of scrap paper.

The sizes of the various background forms required should correspond to the actual sizes of the shapes involved. Therefore, the position of words or phrases on the acetate overlay prepared over the rough will fit the finished background when positioned over it.

The illusion of thickness of depth

FIGURE 4-38 In preparing a frame that will have dimensional forms, the first step is to produce an accurate rough layout in pencil. The forms should be in the same relationship as they will be in the final completed frame.

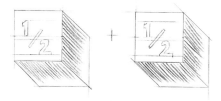

FIGURE 4-39 An acetate sheet can be taped over the rough pencil layout, and type placed where indicated. When the background shapes are cut out and completed, the acetate sheet will position the type in the finished frame.

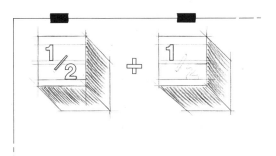

to any form is provided by a back edge and side, usually in a different color. The first step here is to accurately draw the forms on the desired sheet of colored paper. As in the background layout processes described earlier, a base sheet of unmarked colored paper should be prepared and taped down on the desk or working surface. This base sheet should *not* be drawn on or marked because any such marks, even in pencil, can be picked up by the camera and are difficult to erase.

The shapes that are to be placed on this background sheet are measured and drawn *on the back* of separate color sheets (see Figure 4-40). The back of the sheets is used because it is white, and pencil outlines are more visible and therefore easier to cut out. Additionally, pencil marks on the relatively delicate color surface of the sheet may show up around the edges of the cutout form if they are not placed on the back of the sheet.

The outlined forms are then cut out by using a metal-edge ruler and a razor knife. During the cutting process, the colored sheet is kept *face down* (see Figures 4-41 and 4-42). After the shapes

FIGURE 4-40 Geometric forms that are to be cut out are drawn *on the back* of the colored paper sheet. The forms can be placed anywhere on the sheet. *Note:* The sheet shown in this illustration is Pantone brand paper, which has a 1-inch-square grid printed on the back of each sheet.

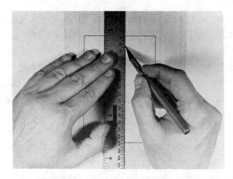

FIGURE 4-41 Using a metal-edge ruler or T square and a razor or stencil knife, the geometric forms can be cut out. Be sure to make the cutting strokes toward you, and use a piece of scrap cardboard behind the sheet you are cutting, to protect the working surface or table top.

FIGURE 4-42 After the cutout shapes have been completed, they are ready for the next step which will add the back edge and illusion of depth to them.

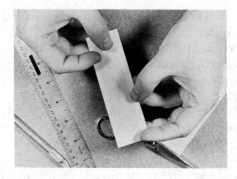

FIGURE 4-43 Apply a strip (or more if necessary) of double-sided tape to the back of each cut shape.

FIGURE 4-44 Tack down the shapes to a sheet of different-colored paper. The shapes can be placed anywhere on this second sheet, but leave some room around all four sides to allow for the cutting of the back edges of the shapes.

have been cut out, some strips of double-sided tape are applied to the back of each piece and the shapes are taped down on a different-colored sheet. The shapes are taped down to the front of the second colored sheet, and all further cutting is done with the sheet face up.

The objective here is to provide a second color shadow or back edge to the original form, thus giving it the illusion of thickness or depth (see Figures 4-43 and 4-44). On rectangular or square shapes, the second edge or side of the shape can appear on one or two sides.

Depending upon the side on which the second edge appears, the raised form will appear to be seen from the right or left side, or above or below.

The illusion of depth to both the shape and the angle of view is provided by a basic application of *linear perspective*. Although an extensive study of the nature and applications of perspective is beyond the scope of this text, the aforementioned shapes can be copied and adapted by eye judgment (see Figures 4-45 and 4-46).

Having taped the original shape down on the second color sheet, the new

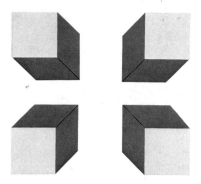

FIGURE 4-45 Depending upon the linear perspective desired, the shape can be made so that it appears to be seen from the left or right side, and from above or below. This option to choose the angle of view for the shapes can be very useful, depending upon the content and purposes of the frame and the shapes appearing in it.

FIGURE 4-46 When a shape has to appear in the center of the frame, (and still be of a dimensional nature), these types of back edges can be used. The angles of the lines receding to the back edge of the shape are both the same.

back edges can be measured and cut. The back edges must be exactly parallel to the edges of the shape, and here a T square or ruler should be used.

Measure and mark two dots parallel to each side in pencil (see Figure 4-47). Then, aligning the ruler with the two marks for each side, cut through the colored paper with a razor knife. The cuts should be longer than each side of the original, and they should meet and cross at one corner (see Figures 4-48 and 4-49).

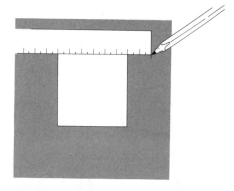

FIGURE 4-47 Having taped down the original shape on a second colored sheet, measure and mark two dots parallel to each side at a distance that will establish the thickness of the form.

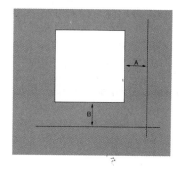

FIGURE 4-48 The distance of the two back edges that are established by measurement (A and B) should be the same.

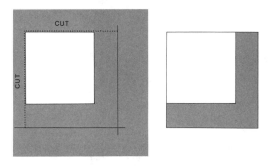

FIGURE 4-49 Carefully cut out the original shape and the two newly established back edges. You will then have a different-colored border on two sides of the original shape.

The distance between the edges of the original shape and the cuts being made to form the back edges of the shape are variable but should be the same on both sides. After these two cuts have been made, the two remaining sides of the shape are cut out. The two sides of the shape that do not have a back edge behind them are cut *along the edges* of the original shape, as illustrated in Figure 4-48.

The final step is to mark off two angles matching the corner angle where the two background edges meet and cut them out. These angles establish the illusion of depth to the shape and usually raise the front face of the rectangle or cube (see Figures 4-50 and 4-51). These two angled cuts can be made by an approximate comparison with the angle at the junction of the two back edges, or they can be measured and marked first with a pencil dot and then cut out. The measurement step is a brief one and guarantees accuracy as shown in Figures 4-52 and 4-53.

FIGURE 4-50 Two angles at the corners of the new shape will have to be carefully measured and cut to produce the final desired dimensional shape.

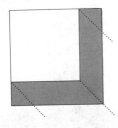

FIGURE 4-51 The corner angles of the cubes will always be the same, regardless of how wide the back edges are when measured and marked.

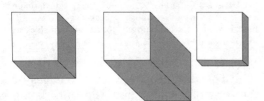

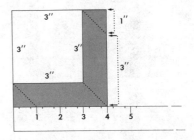

FIGURE 4-52 To establish the proper angles to cut: Along the outer edge of the second color border, measure and mark the length of the corresponding edge of the original shape. The proper angle to cut is the angle formed by a line from a corner of the original shape to the measurement mark for the back edge nearest that corner.

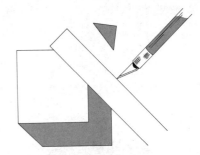

FIGURE 4-53 To produce the final dimensional shape, cut off the corner pieces of extra colored paper with care.

MAKING CURVED OR CIRCULAR SHAPES

The preparation of shapes that are circular, or of shapes that incorporate curves in addition to having depth, is essentially the same process as the one described in the preceding section. The only difference is that when cutting out curved forms, a circle-cutting device is necessary.

The best tool for this procedure is one specifically designed to cut circles in paper or acetate. However, if you have only an occasional need for drawing curved or circular shapes, a substitute cutter can be made from a good-quality, large drawing compass. Since a drawing compass is required to outline all the shapes to begin with, the purchase of such a compass with a stencil knife is desirable because it will perform double duty as a cutter for a nominal extra cost. The type of compass used in these procedures should have a center-wheel width adjustment and an adjustable lead holder on one arm (see Figure 4–54).

Having drawn out the shapes desired on a sheet of scrap paper, this rough is used for the settings of the compass when it is adapted for cutting. In the case of intricate shapes, it is good practice to completely copy the shapes on the back of the colored paper before cutting them out.

When the compass is adapted for cutting, the compass settings must exactly match the compass-made pencil markings of the outlines. As shown in Figures 4–55 and 4–56, if the end result is to be a pie shape with a section separated and retracted, the most accurate method of approach is to first draw a *whole circle* with the compass. After the circle has been cut out, it can be divided

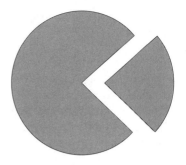

FIGURE 4-55 To produce a pie chart with one or more parts separated out of the whole shape, you will first need to draw and cut out a whole circle.

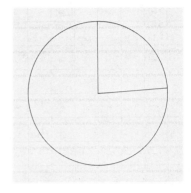

FIGURE 4-56 Begin the pie chart by drawing a circle of the desired diameter *on the back* of a colored paper sheet. Then divide the circle into wedge shapes representing the proportions that will appear in the completed chart.

FIGURE 4-54 A good-quality compass is a useful tool for drawing and (with minor modifications) for cutting out circles.

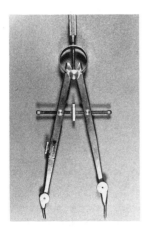

into the desired sections without additional compass measurements.

The next step, therefore, is to adapt the compass for cutting. This is done by substituting a stencil knife blade for the graphite lead, which is normally held in a small clamp at the end of one of the arms.

The stencil knife blade is a small, sharp cutting blade that is attached to, or part of, a thin tubular plastic or metal support. This blade is disposable and quite inexpensive and is usually held in a pencil-type holder. The tubular support that it is attached to is usually narrow enough to fit the graphite holder on larger compasses.

If you do not know whether the blade will fit the graphite holder of the compass you are using, take the compass with you when purchasing the blade so that you can compare them. The installation of the blade is quite simple, but make sure that it is properly seated and aligned in the graphite holder.

Remove the graphite lead by loosening the small screw wheel in the holder and sliding the lead out. Then push the stencil blade support into the graphite holder (being very careful of the sharp blade) and tighten the screw wheel until the tubular shaft of the blade is held firmly in place (see Figures 4-57, 4-58, and 4-59).

The blade should be set in the holder so that its flat side faces the other arm of the compass, and the angled cutting edge faces the direction in which the compass will be rotated to make the cut (see Figures 4-60, 4-61, and 4-62).

The circular cut is made by positioning the compass over the original pencil drawing on the back of the colored paper sheet and adjusting the spread of the arms, if necessary, so that the cutting blade point is exactly on the pencil line.

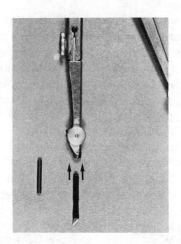

FIGURE 4-58 To adapt the compass for cutting purposes, loosen the graphite-lead holder screw wheel and remove the lead. Then insert the shaft of the small stencil-knife blade into the shaft that formerly held the graphite lead. *Note: Be very careful of the sharp cutting blade during this procedure.*

FIGURE 4-59 When the blade has been set at the proper cutting angle (see Figures 4-60, 4-61, and 4-62), the screw wheel is tightened to hold the blade in place.

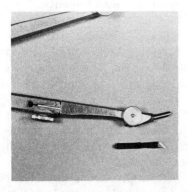

FIGURE 4-57 One compass arm is equipped with a graphite-lead holder, which is held in place by a small screw wheel on the lower part of the arm.

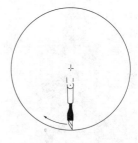

FIGURE 4-60 The angle of the stencil-knife blade must be properly adjusted so that the blade will "track" accurately along the desired cutting path. The blade angle shown here is in proper orientation *when looking straight down at the compass placed in the center of the circle to be cut.*

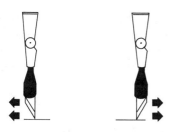

FIGURE 4-61 The stencil-knife blade should be adjusted so that the sharpened edge will face in the direction (clockwise or counterclockwise) in which the circular cut will be made.

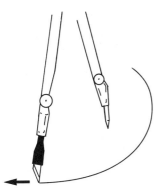

FIGURE 4-62 Insert the pointed pivot arm of the compass at the center point of the drawn circle and position the knife edge along the circle line. Press the compass arm with the knife blade slightly down to force the point into the paper surface, and rotate the compass to cut out the circle.

Applying light pressure, the compass is rotated in the same manner as when the line was drawn, in a smooth, complete rotation. The cutout circle can then be removed from the surrounding sheet.

Some Cutting Suggestions

To keep the colored paper from slipping during the cutting process, and to protect the desk or work surface beneath the paper from damage by the cutting blade, tape the colored paper down, at the corners, to a small sheet of scrap cardboard. Replace the stencil knife blade frequently; a dull blade will not cut a clean edge.

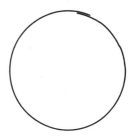

FIGURE 4-63 If (when the compass cutting arm has covered the circumference of the circle) the beginning and end of the cut do not match up, one of two factors can be at fault: (1) too much pressure on the compass cutting arm has caused the stencil-knife blade to wobble out of the proper cutting track; or (2) the center arm-width adjustment wheel of the compass was accidentally turned, causing the compass arms to spread apart during the cutting process.

If, when you have rotated the compass around the circle, the beginning and end of the cut do not meet, the problem can usually be traced to one of two factors: The compass width set wheel was accidentally moved during the cut, or *too* much pressure on the cutting blade was applied, causing it to shift during the cutting stroke. Remember that only light pressure is required to cut through the paper (see Figure 4-63).

Adding Depth to Curved Shapes

After cutting out the whole circle and segmenting it into the desired portions (with a ruler and a razor knife), apply double-sided tape to the back of each piece and tack down on a second colored sheet.

Separate the various shapes enough to allow for the width of the back edges to be cut out. However, to determine the thickness of the back edge of the shapes, position the parts and shapes in the same angles and positions in which they will be placed in the final layout, and draw these on the second background sheet by using a ruler and pencil.

If, for example, a ¾-inch thickness

for the edge of the shapes is chosen, all the lines indicating the thickness—whether at the center or at the edges of the shape—will be ¾ of an inch. Additionally, all the straight lines indicating thickness will be parallel, as shown in Figure 4-64. Note that if the illusion of depth is to work properly for shapes that are circular or have curved parts, *all* of the lines (illustrated in Figure 4-64) *must* be parallel. The *angle* in which these thickness lines are placed in relation to the curved shape is not critical, and eye judgment can be used here.

Having established the lines to indicate the thickness of the shapes, the curves of the back edges of the shapes can be determined. This is done with the compass left at the same width setting that was used to draw and cut out the original shapes.

Place the compass pivot arm at the center point of the original shape and check to make sure that the width setting is unchanged. Then, using a ruler, shift the compass down the same

FIGURE 4-64 After cutting out a circle and dividing it into the desired number of portions, tape down the shapes on a second sheet of colored paper. Place the shapes so that there is enough room around them to allow for the new back edges that will be measured and cut. Place the shapes in the same general orientation or direction to help in the establishment of the lines of the new back edges. Here, all the lines indicating depth are of the same length and are parallel to each other.

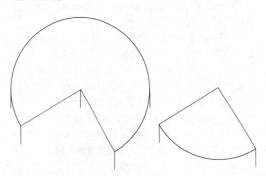

length as the lines that indicate the thickness of the shape. The arc of the compass should intersect the ends of the thickness lines. If it does not, shift the compass slightly until the arc intersects, but *do not* change the width setting.

Draw the required curves, and then add the final straight lines that constitute the back edges (see Figures 4-65, 4-66, and 4-67). Having drawn the curves and

FIGURE 4-65 To draw the parts of the back edges that are curved, keep the same radius setting on the compass. Shift the compass pivot arm and point to the end of the measured depth line that extends down from the center point of the original circle. The new arcs that are drawn will intersect the ends of the other depth-indicating lines that mark the new edges of the back of the shape.

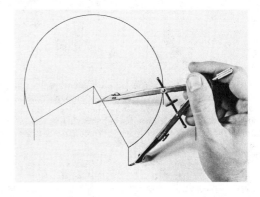

FIGURE 4-66 When the back edges have been measured and marked correctly, the entire shapes can be cut out, and double-sided tape can be applied to the back of each shape.

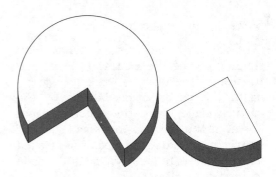

FIGURE 4-67 The completed shapes are positioned and taped down on a new sheet of colored paper that functions as the final background to the dimensional shapes. An acetate overlay can then be added, and whatever type that is necessary can be applied.

straight lines that constitute the back edges of the shapes, they can be cut out and taped to the 10-by-12-inch background sheet as described earlier.

Adding Depth to Irregular Shapes

The addition of a back edge to maps, figures, or other irregular shapes can be quite valuable in separating them visually from the background.

Here again, the shapes are carefully cut out with a stencil or razor knife and are taped down on a separate colored sheet. To avoid confusion, the outline should be sketched lightly in pencil before it is cut out.

A number of variations of the back edge are possible with irregular-shaped forms, and experimentation here can lead to some very interesting possibilities (see Figures 4-68, 4-69, and 4-70).

Save all scraps of colored paper, no matter how small. These will prove quite useful in outlining small shapes, or they can be used to emphasize a single word on the acetate where desired.

FIGURE 4-68 With the creative use of simple graphic elements, not only visual depth but symbolic meaning can be added to the frame content.

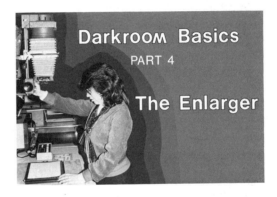

FIGURE 4-69 The use of a back edge in conjunction with a cut photograph or illustration can add visual interest while providing additional space in the frame for type.

FIGURE 4-70 The back-edge concept of working with forms to add dimension can also be used to enhance the instructional nature of an illustration.

RECYCLABLE BACKGROUNDS

Because almost all type that appears in a frame is placed on the overlay, backgrounds can frequently be recycled by using them again in the same or another module.

The same background, however, should not be used more than three times in the same module, as the viewer's attention may be lost even if the information appearing in the frames is quite different. But many backgrounds can be reworked or added to during the course of production of the module to provide an original background for each frame and thus can still save time and expense.

This is also true of type information appearing on the overlay. For example, if the steps of a mathematical problem are being shown, it is not always necessary to reprint all the information

FIGURE 4-71 Frames that are part of a series in which information is added in each successive image need not be produced as five separate overlays and backgrounds. One overlay can be used with the same or different backgrounds. The frame can be photographed, then additional information can be added, and then photographed again.

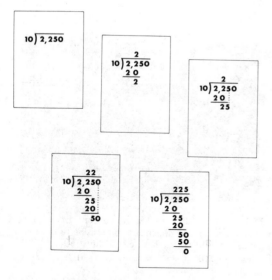

on separate overlays for each frame. In the simple mathematical process illustrated in Figure 4-71, the same overlay is kept throughout the production of *five* separate frames.

The procedure here is to prepare an overlay with the original division problem and place it over a background. It is *then* photographed, rather than waiting until all the graphic designs of the module are finished. After this initial frame of the sequence has been photographed, the overlay is removed and the next stage of additional numbers is added to the original.

The overlay is then reassembled with the same or a different background and photographed to produce the second frame of the sequence. These steps are repeated until the series has been completed.

The obvious advantage to this process is the elimination of the need to repeat the original division problem on four separate overlays. Backgrounds for such a series can be the same or can be varied from frame to frame.

Backgrounds with pictorial material can also be recycled with a minimum of effort. In Figures 4-72A through 4-72D, the background in three frames is the same. The *type* information in each frame is *different*, as is the expression on the face of the person at the bottom of the frame. In these illustrations, the background sheet was prepared in the usual manner. The face appearing at the bottom of the frame, however, was drawn without features. The overlays for each frame was prepared and fitted over the background sheet. The features of the face, which are different in each frame, were drawn *on the overlay* over the blank face with a pen and acetate ink. (A more detailed description of the uses of acetate ink will be given later.) The face and figure were drawn on a

(A)

(B)

(C)

(D)

FIGURE 4–72A–D In the series of frames shown here, the same background was used in each. Three separate overlays were used, one for each frame, and each overlay also contained a different expression drawn for the face in acetate ink on the overlay. The face of the figure was drawn blank, as indicated in the first picture, and was then cut out and taped down to the background sheet.

separate sheet of paper, cut out, and tacked down on the background sheet as in the process described earlier.

If the pictorial material of a frame is to be repeated in other, different colored, backgrounds, the drawing does not have to be recopied. For example, if the face that appears in the backgrounds in Figures 4–72A and 4–72B had to be shown with a different color base sheet for each frame, it would be almost impossible to draw four featureless faces that are exactly alike.

The procedure here would be to draw only one figure and then photocopy the desired number of duplicates required. The duplicates could then be cut out and positioned on the backgrounds.

If you use this method, be sure to draw the original picture in clear dark lines on white paper. A felt-tipped marker reproduces best; pencil lines do not reproduce very well. Use an ordinary office or public-library-type photocopying machine. The photocopies will be the same size as the original.

If the copies are clear, but not as dark as the original drawing, it may be best to use *only* photocopies in the layouts.

The photocopied figures are then cut out and positioned on each of the separate background sheets. Here again, facial or other details should be drawn on the acetate to minimize the time needed for corrections if a mistake is made.

THE ACETATE OVERLAY

Acetate Ink

Acetate inks are specially prepared to draw or paint on the smooth acetate surface. Most conventional inks will "crawl" or bead on the surface instead of staying where they are applied.

Acetate inks are available in a variety of colors and are usually *water soluble*, being removable from the acetate with a damp cloth or cotton swab. The application method is usually by pen or a fine brush (such as a zero or double-zero pointed watercolor brush) and can be done freehand or with the aid of a ruler or other guide. These inks are semitransparent, and broad areas of coverage should be kept to a minimum because they will often show unavoidable application flaws.

Since these colors are semitransparent, however, they can optically change colors when placed over the background sheet. For example, blue lines on the acetate will take on a greenish cast if the acetate is placed over a yellowish background. A red area placed over a green background will appear brown. Only black lines will not change color except to appear sharper against a light color, but less sharp against a dark background.

If a great deal of drawing is to be done on the overlay, and acetate inks are unavailable or do not meet the specific needs of the design being made, *prepared* or *prefixed* acetate sheets should be considered. Prepared acetate is similar to ordinary acetate except that one or both sides have been treated to accept regular inks, watercolors, dyes, and so on. This acetate is available in single sheets or pads in the same variety of sizes as regular acetate. However, it is usually slightly more expensive due to the additional steps involved during the manufacturing process.

As mentioned earlier, freehand and mechanical drawings can be applied to the acetate. The types of pen that work best in this process are the steel drawing or ruling types shown in Figure 4–73.

Drawing and lettering pens are dipped directly into the ink in the bottle. The excess ink is drained off the point by gently pressing it against the inside lip of the bottle. These pen points hold only a small amount of ink and must be refilled frequently. Do not overload the tip with ink, as a large drop will frequently run down the tip from the pen reservoir and ruin the line being drawn.

Practice drawing various types of lines on a scrap sheet of acetate before attempting any formal design applications.

Ruling pens, which are used in conjunction with a ruler or other type of guide, are filled with the aid of a small eyedropper with a tapered tip. Some brands of ink are available in a bottle that has a dropper built into the cap. Ruling pens can also be fitted onto the arm of a drawing compass and used on

FIGURE 4–73 Three types of drawing pens. *Left to right:* a steel point pen in a holder, used for general writing; a steel fine-point pen in a holder; and a ruling pen that has an adjustable line width.

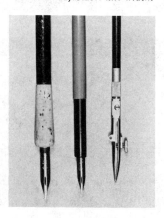

the acetate overlay (see Figures 4–74 and 4–75). The width of the line produced with the ruling pen point can be set with a small adjustment wheel or screw built into the point. This feature can be very advantageous when drawing graph lines or underlining type (see Figure 4–76).

When using ruling or drawing pens on either paper or acetate, certain ap-

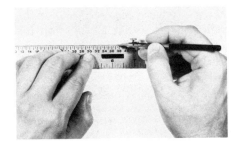

FIGURE 4–76 By a simple adjustment of the pen point, a ruling pen can produce many different line widths.

plication techniques must be observed. One of the most frequent problems in the application of lines is a bleed-under, or smear, caused when ink runs under the edge of the ruler (see Figures 4–77A and 4–77B). The best way to avoid this problem is to use a ruler with a raised edge. If a raised-edge ruler is unavailable, or if the type of guide being used is not manufactured with a raised edge (such

FIGURE 4–74 Ruling pens can be fitted onto the arm of some types of compasses, and they permit the drawing of circles in ink on paper, acetate, or other surfaces. The pen is loaded with a dropper that is built into the bottle cap of some brands of drawing inks (or a medical-type eyedropper can be used).

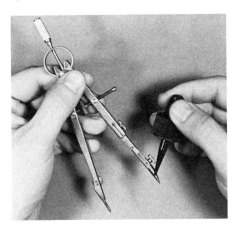

FIGURE 4–77A When applying a line with a ruling pen and a straight-edged or curved guide, one of the main problems encountered is that of *ink bleed-under*.

FIGURE 4–75 When drawing a circle on paper or acetate with a compass ruling pen, use a smooth and continuous hand movement when rotating the compass.

FIGURE 4–77B Ink bleed-under is a smearing of the ruled line caused by ink from the pen point running under the edge of the ruler or guide. When the guide is removed or shifted, the still wet ink is pulled from the ruled line and smeared.

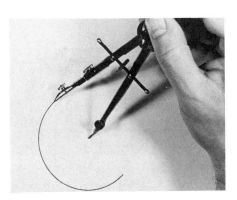

as French curves), the tool can be adapted.

Cut small rectangular or square pieces of thin cardboard and mount them on the bottom of the ruler or other drawing guide with double-sided tape. Place these small pieces of cardboard at regular intervals along the bottom edge of the guide, as shown in Figure 4-78. During the application of the stroke, keep the movement of the pen smooth and continuous. A blob or bead of ink on the surface at the beginning or end of a line is an indication that the pen point was allowed to rest against the surface of the acetate too long at that point.

Make sure that the edges of rulers and other drawing guides are protected from accidental taps or blows during handling, as dents on the drawing edge will produce flawed lines. Never use plastic or wooden rulers as cutting guides—the edges can easily be ruined by sharp blades (other application techniques will be covered in the next chapter).

FIGURE 4-78 When using a ruling pen, the best way to avoid ink bleed-under is to use a raised-edge ruler. If you wish to use a French curve, protractor, or other guide that is not available with a raised-edge, the guide can be raised from the paper or drawing surface by taping small pieces of thin cardboard to the bottom of the guide.

Charting Tapes

When thick lines or extensive numbers of lines are needed, such as in the preparation of charts, charting tapes can be utilized.

Charting tapes are available in a variety of widths and colors in both an opaque and a transparent form, as well as a glossy or matte surface finish.

The best charting tapes for slide graphics are opaque and have a matte finish. Any color may be utilized, and these tapes can be stretched and bent during application to produce curved lines.

Charting tapes can be applied to either the acetate overlay or the background sheet. The tape is self-adhesive and can be repositioned quite easily if placed on the acetate.

Straight tape lines can be applied with the aid of a T square or ruler. A strip of tape is butted against the edge of the ruler or guide and then pressed down (see Figures 4-79 and 4-80).

FIGURE 4-79 To apply a straight line with charting tape, position the tape gently on the paper or acetate surface. Butt the length of tape against a positioned T square shaft and press it down firmly to adhere to the surface.

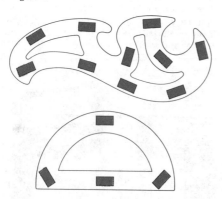

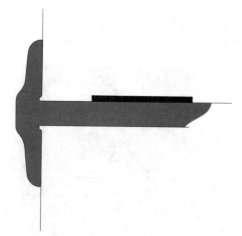

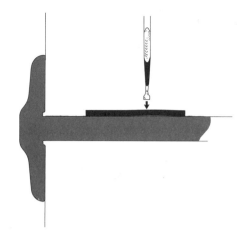

FIGURE 4-80 The length of charting tape can be gently tapped into alignment along the T square shaft with the aid of a type burnisher or flat-tipped tweezers.

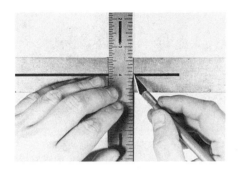

FIGURE 4-81 The proper method of cutting charting tape is to use a razor knife and a metal or metal-edge ruler. The tape should be applied to a hard cutting surface, such as the back of a ruler, to keep it from shifting during the cutting process.

FIGURE 4-82 Ragged or odd angles at the cut ends of a strip of charting tape are quite noticeable, especially in short pieces of tape or thick strips of tape.

Butting the tape against the ruler or T square shaft is accomplished with the fingers, or the tape can gently be *tapped* into position with a type burnisher or other tool. When the tape is positioned properly, the ruler can be removed and the tape can be pressed down along its length to ensure proper adhesion. *Do not* press the tape down with too much pressure, as this may cause it to shift.

If a strip of tape is to have properly squared ends, it must be cut with a razor knife rather than with a scissors. To accomplish this, first cut a strip of tape from the roll that is an inch or so longer than needed. *Gently* press the tape down on a hard glossy surface, such as a piece of scrap acetate or the back of a metal ruler. Then, using another ruler and the razor knife, align and cut the ends of the tape to the desired length (see Figures 4-81 and 4-82). Ragged or improperly cut ends on a strip of tape are quite noticeable, especially on short strips or the wider tape sizes. Small pieces of tape are sometimes difficult to hold and manipulate. *Flat-tipped tweezers*, such as those used by stamp collectors, can be a very useful tool. The tweezers hold the end of the tape securely without damaging it and allow positioning of the strip with a minimum of difficulty (see Figures 4-83A and 4-83B).

The tweezers are used for the initial placement and alignment of the strip of tape while the loose end is being held down with a finger. After positioning the strip, the tweezers are removed, and the tape is pressed down in the usual manner.

Charting tapes are easiest to use on the acetate overlay, as they can be removed or repositioned without damaging it. Charts, graphs, grids, and other graphics that are part of the background sheet can be preserved and reused if all the lines, indicators, and type are kept on the overlay sheet.

Charting tapes are also manufactured in a transparent form. Transparent

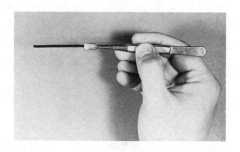

FIGURE 4-83A Flat-tipped tweezers, such as those used by stamp collectors, are very useful for manipulating small pieces of charting tape.

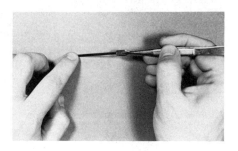

FIGURE 4-83B To position a piece of tape using the flat-tipped tweezers, hold down the loose end against the paper or acetate surface with a finger. While tacking one end of the tape down, the rest of the strip is kept clear of the surface by the tweezers until it is properly positioned. The tape can then be released from the tweezers and pressed down into firm contact in the usual manner.

tapes can be placed over other printed matter that must still remain readable. Transparent tapes are also used in the production of transparencies for an overhead projector (see Chapter 10).

Register Marks and Final Flat Assembly

The acetate overlay and the background sheet can be held in place, and in relation to each other during the preparation of the flat, by taping them to the work surface or desk. However, when the flat is completed and ready to photograph, or be removed and stored while the next flat is being produced, a reassembly method must be established.

When the overlay and the background sheet are removed from the work surface and transferred to the copystand for photographing, it is important that they retain their exact relationship. Here, the use of register marks is required.

Register marks are small guides consisting of two crossed lines, centered in a small circle. Register marks are available in a transfer-type format or printed in rows on transparent tape. For the kind of process described here, the transparent-tape register marks are recommended as being easier to use.

When the flat has been completed, lift and gently fold back the acetate overlay sheet to expose the background sheet. *Do not* detach the overlay sheet from the tape along its top edge, but use the tape as a hinge, keeping the acetate still attached to the work surface or desk (see Figure 4-84).

Peel off a strip of tape with two register marks and cut them off the roll with a scissors. Separate the two register marks. Place one register mark, on its slip of tape, in the *upper-left-hand corner* of the background sheet, and the other in the lower-right-hand corner. At this

FIGURE 4-84 When the type application to the acetate overlay has been completed, fold back the overlay and expose the background sheet. Do not detach the overlay sheet from the desk or working surface, but let the masking tape holding down its top edge act like a set of hinges.

point, the acetate overlay may be folded back down to its original place.

Before placing the register marks on the acetate overlay, check to see whether it is in the proper position against the background. If you wish to shift the acetate sheet—for example, to balance type or move a caption on the acetate closer to an illustration on the background sheet—detach the overlay sheet from the work surface.

If you reposition the acetate sheet, be sure to use a T square and retape the sheet to the work surface before continuing. When the acetate is in its final position, cut out two more pieces of register tape and place them in the upper-left-hand and lower-right-hand corners of the acetate sheet *exactly over the marks on the background sheet* (see Figure 4-85). This action is done by hand or with the aid of the flat-tipped tweezers. The goal here is to place the register marks on the acetate so that they are exactly aligned with those on the background sheet and appear as a single mark in each corner. The best way to accomplish this is by leaning forward and positioning your eyes directly over the flat when applying the second set of register marks.

When reassembling the overlay and background on the copystand at a later point, simply shift the two sheets until the register marks match up and the original relationship is reestablished.

Labels

To avoid confusion, a small label should be attached to each overlay and background. This is especially valuable when you are preparing and storing a large number of flats or several different modules.

A quick label can be made by folding a small self-adhesive label in half. This kind of label is available on a wax paper sheet. The folded label is attached to the lower edge of each sheet at approximately $\frac{1}{4}$ inch onto the sheet (see Figures 4-86 and 4-87).

FIGURE 4-86 A small, rectangular self-adhesive label can be attached to both the overlay and the background sheet to help avoid confusion, especially if the backgrounds and overlays are being stored separately. The label is folded in half, with the adhesive sides facing each other, and positioned near the edge of the background sheet or overlay sheet.

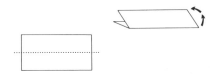

FIGURE 4-87 The background sheet or overlay sheet is inserted only $\frac{1}{4}$ inch or so into the folded sides of the self-adhesive label, and then it is pressed down. This process allows the label to be attached to the background or overlay sheet without interfering with the images or layouts on it.

FIGURE 4-85 A register mark (seen enlarged at the left) is placed on the upper-left-hand and lower-right-hand corners. The acetate overlay is then replaced over the background sheet and another set of register marks is placed on the acetate, *exactly over the set on the background sheet.*

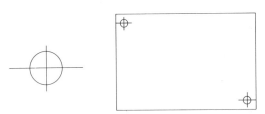

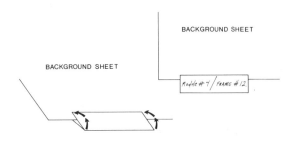

A 1-by-2-inch self-adhesive label is a good size for this process. When folded in half and applied to the overlay or background, it will provide a ½-by-2-inch tab on which the module name or number and the frame number can be written. Neither the label tabs nor the register marks will interfere with the photographing of the frame in any way.

GLOSSARY

Acetate ink A water-soluble ink specifically formulated for use on the surface of an acetate sheet. Available in a variety of colors.

Background sheet A sheet of paper, usually colored, that acts as a base for pictorial material and the type appearing on the acetate overlay.

Bleed-under This problem occurs when using a drawing or ruling pen with a ruler. Small amounts of ink run under the ruler edge, ruining the line. The usual solution to this problem is to use a metal-edge ruler or tape small squares of cardboard to the underside of the drawing guide to raise the edge away from the surface.

Cellophane tape Transparent plastic tape with either a matte or glossy finish.

Charting tapes Flexible, self-adhesive tapes that can be applied to any paper or graphic material surface. Available in a wide variety of colors and widths in either a matte or glossy finish. These tapes are also available in a transparent, as well as an opaque, format.

Color Aid papers A brand name of colored papers available in a wide range of sizes and colors.

Compass A device fitted with two arms attached to a pivot joint and equipped with a pen or pencil lead at the end of one arm and a steel point at the end of the other. Used to draw or cut curves and circles of various diameters.

Contrasting colors Color combinations that enhance each other. Red and yellow, yellow and green, red and green are examples of contrasting color combinations.

Cropped image An image that is altered by either cutting it down or enlarging part of it to focus attention on a specific section of it.

Dimensional backup form An additional colored shape placed behind a geometric form or picture to create the illusion of thickness or depth in the layout.

Double-sided tape A thin masking tape that is coated with adhesive on both sides. This tape is available in various widths.

Drawing pen point A pen point usually made of a piece of thin flexible steel. This point is filled by dipping it directly into the ink. Drawing pen points are held in a pencil-shaped holder and can be used freehand or in conjunction with a ruler or other guide. Line thickness is changed by increasing the pressure of the tip against the surface of the drawing.

Edge coloring Painting or otherwise coloring the edges of cut graphic materials or pictures to make them less noticeable when placed within a layout design.

Film format The size of the image produced on a type of film with a specific kind of camera. A standard 35-mm camera will produce a 24-by-36-mm film image (a ratio of 2 to 3).

Flat-tipped tweezers Tweezers that are equipped with small, flat rectangular clamps instead of the usual points. Although designed for stamp collectors, these tweezers can help the graphic artist manipulate tape and other small, hard-to-handle materials.

Floated material Pictorial material that is superimposed on a colored background sheet or other pictorial images.

Labels Self-adhesive slips of paper usually available in a square, rectangular, or round format in a wide range of sizes and some colors. These materials have many applications in graphic design.

Mechanical drawing A drawing produced with the aid of a T square, ruler, protractors or curves, a compass, or other kinds of guides.

Metal-edge ruler A ruler or T square with a strip of metal embedded along one edge. The metal edge protects the ruler from damage when used in conjunction with a cutting tool.

Opaque Nontransparent.

Optical color change Occurs when a transparent colored material is placed over another colored material and the two colors mix optically to produce a third color.

Pantone paper A brand name of colored paper available in a wide range of sizes and colors.

Paper cutter A flat platform (usually wood) on whose edge is attached a knife-edged cutting arm. These devices are used to trim paper or other thin graphic materials to the desired size while keeping the edges of the material parallel.

Partial background A sheet of colored paper used to fill out the rest of the frame area where an odd-sized illustration has been used (see *floated material*).

Pen stroke A line or mark made on the drawing surface with a single movement of the pen.

Perspective The process of arranging the lines and curves constituting a shape in such a way as to create the illusion of depth to the shape and receding space to its environment.

Photocopy The process of making a duplicate of any graphic material by taking a picture of it.

Pictorial material Photographs, maps, graphs, charts, or any artwork that is used in production of a frame layout.

Prepared or prefixed acetate Acetate sheets that are manufactured with a treated surface that will accept inks, paints, and watercolors. Available in the same size ranges as untreated acetate.

Recyclable backgrounds Background sheets for frame layouts that can be used for the design of more than one frame.

Register marks Small guides consisting of two crossed lines centered in a small circle. Used to align and keep the proper relation in graphic layouts consisting of more than one sheet of material. Register marks are available in a transfer-type format or printed on a roll of transparent tape.

Rubber cement A liquid adhesive with a viscous, or syruplike, texture. The liquid base of rubber cement is a highly volatile and flammable petroleum distillate. Rubber cement is not considered a permanent adhesive.

Ruling pen point A bow-shaped pen point used in conjunction with a ruler or attached to a compass arm. Ruling pens are usually filled with the aid of a fine-pointed eyedropper. Most ruling pen points are equipped with a setscrew or threaded shaft between the blades of the point which is used to set the thickness of the line.

Self-adhesive materials Tapes, labels, or any graphic material that is designed to adhere to a surface without having to be wet or coated with glue.

Silhouetting The process of outlining or cutting out the outlines of a two-dimensional image. Separating part of an image from the surrounding material.

Simultaneous contrast colors Color combinations that are optically opposite each other and, when placed in proximity to each other, produce a shimmering or vibrating visual effect. Red and blue, orange and green, yellow and violet are examples of simultaneous contrast colors.

Single-edge razor blade A small disposable cutting blade with one sharpened edge. Useful for many graphic arts purposes, such as cutting paper, cardboard, acetate.

Stencil knife A small cutting blade set in a pencillike handle. Some stencil knives have blades that swivel in the direction of the cutting stroke. These are very useful for intricate cutting jobs.

Water soluble A term applied to a substance that can be mixed or diluted with water.

X-Acto knife A brand name of a graphic-hobby tool. These knives have replaceable blades that are available in a variety of shapes.

5
ART AND ILLUSTRATIONS

ART AND ILLUSTRATIONS

In the preceding chapters we have seen that the illustrations, pictures, and visual representations of both physical processes and abstract concepts are part of the main foundations of the sound-slide method of instruction.

The generation of the illustrative materials needed for a module is a relatively simple task if you already have the skills needed to paint, draw, or otherwise produce them. However, you do not actually need to have talent or even extensive training to produce perfectly acceptable and usable illustrative materials.

There are several methods by which art can be generated to fit the demands of a particular subject, and only average hand and eye skills are necessary. Individuals who have not been trained in the specific skills will, when confronted with the need to produce a picture of a house or a person or a machine part, be faced with a nearly impossible task if they must rely solely on their own imagination.

Many difficulties disappear when there is a model available to copy and adapt. Rendering a three-dimensional solid object into a two-dimensional representation is much less difficult if you have a model before you that has already accomplished this transformation, such as a photograph, diagram, or other kind of illustration.

When confronted with the need to display a complex object or make a clear and accurate representation, it is best to take a photograph of the subject and then modify it to the requirements of the module being prepared.

Modern illustration styles vary a great deal as to medium and approach. By scanning through several illustrated books and magazines, you will find a number of examples of different illustration styles and techniques, and it is perfectly valid to borrow some of these design ideas and adapt them to your own graphic projects.

One universal observation can be applied to all illustrative matter: A picture, no matter how accurate or complete, still relies heavily on the viewer's imagination to be accepted, perceived, and understood. A picture is only a representation of something else, no matter how well it is done. Therefore, when illustrating a physical object or process, keep the forms and shapes simple and delete superfluous visual details.

In some module subject areas, the

written information presented is more important than the illustrative. In such instances, the illustrations function as a tool to keep the viewer's attention, rather than having a strictly instructional purpose. Most illustrations, however, serve a decorative purpose as well as an instructional one, and both are equally important. Therefore, the approach to the process of making pictorial material for modules should be a blend of decorative and instructional motivations (see Figure 5-1).

The best way to begin the preparation of original illustrations is to consult what is known in the commercial art field as a "snitch" file. Seek out existing publications, such as books and magazines and catalogs that have illustrative material similar to the needs of the module subject that you are creating. These illustrations or photographs can be cut out or photocopied and kept as an idea file that you can refer to when you are generating your own art ideas. The snitch file can be as extensive as you wish and can also include examples of interesting type layouts.

FIGURE 5-1 Illustrations, besides being a source of instruction, can function as a means of keeping viewer attention, as well as having a decorative purpose. Ideally, the illustrative part of a frame should amplify and clarify the text.

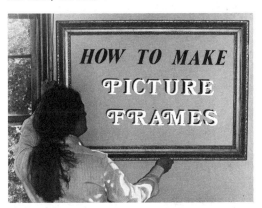

A NOTE ABOUT COPYRIGHTS

The snitch file can be a very useful tool, but it should be used *only* as a source of ideas and *not* for actual illustrations used in the sound-slide module. Virtually all written and pictorial matter that is published is covered by a copyright. The copyright represents a legal ownership by the author, artist, or publisher of the printed material. To use existing printed illustrations, whole or in part, in a slide module without the written permission of the copyright holder is an infringement of the law. By respecting the copyright rules, a great deal of time and trouble, as well as possible legal problems, can be avoided.

PRODUCING LINE ILLUSTRATIONS ON ACETATE

The best medium for line illustrations, whether produced freehand or with the aid of mechanical drawing tools, is pen and ink. Pencil, charcoal, or other drawing materials will often produce a line that is too delicate or broken to be faithfully reproduced when photographed.

A felt-tipped marker with black or another dark ink color is also suitable for drawing line illustrations.

Whether using pen and ink or a marker, try to avoid thin, delicate lines because these may be difficult to see, especially against a brightly colored background. Line illustrations can be placed on either the acetate sheet or the background sheet, but they are easier to produce on acetate. Because the best kind of line is a fairly heavy one, the drawing produced will work best if kept simple and as large as space permits. When a line illustration for a complex or difficult-to-draw object is needed, the snitch file can be searched for an existing illustration that can be adapted by a tracing technique.

The first step is to find a suitable picture whose dimensions are as close as possible to those of the drawing that must be fitted into the frame layout. This sizing process consists of a simple comparison of the open space available for an illustration in the layout and the size of the image on the existing pictorial material, and it can be made by eye judgment or by actual measurement with a ruler (see Figure 5-2). When a proper-

sized picture has been found, tack it down on the work surface or desk top with a few pieces of masking tape. Then position the acetate overlay on the picture so that its image fits within the open area where the line illustration is desired. Tape the top of the acetate down to the work surface (see Figure 5-3).

The next step is to trace the outline of the object on the acetate by using either acetate ink or a felt-tipped marker (if the acetate being used is of the prefixed or prepared kind). See Figures 5-4 and 5-5. Try to follow the outlines of the original picture in smooth, heavy lines. Do not go over the outline more

FIGURE 5-2 Having found a suitable illustration or picture to trace, measure the part of the image you wish to use and compare it with the open area on the acetate overlay carrying the text for the frame.

FIGURE 5-4 Trace the outlines of the image with acetate ink and a dip-type or technical fountain pen.

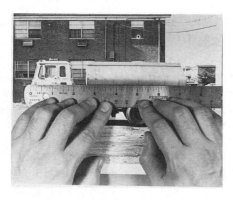

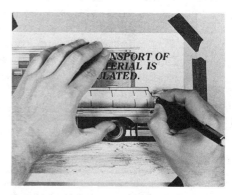

FIGURE 5-3 Tape the illustration down to the desk top or work surface.

FIGURE 5-5 After the tracing process has been completed, a suitable background of colored paper can be added to complete the frame.

than once, as this gives it a rough, inaccurate look. A wide variety of simple line illustrations can be produced with this tracing process.

The backgrounds for overlays that contain line illustrations should be kept bright and simple to emphasize the drawing. Additional localized color can be added to line drawings with the aid of a graphic material called *shading film*, which will be described later in this chapter.

SOLID SILHOUETTES AS ILLUSTRATIONS

Simple illustration forms can be created for placement on the background sheet with a tracing and cutout process that produces solid-color silhouettes. The initial preparation steps are the same as those for the acetate tracing process just described.

First, find a suitable picture whose image is of a size that will fit the area open in the background sheet. When determining the size of the area in the layout that the silhouette will fit into, it may be helpful to place the acetate sheet with type over the background sheet first, before taking any measurements (see Figure 5–6).

After you have found a proper-sized original picture in your snitch file or another source, the next step is to tape a sheet of *typewriter carbon paper* to the back of the picture (see Figures 5–7 and 5–8). Note that the silhouette-tracing process will ruin the original picture because it must be drawn on with a pencil or ball point pen. If the original picture must be kept intact and unmarked, you should make a photocopy of it and tape the carbon paper sheet to the back of the duplicate.

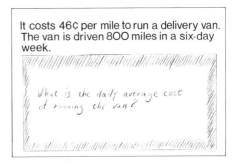

FIGURE 5–6 First, determine the total amount of space on the acetate overlay that an illustration can be fitted into.

FIGURE 5–7 Next, locate an illustration of the subject and size needed for the layout.

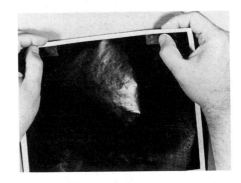

FIGURE 5–8 Tape a sheet of typewriter carbon paper to the back of the illustration or picture that will be silhouetted.

Place the original picture, with the carbon paper backing, *against the back* of a sheet of Pantone or Color Aid paper and tack it down to the corners with small pieces of tape (see Figure 5-9). Then, with a sharp-pointed pencil or ball point pen, trace the outlines and larger details of the image of the original picture (see Figure 5-10).

After tracing the complete outline with a firm, constant pressure on the pencil or pen point, gently remove the original picture and carbon paper from the back of the colored sheet. The result will be an accurate tracing of the desired outline in blue-black lines on the back of the colored paper (see Figure 5-11). Place the colored paper on a sheet of scrap cardboard, and cut out the outline with a stencil knife or single-edge razor blade (see Figure 5-12). When the cutting process has been completed, the remaining shape is ready to be placed,

with the use of double-sided tape, where desired on the background sheet (see Figures 5-13 and 5-14).

When the cutout shape is turned over so that the colored surface is face up, it will be a reverse of the original shape from which it was traced. This reversal is unavoidable because if the colored paper is left face up during the tracing process, the lines from the car-

FIGURE 5-11 The tracing process should produce a clean outline in a blue-black carbon line on the back of the colored paper sheet.

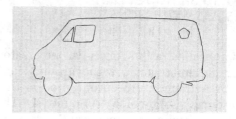

FIGURE 5-9 Place the original picture, with the carbon paper taped to its back, face up on top of a sheet of colored paper that is *face down* on the desk or work surface, and tape in place.

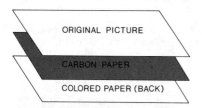

ORIGINAL PICTURE

CARBON PAPER

COLORED PAPER (BACK)

FIGURE 5-10 With a pencil or ball point pen, firmly trace the outline of the original picture you wish to silhouette.

FIGURE 5-12 Place the colored paper sheet with the carbon outline on it, on a sheet of scrap cardboard and carefully cut it out with a stencil knife or razor blade.

FIGURE 5-13 Apply double-sided tape to the back of the cutout shape, along its edges.

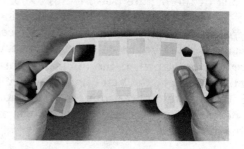

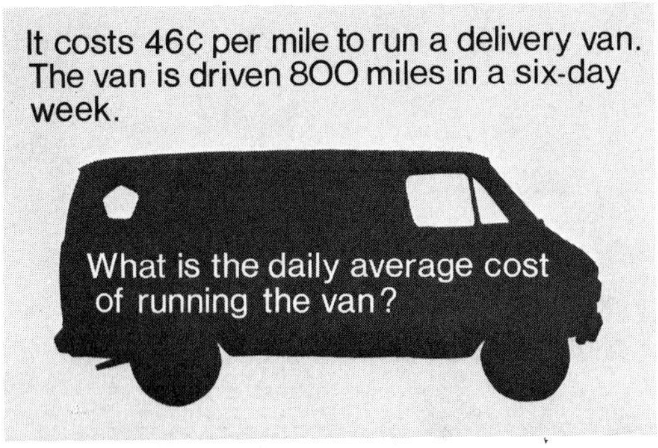

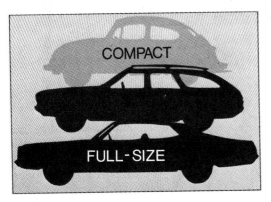

It costs 46¢ per mile to run a delivery van. The van is driven 800 miles in a six-day week.

What is the daily average cost of running the van?

FIGURE 5-14 Position and tape down the finished cutout shape on a background sheet of colored paper. Position the acetate overlay with the type text to complete the frame.

COMPACT

FULL-SIZE

FIGURE 5-15 More than one silhouette shape can be used successfully in a single frame design. Silhouettes can be used as is demonstrated here, in conjunction with printed texture sheets or shading sheets.

HOW TO COMPUTE

COMPOUND INTEREST

FIGURE 5-16 Cutout silhouette shapes can be drawn on, or added to, to create arresting and decorative illustrations.

bon paper will appear around the edges of the finished cutout. These will be difficult to erase without damaging the paper surface.

Silhouetted shapes can also be combined and overlapped to create diagrams and other instructional and decorative forms (see Figures 5-15 and 5-16).

ADDITIONAL GRAPHIC MATERIALS

Line illustrations and solid-color silhouettes as well as other kinds of illustrative material can be combined with printed textures, patterns, and colors if desired. Specially prepared self-adhesive sheets containing a wide variety of textures and patterns are manufactured by a number of firms. These sheets, available in several sizes, consist of a thin, transparent or semitransparent plastic sheet (upon which the pattern is printed), with a paper backing to protect the adhesive coated side.

The thin plastic sheet can be drawn upon or traced through and cut with a stencil knife to any desired shape. The cut shape is then peeled off the protective paper backing and positioned within the outlines of a drawing, over a drawing, or under a drawing done on the acetate overlay. Because the sheets are semitransparent (depending upon how dense the printed pattern is), color will usually show through the pattern. The positioned pattern shape is then burnished gently down with the *bone* end of the type burnisher.

The patterns available include parallel lines of various thicknesses, concentric circles or curves, broken lines, dots, crosses, small squares and rectangles, stars, wavy lines, and so on. Most of the patterns are printed in black; however, some white patterns are available (see Figures 5-17A and 5-17B for just a few

FIGURE 5-17A, B A wide variety of self-adhesive, printed texture and pattern sheets are available from a number of manufacturers. Here is a small sampling from the catalogs of Letraset brand (A) and Chartpak brand (B) graphic products. By permission of Letraset USA Inc. and Chartpak Graphic Products.

(A)

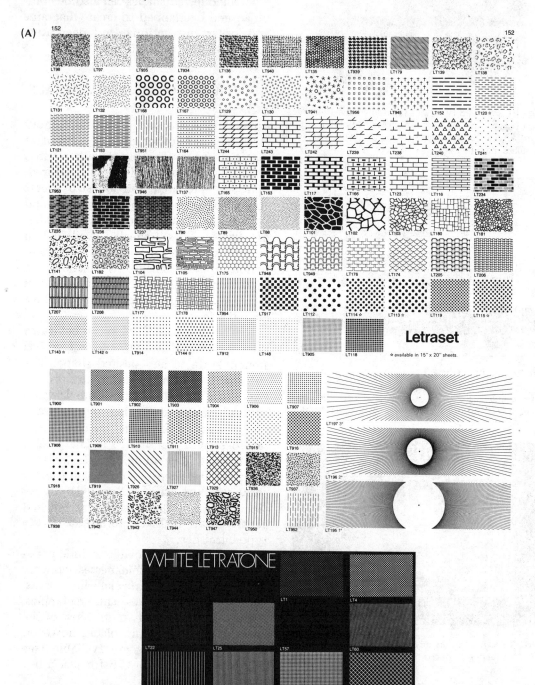

(B)

LINE TINTS

chartpak·

10 1/2" × 13" $1.75 each

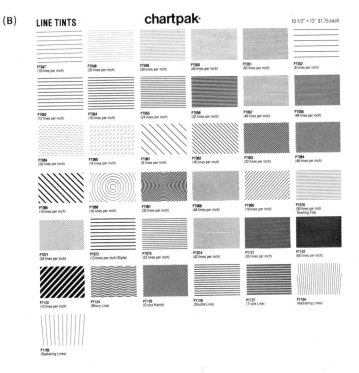

GRIDS AND TEXTURES

chartpak·

10 1/2" × 13" $1.75 each

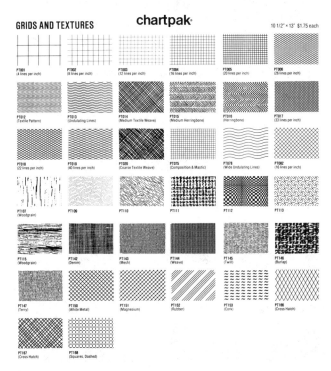

examples). Letratone brand shading films, Chartpak brand pattern films, and Zip·A·Tone brand films are illustrated in these manufacturers' catalogs, and other manufacturers of graphic arts materials offer similar products. These patterned sheets can be very valuable in emphasizing and separating the elements of an illustration or picture visually (see Figures 5-18 and 5-19).

Color can be added to line drawings and other black-and-white pictorial

FIGURE 5-18 With the exception of the oil rig (drawn freehand), all the other elements in this illustration were produced with transfer illustrations or shading sheets.

FIGURE 5-19 The use of various textures in addition to a simple, clear drawing can greatly aid the viewer's understanding of an illustration.

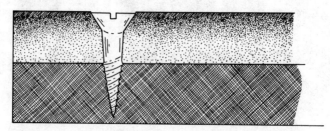

materials by the use of color film sheets similar to the pattern-printed ones. These sheets can be cut to any desired shape and positioned over drawings on the background sheet or behind drawings on the acetate overlay. Letratone sheets and Chartpak matte acetate color films, as well as color films produced by other manufacturers, are available in a number of colors and sizes.

The pattern films and color film sheets work best when placed on the background sheet. Although they will adhere to the acetate overlay, this should be avoided.

The differences in surface texture and reflection between the graphic films and the acetate surface can be detected by the camera if the films are placed on the front of the overlay.

Because of the wide selection of color film sheets available, you should collect the catalogs issued by the various manufacturers if you plan to use these materials often. These catalogs can be purchased or obtained free by inquiring at a large art materials store or by writing directly to the manufacturer.

There are many applications and possibilities for color and texture in combination with line drawings. However, color and texture alone can also be useful for illustrative materials. The visual difference between one area of color or texture and another area or a surrounding area can effectively produce a separation or emphasis without any outlines (see Figures 5–20 and 5–21).

FIGURE 5–20 Drawn outlines are not always necessary to separate one area visually from another. By using different colors or shades to achieve area separations in an illustration, an overall simplicity can be achieved and the viewer's attention can be directed to desired parts of the image.

FIGURE 5–21 Texture and line alone, with a total absence of color can also be a very effective pictorial medium.

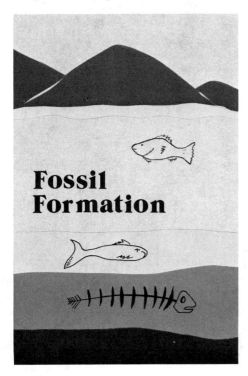

FULL-FRAME PHOTOGRAPHS

If the subject of a module or an individual frame calls for an illustration of great complexity or realism in conjunction with written material, a modified photographic enlargement can be used.

An 8-by-10-inch black-and-white or color enlargement with an acetate overlay for the type can be rephotographed into a slide by the same procedure as that used to photograph a standard layout. The camera distance is slightly adjusted during the photography process, so that the entire slide frame is filled by the enlargement image, thus eliminating the need for a background color sheet. When projected, the type appears superimposed, and floating over the photographic image or scene, in the same way that it does in a conventional layout.

The use of large photographs in frame design is especially valuable when it is necessary to show an object in its environment, a group of objects that have a complex relationship, or a large

FIGURE 5-22 Full-frame photographs can be used to produce viewer interest or to provide decorative or instructive elements to a frame. The photographs (subject permitting) can be made with open spaces for text, which is placed on a conventional acetate overlay, and then the entire composite image is rephotographed into a slide.

environment (such as a room or outdoor scene), which would be difficult or time consuming to draw or otherwise represent (see Figures 5-22, 5-23, and 5-24). The layout for full-frame photograph slides is similar to the procedures for frames that utilize colored paper backgrounds.

The first step is to affix the photograph to a cardboard backing that is at least 1 inch larger on all sides (10 by 12

FIGURE 5-23 Complex actions or relationships, which would be difficult to describe in a written text or drawn, are rendered quite clear with the use of a full-frame photograph and overlaid type.

FIGURE 5-24 Photographs have a documentary value that cannot be matched in terms of viewer impact or recognition.

inches). This will keep the photograph flat and stable during type application to the overlay while supplying a border to which the overlay can be taped. The photograph can be glued down to the cardboard with rubber cement, taped along the edges with photographic masking tape, or dry mounted with a heat press if one is available to you. If the photograph you are using has a very bad curl or buckles in the surface, it may be best to dry-mount the enlargement to a stiff piece of cardboard or mat board.

If a dry-mounting heat press is not available (this kind of press can be quite expensive), try to have the print mounted at a local photo studio or film-processing service store. If the enlargement is not curled or badly buckled, it can be taped down to the cardboard backing with strips of photographic masking tape.

Photographic Masking Tape

Photographic masking tape is an opaque paper tape with a wrinkled, crepelike surface texture. It is coated with an adhesive that allows it to be used on prints and other photographic materials, and it can be removed without damaging the delicate surface of these materials.

Photographic masking tape is available in several widths, but the ¾-inch width is recommended as being the most universally applicable for the processes described here.

Strips of tape can be placed across the top and bottom edges of the enlargement and can overlap the print surface by about ¼ inch. If desired, strips of tape can be placed on all four sides of the enlargement if the edges are slightly curled up (see Figures 5–25 and 5–26).

Double-sided tape such as that described earlier is not recommended to

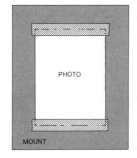

FIGURE 5-25 A photograph can be mounted to a board by placing a strip of tape across the top and bottom edges, or strips of tape across all four edges if the photo is slightly curled or warped.

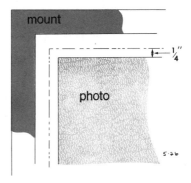

FIGURE 5-26 The photographic masking tape is placed so that the strip overlaps the surface of the print about ¼ inch. The rest of the tape width will hold the print to the mounting board.

adhere the enlargement to the cardboard because this tape will tear the back of the enlargement paper if the print has to be removed from the cardboard for repositioning. Rubber cement mounting of the enlargement to the cardboard should also be avoided if the print is to be removed later.

After the enlargement has been taped down to the cardboard mount, a sheet of acetate large enough to cover the entire image area is placed over it and taped along the top edge on the cardboard border (see Figure 5–27). The acetate overlay can then have type applied to it by using the T square and

FIGURE 5-27 After the enlargement has been taped down to the mount board, a sheet of acetate large enough to cover the entire image area is taped over it.

slipsheet method described in earlier chapters.

The overlay should be left taped in place until the frame is photographed. However, register marks should be applied to the overlay and the cardboard mount to make sure that the realignment is accurate (if the overlay should accidentally become detached from the cardboard mount). *Remember* that the register marks should not be mounted

FIGURE 5-28 Depending on the subject of the module, a wide range of illustrative materials can be drawn from unexpected sources (such as a family album) to produce interesting visual results.

over or on *any* part of the photographic image because the whole image will be used later when photographing the slide. Both black-and-white and color enlargements can be used for this process, and many images can produce striking visual effects when combined with type (see Figures 5-28, 5-29, and 5-30).

FIGURE 5-29 In the original photograph, the chalkboard was blank. The "chalk" printing was achieved by writing on the acetate overlay with a white grease pencil.

FIGURE 5-30 Photographs can also be used to create a mood or produce a desired emotional response in the viewer.

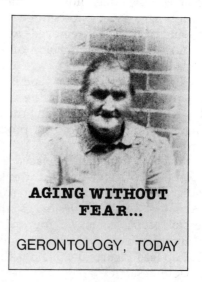

Selective Focus on Photographs with Frosted Acetate

When using photographic enlargements for full-frame layouts, there are two primary ways to focus the viewer's attention on specific areas of the image.

The first way is to use arrows, which can indicate direction or motion. Arrows can also be valuable in singling out a specific detail or in demonstrating an interrelationship of areas, such as in the movement of machine parts (see Figure 5-31).

The second way is to use an acetate overlay made from a sheet of frosted acetate. *Frosted acetate* is a translucent plastic sheet that is available in the same sizes and thicknesses as the clear acetate sheets used for type overlays.

When a sheet of frosted acetate (sometimes called *matte acetate*) is placed over a photograph or an illustration, the image will show through but will be slightly diffused and less distinct.

FIGURE 5-31 One way to focus the viewer's attention to specific areas of the full-frame photographic image is with the use of arrows.

Two sheets will produce a greater diffusion effect. The frosted acetate sheet will usually have one glossy side and one frosted, or matte side. Either side can be placed down, and this acetate, like clear acetate, can take both type and acetate inks.

A specific area of the photograph or illustration can be emphasized by cutting a *window* in the acetate and exposing the illustration beneath it. These windows can be square, rectangular, circular, or any shape desired. When the window has been cut and the center piece of acetate removed, the area within the window will be sharper and more distinct than the surrounding image that is still beneath the overlay. In this way, the viewer's attention can be focused on a specific area of the image without any part of the total image being lost or obscured. For additional emphasis, the window cutout can be outlined with an ink or tape line.

The best way to cut window shapes out of a frosted acetate sheet is to tape the sheet temporarily over the photograph and outline the window area by using a pencil or felt-tipped marker. Then remove the acetate sheet to a piece of scrap cardboard for the cutting process (see Figures 5-32A and 5-32B).

With most brands of acetate, it is usually not necessary to cut all the way through the sheet to effect a cutout separation. Using the stencil knife or razor blade, score the acetate deeply along the guidelines for the window (see Figure 5-33). Then pick up the whole sheet, and with one hand under the sheet and one hand on top of the sheet, repeatedly pinch and fold the scored lines one at a time until they break through and separate. Repeat this process on each of the separate cuts until

FIGURE 5-32A The viewer's attention can be directed to larger areas on the image with the use of the frosted acetate overlay. Here, the action of removing the engine air filter is to be highlighted.

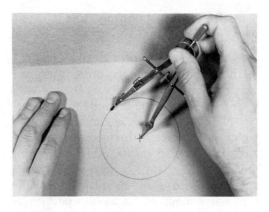

FIGURE 5-33 The frosted acetate sheet is removed and placed on a sheet of scrap cardboard for the cutting process. Score the cut lines (curved or straight) deeply with a razor knife.

FIGURE 5-32B After mounting the photograph, a sheet of frosted acetate large enough to cover the entire image is positioned and temporarily taped down. Next, the size and shape of the desired "window" is measured and marked with a pencil or felt-tipped marker.

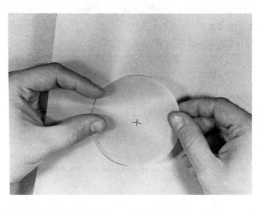

FIGURE 5-34 Flex the acetate sheet along the scored cuts to effect separation of the window from the sheet. If the type of acetate you are using does not separate easily, rescore the original cuts or apply heavy pressure to the cutting knife and cut all the way through the sheet in one or two strokes.

the entire window shape breaks free (see Figure 5-34).

Never try to rip or pull the window shape out of the main sheet. If the folding process for separation does not work after a few attempts, rescore the lines of the cutout shape and try again. Similarly, *never* try to score or cut the acetate sheet while it is still over the photograph, as any cuts that penetrate the

acetate and cut the surface of the photograph will be very apparent and almost impossible to take out or disguise.

A clear acetate sheet for type can be repositioned over the frosted sheet when it has been positioned over the photograph. However, the clear sheet is not always necessary, since the frosted acetate sheet can also accept pressure sensitive type.

The placement of a frosted acetate sheet with a window cutout over a photographic illustration is a simple, quick step that can greatly enhance viewer understanding of the contents of that frame (see Figures 5-35 A and B).

FIGURE 5-35A The cut acetate sheet is repositioned over the image and taped down.

FIGURE 5-35B The window edges can also be outlined in acetate ink if desired.

GLOSSARY

Carbon paper A thin sheet of paper coated on one side with a transferable carbon-based coating. Although designed for making duplicates of typewritten pages, carbon paper is an excellent medium for the transferring of line drawings to another surface (such as colored paper). Carbon paper is used in the preparation of silhouettes (see *Solid-color silhouette*).

Color-shading films Self-adhesive sheets of graphic material available in a wide range of colors. Similar to pattern films in application, color-shading films are used to introduce color to line drawings and other images.

Copyright The legal ownership by an author, artist, or publisher of any printed or pictorial work. It is an infringement of the copyright to reproduce any material, whole or in part, without the written permission of the copyright holder.

Decorative illustrations Pictorial materials whose primary purpose is to attract viewer attention to the frame content, rather than having any specific instructional purpose. Note that decorative illustrations can also be instructional and that the two terms and purposes are not mutually exclusive.

Diffusion A visual blurring or softening of focus caused by viewing an image through a substance that is not completely transparent or clear.

Dry mounting A method of mounting a photographic enlargement on a sheet of cardboard or other flat, thin material. This process utilizes a heat press and a thin, waxlike adhesive sheet that is placed between the enlargement and the mount. When heat is applied in the press machine, the wax adhesive sheet melts and adheres the enlargement to the mount.

Frosted acetate A tough, flexible plastic sheet similar to clear acetate, but with a frosted side. This acetate is translucent, and either side of the sheet will accept transfer type.

Full-frame photograph An 8-by-10-inch color

or black-and-white enlargement that is used instead of a colored paper background for a frame design. Type can be introduced to the image by placing an overlay on the photographic image. When photographed into a slide, the enlargement will fill the entire frame.

Line illustrations Drawings that are composed only of lines in ink, pencil, or another medium.

Pattern-shading film A self-adhesive sheet of graphic material that has a pattern or a tone made up of fine dots printed on the surface. This material can be cut to any desired shape and positioned over or under other illustrative material, such as line drawings. Pattern-shading films function as a source of ready-made patterns for the enhancement of many kinds of pictorial material.

Photocopy A black-and-white reproduction made from an original page by a photocopying machine. Photocopy machines can usually be found in schools, libraries, and offices.

Photographic masking tape A thin, opaque paper masking tape with a wrinkled, crepelike surface texture. Photographic masking tape is available in white or black rolls and in various widths. This tape has a special adhesive coating that allows it to be placed on the surface of photographic enlargements and then repositioned or removed without damaging the delicate image surface of the print.

Selective focus The process of attracting the viewer's attention to a specific area or areas of the frame by the use of color, line, or graphic indicators such as arrows or circles.

Snitch file A resource file consisting of pictorial materials or examples of type layouts taken from books, magazines, or other publications. The snitch file is used as a source of ideas in the generation of original illustrations and layouts.

Solid-color silhouette The shape of an object represented in the format of a cut sheet of colored paper. Any cut paper shape whose outline is taken from an original drawing or tracing.

Tracing The process of placing a translucent material (such as tracing paper) over an image and following the outline of all or a part of the image with a pen line, pencil line, and so on.

Translucent A material that permits light to pass through it. Semitransparent.

Window A shaped opening cut out from a sheet of frosted acetate. When positioned over illustrative material, the acetate sheet presents a clearer, sharper portion of the illustration image where the window opening is. This directs the viewer's attention to that area and therefore acts as an instructional aid.

6
THE CAMERA

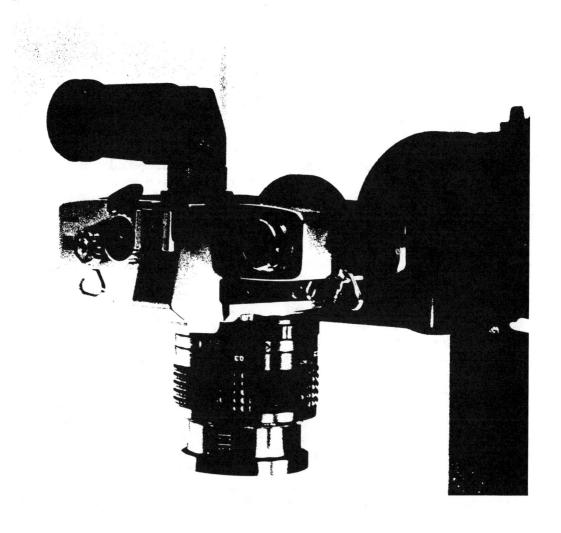

Sound-slide modules and filmstrips that are manufactured by media production companies or book publishers are photographed with the use of expensive and sophisticated copy cameras and lighting systems. The large-scale operations of these companies and publishers call for the production of a large volume and variety of materials and are therefore geared to the mass-production marketplace.

However, the much more common and readily available 35-mm camera, while not being a mass-production tool, is quite capable of producing slides whose professional quality is similar to that produced by equipment of much greater cost and complexity. Before discussing the flat-copy photography process, let us examine the 35-mm camera and needed accessories.

The 35-mm single lens reflex camera with a 50-to-58-mm normal lens is the main tool of the flat-copy photography process. The SLR-type camera is one of the most popular cameras on the market and is extensively used not only by professionals but by amateurs and hobbyists.

The SLR is recommended for flat-copy photography over rangefinder and other types of focusing 35-mm cameras because the SLR views its subject (and therefore allows pictorial composition) through the same lens that is used to take the actual picture. This is a very useful feature, as an important aspect of flat-copy photography is the proper centering and alignment of the image on the film. Because the SLR does not rely on a separate viewing and focusing system (as a rangefinder camera does), there is a reduced margin for error in the area of critical image alignment. The brand of SLR camera is not important as long as the camera and lens meet some basic requirements.

The SLR camera should have an adjustable shutter speed range, and the lens must be of a focusing kind and have an adjustable diaphragm.

An SLR that has a built-in internal light meter, whether coupled to the lens or otherwise, is also worthwhile. A separate, hand-held light meter can also be used, either in conjunction with the camera's meter or alone.

The lens should be the *normal* type—50 to 58 millimeters. Wide-angle lenses should be avoided for copy work because they can distort straight lines into curves. Most telephoto lenses should be avoided because, although they may produce an acceptable image, they must be extensively adapted with the use of extension tubes or bellows before they can do close copy work.

The 50-to-58-mm *normal* lens with a lens speed of $f/1.2$, $f/1.4$, or $f/2$ is the recommended lens for this type of copy work (see Figures 6-1 and 6-2). Most lenses in this range have a maximum close-focusing capability of approximately 1 3/4 to 2 feet.

This close-focusing capability can be increased and extended with the use

of a simple accessory magnifying lens of +1, +2, or +3 power (see Figures 6-3 and 6-4). The accessory close-up lens is a simple magnifying lens in a threaded metal collar. This lens is threaded and screwed into place on the front mount of the normal camera lens. The camera lens is then able to focus on materials and objects that are closer to the camera

FIGURE 6-3 The close-focusing capability of the camera lens can be increased with the use of a simple, magnifying accessory. The close-up lens is a +1, +2, or +3 lens mounted in a threaded metal collar (see Figure 6-4).

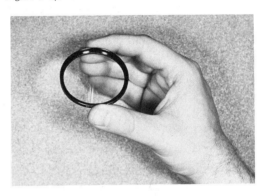

FIGURE 6-1 The best type of camera for photographing slide modules is a single lens reflex that has adjustable shutter speeds. The lens should be a *normal* one (50 to 58 millimeters) with a lens speed of 1.2, 1.7, or 2. An SLR with an internal light meter or automated exposure system is ideal. A few relatively inexpensive accessories for the camera will be needed to adapt it to close-up copy work. These accessories are illustrated and described throughout this chapter.

FIGURE 6-2 If the camera you are using does not have a built-in light meter, you can purchase a small hand-held meter. Hand-held light meters are usually powered by a small battery and are very accurate.

FIGURE 6-4 The close-up accessory lens threads onto the front of the normal camera lens. When purchasing this accessory, be sure to indicate the proper lens millimeter size to the salesperson, or bring the lens with you to the photography store, to ensure a proper fit. Close-up lenses will also thread into each other; thus a +5 lens can be produced by threading a +2 and a +3 together. However, do not thread more than two lenses together at once or image distortion may result.

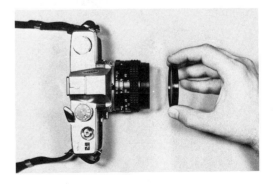

than the minimum distance engraved on the lens barrel.

The exact new close-focus range is dependent on the original maximum close-focusing capability of the lens. However, with the acquisition of two close-up accessory lenses, a +1 and a +2, virtually all the close-focusing requirements of the flat-copy photography process can be met.

The +2 close-up lens can also be threaded to the +1 lens, thus creating a +3 lens that can be threaded to the camera lens to facilitate extreme close-ups. Note that if the camera being used does not have an internal meter and you are using a hand-held meter, the close-up accessory lenses do not significantly affect exposure values.

ADDITIONAL CAMERA ACCESSORIES

During the flat-copy photography process, the SLR is held in position by the

FIGURE 6–5A During the flat-copy photography process, the camera is held in position by the copystand so that it is facing downward. The top of the camera is therefore facing the operator.

copystand so that it is facing downward and the top of the camera is facing the operator (see Figure 6–5A).

This downward camera position can prove difficult when focusing and composing, because the photographer's head must be tilted down and cocked to one side to see properly through the camera viewfinder (see Figure 6–5B). To eliminate this problem, a right-angle viewfinder attachment can be a useful camera accessory.

The *right-angle viewfinder* is a small device that attaches to the camera eyepiece and permits the photographer to see the image in the viewfinder while being at a 90-degree angle to the camera (see Figures 6–6, 6–7, and 6–8).

Right-angle viewfinders are manufactured by a number of camera companies, as well as several companies that specialize in camera accessories. Most right-angle viewfinders are designed to show the camera viewfinder's *entire*

FIGURE 6–5B The camera position can sometimes prove awkward when trying to see down into the viewfinder to focus and frame the picture. This is especially so when the camera has to be raised fairly high on the copystand support in order to ensure that the entire graphic design on the copystand base will appear in the frame.

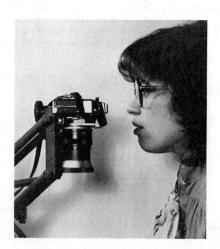

FIGURE 6-6 An angle-finder accessory is a compact optical system that permits the camera operator to look into the camera viewfinder without having to angle his or her head or look down.

FIGURE 6-7 Angle-finder accessories are available for most major brands of SLR cameras. Your local photographic supply dealer or camera store can supply specific information on the availability of this accessory for your camera. The angle finder attaches to the outside of the camera viewfinder slot on the back of the camera.

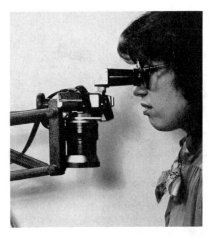

FIGURE 6-8 By bending the light passing through the optical systems of the camera, the angle finder allows the viewfinder image to be seen while keeping the operator's head at a comfortable, normal angle.

image. This is an important point to check when purchasing a right-angle viewfinder, as it is necessary to see the entire image when photographing flat copy.

The right-angle viewfinder attaches directly to the camera viewfinder opening. Most major brands of SLRs are built with a set of slots or some other kind of attachment provision for an angle viewfinder. For specific details, check your camera instruction booklet or consult the dealer from whom you purchased the camera.

The Cable Shutter Release

In any kind of still photography, avoiding camera vibration during exposure is necessary for the production of a clear, sharp image. The vibration factor is especially important in flat-copy photography, and all sources of possible camera vibration should be reduced or eliminated.

The copystand should be placed on a solid table or other support, and the camera shutter should be tripped by using a cable-type release or bulb-type release (see Figure 6-9). Most SLR cameras do not require a great deal of pressure when releasing the shutter. However, any time the hand comes in direct contact with the camera during exposure, there is an increased risk of accidental vibration.

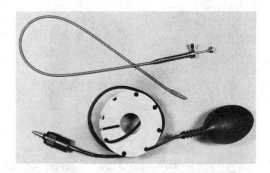

FIGURE 6-9 Two "long-distance" methods of tripping the camera shutter. Above, the cable-type shutter release. Below, the bulb-type, air-pressure shutter release. The flexible rubber tubing is wound around a plastic core spool.

The *cable shutter release* is a flexible metal shaft of up to 20 inches in length, with a spring-loaded wire at its core. One end of the cable has a small button plunger that is held in the hand, and the other end has a threaded adapter that screws into the shutter release button on the camera. When the button plunger held in the photographer's hand is depressed, a small metal probe on the camera end of the cable extends into the camera shutter release button and trips the shutter. This system produces little or no vibration and eliminates the problem of groping for the camera shutter release while looking through the viewfinder.

Another long-distance method of shutter release is with an *air-bulb release.* The air-bulb release consists of a long, thin flexible rubber or plastic tube. One end of the tube has an adapter that screws into the shutter release button on the camera, and the other end has a small rubber air bulb. When the air bulb is squeezed, the increased air pressure along the tube to the adapter at the camera end will trip the shutter.

Air-bulb shutter release units with a tube length of up to 20 feet are available.

The air bulb can be squeezed with the hand, or the photographer can place the bulb on the floor and step on it when tripping the shutter. Having the bulb on the floor is a distinct advantage, as it allows the photographer to keep both hands free during the exposure, to hold down or position the flat copy (see Figures 6-10, 6-11, and 6-12).

FIGURE 6-10 The cable-type shutter release and the bulb-type shutter release are attached to the camera body, usually through the shutter release button.

FIGURE 6-11 The bulb-type, air-pressure shutter release is activated by squeezing the rubber bulb. The resulting increase in air-pressure causes a small probe to extend into the camera body through the shutter button and trip the camera shutter.

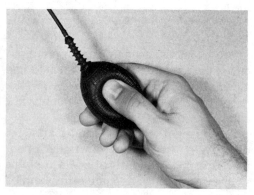

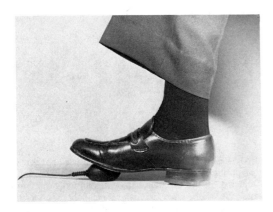

FIGURE 6–12 An advantage of the bulb-type shutter release is that the bulb can be placed on the floor, and the shutter can be triggered by stepping on the bulb. This method allows both hands to be free when adjusting the camera controls, the copystand controls, and the alignment of the flat on the copystand baseboard.

The Slide Duplicator

Another useful camera accessory is the *slide duplicator* (see Figure 6–13). As with other equipment elements of the flat-copy photography process, some very expensive and sophisticated slide duplicators are available on the market. However, very acceptable and usable slide duplicates can be produced by a much less expensive extension tube-type

FIGURE 6–13 The slide duplicator is a camera accessory that allows the rephotography of a slide or an entire module.

slide duplicator. This duplicator consists of a metal tube approximately 6 inches long. One end of the tube has an adapter that permits the duplicator to be attached to the camera body.

The duplicator is used *instead* of the normal camera lens. The other end of the tube has a head containing slots that hold a 35-mm slide and color correction filters if desired, and it has a plate of frosted glass or white plastic to ensure even illumination of the slide image during the exposure.

The lens in this type of duplicator is built into the barrel and has a fixed focus. Most duplicators do not have a lens diaphragm, and exposure adjustments are made by changing shutter speeds or by increasing or decreasing the distance that the duplicator is held in relation to the light source.

The slide-copying procedure is relatively simple. After attaching and aligning the duplicator to the camera body (as per the manufacturer's instructions), the camera is loaded with slide film.

The kind of slide film used to produce the duplicates depends on the kind of light source used in conjunction with the duplicator (see Figure 6–14).

If a tungsten photoflood bulb is used as the light source, a tungsten light-type film must be used (see Figure 6–15). If the duplicator is used with an electronic flash unit as the light source, a daylight-type film must be used (see Chapter 7).

After the camera has been loaded, the slide that is being copied is placed into the slotted holder at the far end of the duplicator. The duplicator and camera are then aimed at the light source and the shutter is released.

Because of the duplicator's small lens and fixed aperture, it is difficult to

FIGURE 6-14 The slide duplicator attachment connects directly to the camera body, in place of the regular lens. The camera is loaded with slide film that is compatible with the type of light being used as an illumination source. The slide to be duplicated is placed in a slot at the front end of the duplicator and pushed into alignment with the optical system inside the duplicator.

FIGURE 6-15 When using tungsten light-type film, the duplicator can be aimed at a photoflood bulb as an illuminaton source. At a fixed shutter speed, and with a fixed aperture in the duplicator optical system, the exposure is adjusted by the distance between the duplicator front and the bulb.

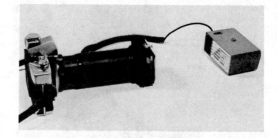

FIGURE 6-16 The best and easiest-to-use light source for duplication is the electronic flash. The exposure is adjusted by the distance between the duplicator front and the flash unit. By using this light source and daylight-type film, very consistent and evenly illuminated duplicates can be produced. The problem of excessive heat, such as that produced when using a large photoflood bulb as a light source, is eliminated when using an electronic flash.

use the camera's internal light meter when the duplicator is attached to the camera body. This makes the viewfinder image quite dark, and consequently the camera meter needle and other exposure information are often difficult to see.

The best light source for slide duplication is an electronic flash unit. Although a photoflood bulb can be used as a light source, the electronic flash produces duplicates that compare favorably

with the original slide—there is less contrast, better overall illumination, and closer color saturation.

The duplicator is aimed directly at the light source, and the distance between the front of the duplicator and the light source, coupled with the ASA speed of the film being used, determines the proper exposure of the new copy slide (see Figure 6-16).

It is usually necessary to calibrate the distance between the light source and the duplicator and keep accurate records for the first roll of slide duplicates. The calibration consists of shooting a series of test exposures using the same shutter speed and light source. Each successive exposure is made with the duplicator moved back an inch or two from the light source. When the slides have been developed and examined in terms of brightness of image and color saturation, the best exposure can be chosen and compared with the information recorded about its exposure, and that exposure process can be repeated to produce good duplicates when needed. Calibration notes can be tabulated as follows:

EXPOSURE CALIBRATION

Film—Ektachrome ASA 64 (daylight)
Light source—electronic flash
Shutter speed—one-sixtieth of a second

DISTANCE BETWEEN LIGHT SOURCE AND DUPLICATOR (INCHES)	EXPOSURE NUMBER	SLIDE QUALITY (EXPOSURE AND COLOR SATURATION)
2	1	Much too light and bleached out.
3	2	Images too thin, color weak.
4	3	Acceptable.
5	4	Excellent; color rich, exposure bright
6	5	Slightly too dark

The distance column, listed in 1-inch increments, indicates the distance between the *front* of the electronic flash unit and the *front* of the duplicator where the slide is held, which usually has a hinged plate of white plastic or frosted glass to diffuse the light during the exposure.

After the slides have been developed, they are inspected as to general brightness and color saturation (the richness of the colors). It is good practice to project the slides for this comparison, as a slide that may look too dark to the naked eye can be correct when projected with 300 or 500 watts of brilliant light passing through it.

Having selected the best-exposed slide, the calibration list can be consulted to determine the exact distance between the light source and the duplicator for that exposure. From that point, duplicates can be made without further calibrations, as long as the same light source, distance, film, and shutter speed are maintained. Note that if you change to a different ASA film speed or use a different shutter speed or light source, it will be necessary to make up a new exposure calibration list.

All types of films have two sides. The dull side, called the *emulsion side*, carries the actual image, either a positive image such as that found on slides or a negative image such as that found on black-and-white or color negative films from which prints are made.

When looking at a color slide, *the image is correct when the glossy, non-emulsion side is toward the viewer.*

When making a copy slide with a slide duplicator, the *original* slide is placed in the duplicator, with the *glossy side* facing the camera and photographer.

The Importance of the Slide Duplicator

One of the recommended procedures when producing a sound-slide module is the preparation of a master set of slides.

The *master set* consists of a set of properly exposed slides representing the entire module, which are preserved and stored strictly for the production of duplicate sets. The master set is kept separate from other slide set copies of the module and is never projected or used.

The master set is produced when

the original module is photographed from the flat copy by taking an extra slide of each frame, in addition to any other shots of that frame. This produces an extra set of slides of the entire module, which, after processing, are carefully stored away in plastic slide-file pages (see Figure 6–17).

The reason for preserving a master set of slides for each module is that slides lose their color integrity when they have been projected for a few hours. Slide colors are produced with dyes that can fade or change color when the slide has been projected for some time. Even intermittent exposure to the heat and bright light of projection or viewing equipment will cause noticeable changes. Repeated use of a slide set can cause buckles and warping of the film base as well as wear and tear on the cardboard

FIGURE 6–17 A master set of slides is never used for projection. The master slides are placed in plastic pocket pages and stored so that duplicate sets of the module can be made from them as desired. The slide pages are usually made so that they can be placed in a standard three-ring loose-leaf binder.

slide mount. The combination of these factors results in a relatively short life span for a slide set that is exposed to heavy usage. By keeping a master set for each module, any number of additional copies of the module can be prepared by the duplication process whenever desired. Producing additional copies of a module by the slide duplication process is much easier and less time consuming than reassembling and rephotographing the original flat-copy layouts.

More sophisticated versions of the slide duplicator are available for photographic applications that require the duplicate slide to be altered. Some duplicators have an adjustable image magnification feature that enables the photographer to enlarge a small area of the original slide to full-frame size in the copy.

There are many possible applications for the zoom magnification feature in cropping and balancing the image in the copy slide, which may be incorrect in the original.

Some slide duplicators are available in complete sets consisting of a duplicator, an adapter for your type of camera, an electronic flash unit, and a printed distance calibration card. Additional information about any of these accessories can be obtained at a camera store or by writing directly to the manufacturer. Check the advertising sections of popular photography magazines for prices and manufacturers' addresses.

GLOSSARY

Accessory close-up lens A simple magnifying lens of +1, +2, or more power that is set into a metal collar that threads into the front of the camera lens. This attachment is frequently used to extend the close-focus capability of the camera lens.

Air-bulb shutter release A camera attachment consisting of a length of rubber or plastic tubing with a hollow squeeze bulb at one end and an adapter that fits into the camera shutter button at the other end. When the bulb is squeezed, the increased air pressure in the tubing will trip the shutter. With this attachment, the photographer can trip the camera shutter with his or her foot, allowing both hands to be kept free during exposure.

ASA film speed A number designation representing the light sensitivity of a photographic film as determined by the American Standards Association. The higher the ASA number, the more sensitive the film is to light.

Cable shutter release A camera attachment consisting of a flexible metal cable with a small finger grip plunger at one end and an adapter that fits into the camera shutter button at the other end. This device is used to trip the camera shutter with reduced vibration and without the hand touching the camera body.

Color correction filters Small, transparent sheets of plastic or glass that are tinted different colors. Used in conjunction with a slide duplicator to correct the color content of the duplicates. If the original slides have color problems such as a pale, bleached image, or if the originals were photographed with an improper light and film combination that produces an unwanted bluish or yellowish tint, the color correction filters can be used to correct the colors in the duplicate slides.

Color saturation The visual brightness or richness of the colors in a slide or print as compared with the original scene or object photographed.

Copy slide A slide that has been photographed from another slide.

Electronic flash unit A photographic light source that produces illumination similar to that of a flash bulb but has a permanent flash bulb capable of extended use. Electronic flash units are usually battery operated, or on house current with an adapter.

Film emulsion A chemical coating on one side of film that is light sensitive and carries the actual image in either a positive form (as with slides) or a negative form (from which prints are made).

Fixed aperture diaphragm A lens that has a preset and nonadjustable opening.

Fixed-focus lens A lens that has a set, nonadjustable focus.

Hand-held light meter A light-measuring device used to calculate proper film exposure.

Internal light meter A light-measuring device used to calculate proper film exposure. Internal light meters are built into the camera body and directly measure the amount of light that is passing through the lens into the interior of the camera.

Lens barrel The body or external shell of a camera lens.

Lens close-focus capability The exact minimum distance at which a lens is capable of focusing without special attachments.

Lens diaphragm An iris similar to the one in a human eye. Due to the adjustable diameter of its opening, the lens diaphragm can control the amount of light passing through the lens to the film. The diameter of the diaphragm opening, from the largest opening to the smallest, is divided into logical increments called "f/stops." The higher the f/stop number, the smaller the opening in the diaphragm, and the less the amount of light that passes through the lens.

Master slide set A set of slides representing a complete module. The master slide set is never projected and is preserved as a source from which additional copies of the module can be photographed by a slide duplication process.

Normal lens A camera lens with a 50 to 58-mm designation.

Photoflood bulb A standard-looking light bulb that produces an intense, bright light that is compatible with tungsten light-type photographic films. Photoflood bulbs usually have a much shorter life than regular light bulbs.

Rangefinder camera A camera, 35 mm or otherwise, that uses a separate rangefinder viewing system to focus the lens.

Right-angle viewfinder An optical device that attaches to the viewfinder window of a camera. This attachment allows the photographer to see into the viewfinder while at a 90-degree angle to the camera body.

Single lens reflex camera Usually referred to by the abreviated term *SLR*, this type of camera views the subject through the same lens that is used to take the picture.

Slide duplicator An attachment used instead of the camera lens to duplicate slides by re-photographing the original image.

Slide-file pages A flexible plastic page consisting of small clear pockets attached to a frosted backing sheet. The pockets in the slide-file page hold up to twenty mounted slides and are used for quick viewing of groups of slides, as well as for protecting the slides from dust and fingerprints. Slide-file pages are usually produced with adapter holes along one side so that the pages can be placed in a standard three-ring loose-leaf binder.

Shutter speed The amount of time that the film is exposed to light. Most modern cameras have a shutter speed range from one second to one thousandth of a second.

Telephoto lens A camera lens that has a long focal length and is used to produce enlarged images of distant objects. A 135-mm lens is an example of a telephoto lens.

Thirty-five-millimeter camera A camera that uses 35-mm film.

Tungsten light Artificial light produced by a light bulb that has a tungsten filament.

Wide-angle lens A camera lens that has a short focal length and a wide angle of view. A 28-mm lens is an example of a wide-angle lens.

Zoom magnification lens A lens that can be adjusted to change its focal length without affecting the focus clarity at which it is set.

7
THE FILM

Despite the number of slide films available, the somewhat more demanding needs of flat-copy photography for slide modules makes the choice of a proper film crucial to the quality of the final desired presentation.

Slide films are frequently referred to as *direct positive* films. This means that a positive image representation of the original object or scene is produced directly on the film by the development process, rather than being printed from a negative.

Many factors can affect the direct positive image. Different slide films have different color characteristics. This means that some kinds of slide films may render colors that are more reddish or bluish than those appearing in the original scene. Slide films can be affected by the type of light present when the exposure was made, as well as the type of processing used to develop the image.

As already mentioned, slide films fall into two main categories: tungsten and daylight-type films. Tungsten films are designed to be used with tungsten-film light bulbs as a light source. Daylight films are color balanced to work with either daylight, blue flash or daylight-type photoflood bulbs. Neither of these films will produce an acceptable color image when used with fluorescent lights unless a special filter is placed over the camera lens during exposure.

Daylight film can be used with tungsten light, and tungsten film can be used with a daylight light source if special camera filters are used. However, because of the additional expense of the filters, and having once set up a flat-copy photography system, the light source is already matched to the film being used. There is no need to complicate the system by using special filters.

While virtually any slide film will produce a clear, readable image, the best type of film for modules should be one of relatively low contrast that projects well in terms of both color and grain and can be successfully duplicated when additional copies of the module are made.

The recommended film for slide modules is *Kodak Ektachrome slide film ASA 64, or ASA 200 for daylight, and ASA 160 for tungsten light*. Ektachrome ASA 400 for daylight may also be used, but a film of this sensitivity is not needed for this type of photography. All of these films are available in twenty- and thirty-six-exposure rolls. The ASA film speed number designates the light sensitivity of a film (*ASA* in an acronym for *American Standards Association*).

If your camera has an internal light meter, it will have a range of ASA settings for adjusting the light meter. Some cameras also have a set of film-sensitivity markings with the designation DIN. The letters DIN are an acronym for Deutsche Industrie Norm, and this film light-sensitivity designation is used in Europe. American films, however, are usually rated by the ASA system.

The higher the ASA number of a film, the greater the film's sensitivity to light. The ASA speed of the film is an indication of the film's versatility under different light conditions.

The film speed is directly related to the range of shutter speeds and aperture settings that can be used in a given light situation. The shutter speeds and aperture setting profoundly affect the photographic image not only in relation to proper exposure but also in relation to the depth of field of the camera lens which can affect image clarity. (Shutter speeds and aperture settings and the depth of field of the camera lens will be discussed in the next chapter.)

All photographic films, whether black and white or color, possess an image composed of very tiny particles referred to as the *image grain*. The image grain of slide films is usually extremely fine and is not noticeable under normal viewing or projection. It is related to the light sensitivity of the film. Films with a low ASA speed have a finer image grain than those with a high ASA speed. Under normal exposure and processing circumstances, however, all the slide films mentioned earlier have an acceptable image grain.

Most Ektachrome films can be *push-processed* to increase their ASA speed. With push processing, a film with a normal ASA speed of 160 can be made to achieve an effective film speed of ASA 320. An ASA 200 film can be push-processed to a film speed of ASA 400.

Push processing is used to increase the film light sensitivity when it is necessary to make exposures under low-light conditions. This type of processing increases the apparent grain of the photographic image and *should be avoided in the flat-copy photography process*. When photographing the slides of a module, a properly set up lighting system will provide enough illumination to make push processing of the film unnecessary.

BLACK-AND-WHITE TYPEWRITTEN SLIDES

As mentioned in Chapter 2, there is a process by which black-and-white slides can be produced from a typewritten layout. These slides have an all-black image with the type appearing in white (see Figure 7-1).

It is not recommended that entire modules be produced with these slides—the image would lose its impact if repeated too often. Because of their stark visual impact, however, high-contrast black-and-white slides can be used for question sequences or for information that needs special emphasis. The film used for this process is Kodak Technical Pan 2415 (Estar-AH base). This film is available in thirty-six-exposure rolls, and you can process it yourself or you can use any black-and-white processing service.

The layout for this kind of slide is produced with a typewriter, centered on a smooth, clean sheet of white paper. The best kind of typewriter for this purpose is one that has a large type style

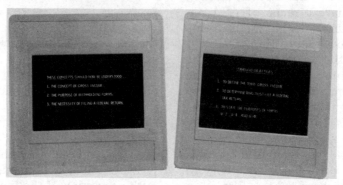

and uses a carbon ribbon that produces clear, sharp characters. It is good procedure to use all capital letters whenever possible. If the type characters are blurred, smudged, or incomplete, the photography process will pick up these flaws and magnify them.

Keep the typewritten copy in the center of the sheet with as much white space around all four sides as possible. Keep double-spaced lines between the lines of type, and typed lines should not exceed six words or so in length. Four or five lines of actual type would be the maximum amount that could be fitted onto the slide while still retaining clarity.

When photographing the layout, use the same procedures described in Chapter 8 with regard to the copystand. Any type of light can be used with this film as long as it is bright.

The ASA speed of copy films is usually low, and to produce a solid-black background it is often necessary to overexpose the film by two or more f/stops than those indicated by a light meter. It is good practice here to shoot an experimental roll of film, retaining the same shutter speed but increasing or decreasing the f/stop for each exposure.

After this first roll has been developed, the frame that has a very dense black background with clear white type can be selected, and the exposure information for that frame is then used for future shots.

Depending on the type of camera lens used, a +2 or +3 close-up accessory lens will be necessary to enlarge the typewritten copy to fill the slide frame.

After the film has been processed, the frames can be mounted in conventional cardboard slide mounts or in thin plastic slide mounts that are available from most camera stores or photographic supply houses.

Limited color can be added to black-and-white slides by placing small, narrow strips of clear, colored mapping tapes to one side of the slide over the clear, white type lines.

PROCESSING, MOUNTING, AND MARKING COLOR SLIDES

Color slide films can be processed through a camera store service, or they can be mailed to the film manufacturer.

Many custom film-processing service firms also offer fast, highly competent film processing. Consult a local telephone directory for custom film-processing services in your area. You can also process color slide films yourself if you have the time and the inclination to do so.

When slide film is returned from the processor, it is usually mounted in numbered cardboard mounts. These numbers stamped on the slide mount may or may not reflect the actual frame number of a given slide in the module you are preparing.

As soon as all of the slides of a module have been processed, assemble them in a row in numerical order from left to right, on a clean dust-free surface. The images should be face up, with the glossy side of the slide film toward you.

The first slide of most modules is the title slide, and this should be marked on the top of the cardboard or plastic slide mount in permanent ink with a fine-pointed marker or ball point pen. Each successive slide should then be marked with the module name or number and the frame number. This step will avoid confusion if the slides of the module are accidentally mixed out of sequence or, in an extreme case, if the slides of two or more modules are accidentally mixed together. Always handle slides by the cardboard mount to avoid getting fingerprints on the film surface.

Fingerprints can be removed from the glossy side of the film surface with a soft paper tissue or a small medical-type cotton swab. Particles of dust can be removed from both sides of the film surface with the aid of a squeeze-bulb duster brush, such as the kind available from camera stores for cleaning lenses and dusting negatives prior to enlargement (see Figure 7–2).

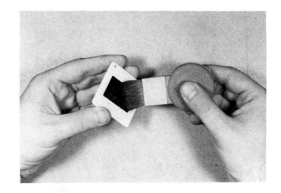

FIGURE 7–2 A squeeze-bulb-type dusting brush, such as those used to clean negatives in the darkroom, is an excellent way of cleaning dust particles off the slide-film surface. Be sure that your fingers do not come into contact with the film, as this can cause smudges and smears.

SLIDE STORAGE

Heat and humidity are the enemies of all types of films. When not in use, slides should always be stored in a cool, dry, dust-free environment.

Although slide-file pages are an excellent way to store slides, this can sometimes be impractical. If the module is used frequently, it is somewhat time consuming to remove and replace slides from the file pages. Therefore, slide sets can be stored in the original boxes supplied by the film processor or in slide-file cases, such as the one shown in Figure 7–3.

Slides can also be stored permanently in the projector tray. This is a particularly good storage system, as the module is then always ready to be used in a personal viewer or projector. Most slide projectors use a circular tray magazine that holds up to 140 slides in sequence. In some projectors, such as the Kodak brand models, the circular tray magazine is on top of the projector. In other projectors, the circular tray is

FIGURE 7-3 Slide-file cases made of metal or plastic are a good way to store large quantities of slides in a relatively clean environment.

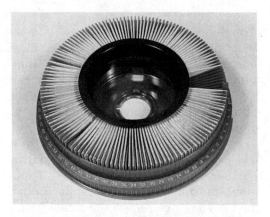

FIGURE 7-4 After placing the slides in a magazine in the desired sequence, run them through a projector to ensure that none have been accidentally reversed or placed upside down.

held in a channel along one side of the projector.

Regardless of the type of projector and circular tray magazine being used, the slides in the tray can be marked for quick loading and sorting. This simple procedure can save a great deal of time and effort when loading a module into a tray for projection.

The first step is to load the module into the magazine tray, orienting the slides according to the manufacturer's instructions for that type of projector. After loading, run the entire module through the projector and check the projected images to make sure that you have not accidentally placed a slide in backwards or upside down (see Figure 7-4).

After checking out the slides by projection, remove the magazine from the module and place it on a table or other surface, face up, with the tops of the slides in the same position as they were when the magazine was being loaded originally. Then, using a large felt-tipped marker with permanent ink, place a large colored dot on the edge of each slide. The dots should be placed

either on the right-hand edge *or* the left-hand edge of the exposed top of each slide mount. *Do not place the dots in the middle of the slide mount.* If you begin marking on the right-hand edge of the first slide, mark *all* the slides on that edge, likewise for marks on the left side (see Figures 7-5 and 7-6).

Once you begin marking the slides in the tray, *always* mark them on the same side and mark all future slides and modules on that side of the mount. If the slides of a marked module are ever removed from the magazine tray, they can be put back without your having to inspect each image *because you will know that having all the dots lined up on that side of the mount means that the slides are in the proper orientation for projection.*

The reason that the slide mounts *should not* be marked in the middle is that although it would indicate that the image is not upside down, it would not indicate whether the slide image is reversed.

By always marking the slide mounts on the left-hand *or* right-hand side, the proper orientation is automatic. The

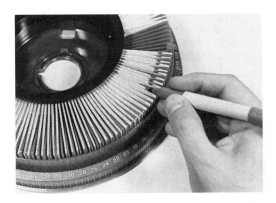

FIGURE 7-5 Using a permanent ink felt-tipped marker, put a dot or mark on the right-hand or left-hand edge of each slide. If you begin marking on the right-hand edge of the mounts, continue on that side throughout the module.

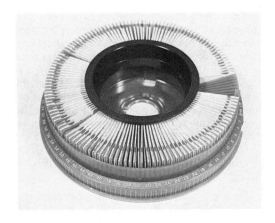

FIGURE 7-6 The marking process will aid in reassembling the module if it is taken out of the magazine at some point for storage or cleaning.

only other element to be checked when loading slides into the magazine is whether they are in the proper numerical order.

To avoid dust and excess humidity, always store the slides in their magazine tray in a tight box or container when not in use.

GLOSSARY

ASA film speed (American Standards Association) A number designation representing the light sensitivity of a photographic film. The higher the ASA number, the more sensitive the film is to light.

Black-and-white slides Slides produced with a black-and-white film (see *typewritten slides*).

Cardboard slide mounts Thin cardboard frames that hold the slide films for projection and viewing.

Cotton swab Designed primarily for medical use, the cotton swab consists of a thin plastic or cardboard tube with cotton fibers wound into a tip at both ends. A swab is very useful for small cleaning jobs on film and camera lenses.

Daylight film A film whose emulsion is designed to produce proper color and tone values when used in conjunction with day-

light, an electronic flash unit, daylight-type flash bulbs, or daylight-type photoflood bulbs.

Daylight-type photoflood bulb A photoflood bulb with a colored glass shell that produces a light that approximates daylight.

DIN Acronym for Deutsche Industrie Norm. A number designation representing the light sensitivity of a photographic film. The DIN system is used primarily in Europe.

Direct positive film A film on which a positive image representation of the original object or scene is produced directly by the development process, rather than being printed from a negative. Slide films are direct positive films.

Fluorescent light Light produced by a fluorescent-type tubular bulb. This light source cannot be used with either daylight- or tungsten-type films unless a special camera filter is used.

F/stop A number representing the size of the opening of the diaphragm in a camera lens, and therefore the amount of light passing through the lens to the film. An *f*/stop number range on a typical 35-mm camera lens would be 1.7, 2.8, 4, 5.6, 8, 11, 16. The smallest number (in this case 1.7) indicates the largest aperture that can be used. The largest number (16) indicates the smallest aperture that the lens is capable of. The lower the *f*/stop number, the greater the amount of light passing through the lens. The higher the *f*/stop number, the less the amount of light passing through the lens.

Lens aperture setting The size of the opening of the diaphragm of a camera lens as indicated by the number of the *f*/stop (see *f/stop*).

Low-contrast image In photography, an image in which the constituent colors or light and dark values are not sharply differentiated.

Overexposure The process of accidentally or deliberately exposing film to more light than would normally be needed to record an image. An overexposure effect can also be produced by extended film-processing times.

Photographic image grain Tiny particles that make up a photographic image. The image grain can usually be seen only under extreme magnification.

Plastic slide mounts Frames of thin, rigid plastic for 35-mm or other types of slides. Plastic slide mounts are used instead of cardboard mounts when the slides are expected to have continuous or rough usage.

Projector circular magazine tray A plastic wheel-shaped tray that can hold up to one hundred slides for projection. Slides can also be permanently stored in the magazine.

Push processing A film development process that increases the light sensitivity of a film. Push processing is often used to improve the photographic image of films that were exposed under very low light conditions.

Slide-file cases Plastic or metal cases used to store and file up to three hundred or more slides.

Slide-film processing The chemical development of direct positive films.

Slide sequence The proper numerical order of the slides of a module for projection and viewing.

Squeeze-bulb duster brush A small hollow rubber bulb with a short rigid tube attached, ending in a soft hair brush. By gently brushing and squeezing the bulb at the same time, dust and heavier particles can safely be removed from slides and other films.

Tungsten light film A film whose emulsion is designed to produce proper color and tone values when used in conjunction with a tungsten light source.

Typewritten slide A black-and-white slide produced from a typewritten layout and photographed on high-contrast copy film. The slides produced by this process have a black background and white type.

8

THE COPYSTAND
AND LIGHTING

THE COPYSTAND AND LIGHTING

The copystand is the heart of the flat-copy photography process because it incorporates a system for the generation of slides that are of consistent quality.

The copystand is a rigid support device that suspends the camera over the flat copy and permits its being photographed under conditions of controlled lighting, minimum camera vibration, and simplified viewfinder framing as well as proper camera-to-copy alignment. These elements are an absolute necessity if properly composed and exposed slides are to be produced.

FIGURE 8-1 A copystand consists of *A*, the flat baseboard; *B*, the vertical support (usually tubular metal); *C*, the camera support-stage arm; and *D*, the camera platform. Although design differences such as height-adjustment cranks and fine-focus rails may appear in different models, all copystands will have the four listed features in the configuration shown.

The copystand consists of a flat baseboard, a rigid vertical support (usually tubular) of 2 feet or so in height, and a camera support-stage arm, whose distance to the baseboard is adjustable (see Figure 8–1).

Copystands are produced by many manufacturers of 35-mm cameras and are also available from companies that manufacture camera accessories and lighting equipment. Many types of darkroom photographic enlargers can be adapted to copystand use by the removal of the enlarger head (see Figure 8-2).

FIGURE 8-2 Some brands of photographic enlargers have a design provision that permits the removal of the enlarger head and the use of the remaining support structure as a copystand.

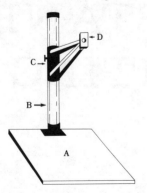

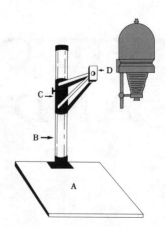

Some copystands have additional features, such as spring-loaded camera support stages and other design variations. Although these can be considered when purchasing a copystand, it is more important to look for the basic structural requirements involved in proper photography.

BASIC STRUCTURAL REQUIREMENTS

The first basic structural requirement for a copystand is rigidity of construction. The copystand should have a solid, heavy baseboard of plywood or particle board, ¾ to 1 inch thick and large enough to easily hold the flat copy that is to be photographed. A baseboard size of approximately 16 by 20 inches is recommended, and the board should be smooth and flat. The copystand vertical support can also be bolted to a desk top or other surface instead of a baseboard if desired.

The vertical support and camera support arm structures should be of an all-metal or predominantly metal construction. The tubular vertical support should be at least 1½ inches in diameter and held to the baseboard.

The camera support stage is usually clamped around the vertical support and, when a setscrew knob is loosened, is adjustable in its height relationship to the baseboard.

The entire camera support-stage assembly should be inspected to make sure that it is rigid and does not slip down the vertical support pole when a downward pressure is placed on it, such as that approximating the weight of a camera.

The entire copystand unit should be placed on a solid support such as a desk top or heavy table to avoid vibration and accidental shifting during use.

The camera is held in place on the camera support-stage arm by a large threaded bolt that extends through the support stage and into the tripod socket on the bottom of the camera. When the camera is bolted into place on the support stage, it will be exactly parallel to the copystand baseboard (see Figures 8–3 and 8–4).

When the camera is in position on the support stage, check the front parallel angle by facing the top of the

FIGURE 8-3 A side view of the copystand and camera indicates how the camera and baseboard (on which the copy to be photographed is placed) are kept in a parallel alignment. This alignment remains the same no matter how near or far from the baseboard the camera is placed.

FIGURE 8-4 When the camera is attached to the copystand support stage, *it points straight down with the top of the camera facing the photographer.* This front-view diagram of the camera on the copystand indicates how the film plane in the camera is kept in parallel alignment with the copystand baseboard.

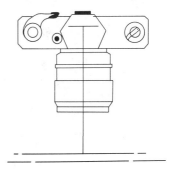

camera at eye level. The camera body and lens *must not* be angled to the left or right, as this will bring about distortions in the slide image (see Figures 8-5 and 8-6). This alignment can be done as an eye judgment. If the camera has to be realigned, it is good practice to loosen the support-stage bolt, straighten the camera, and then tighten the bolt. Do not try to shift the camera by using manual force if the bolt is tight, as this could not only misalign the support stage but damage the camera.

Some cameras have their light meter switches on the bottom plate, near the tripod socket. If this is the case, the meter should be turned on before bolting the camera to the support stage, as the support stage will block access to the switch. The film may be loaded into the camera either before or after it is attached to the copystand.

FIGURE 8-6 Correct camera alignment for the front parallel angle is not automatic when the camera is attached to the copystand support arm as it is with the side parallel angle (see Figure 8-3). Proper front parallel angle alignment for the camera is achieved by eye judgment and careful manual adjustment (see Figure 8-4).

THE LIGHTING SYSTEM

The light sources used in conjunction with a copystand are usually photoflood bulbs. The support system for the light sources can be part of the actual copystand or a separate system.

The main requirements for proper lighting of flat-copy photography are bright, even light and a correct angle of illumination.

Two bulbs, one each on the left and right of the copystand, will provide enough illumination. The bulbs can be operated both through a common switch or individually by a switch on each socket.

Photoflood bulbs generate a great deal of heat during use, and the bulbs should be used only in properly insulated

FIGURE 8-5 After the camera has been attached to the support stage, check the front parallel angle by facing the top of the camera at eye level. The body and lens *must not be angled* to the left or right, or image distortions will appear in the slide (see Figure 8-24). This is an example of improper alignment.

sockets. The bulb sockets should be either ceramic or metal sockets that are held by clamps or a flexible metal gooseneck tube (see Figure 8-7). With properly insulated bulb sockets, there is no danger of burning your hands should the lights need to be repositioned during use.

The photoflood bulbs may also be used in conjunction with a metal reflector dish that threads onto the socket (see Figures 8-8 and 8-9). The reflector dish offers the advantages of increased reflected light in the direction of the

FIGURE 8-7 Photoflood bulbs generate a great amount of heat during use. Be sure that such bulbs are used in ceramic or metal sockets and held by a metal gooseneck or an adjustable metal clamp.

FIGURE 8-9 A reflector dish and socket attached to an adjustable clamp that can be used to hold the lamp to any convenient support.

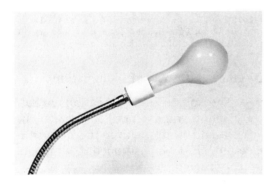

FIGURE 8-8 Photofloods may be used in conjunction with a metal reflector dish that threads onto the socket. The reflector aids in directing the light toward the copy being photographed, as well as providing additional protection from the heat of the bulb.

copy, as well as additional protection from the heat of the bulb. *Always make sure that the photoflood bulbs are not used near materials that can be damaged by heat or catch fire.*

The reflector dishes are not absolutely necessary for proper lighting and can be dispensed with if the bulbs are positioned at a sufficient distance to dispel their heat.

As mentioned earlier, the lighting system can be part of the actual copystand (Figure 8-10), a separate system attached to the baseboard (see Figure 8-11), or a separate free-standing system (Figure 8-12).

Copystand manufacturers usually offer lighting systems for their units. You may wish to make your own lighting system by using clamp-type lights or gooseneck lamps. Making your own system is perfectly acceptable from the standpoint of producing proper illumination, but you must be sure that all the parts are insulated and heat resistant.

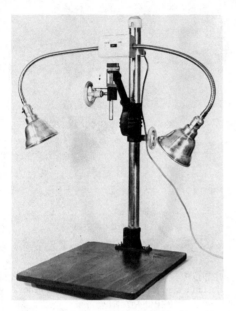

FIGURE 8-10 A copystand with a lighting system attached to the vertical support pole. With this arrangement, the lighting system can be raised and lowered in the same manner as the camera support-stage arm.

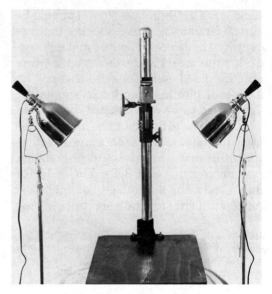

FIGURE 8-12 The copystand can also be used with an entirely separate lighting system, as long as the angle and height of illumination are adjustable.

Distance and Angle of Illumination

The source of illumination in flat-copy photography not only must be intense and uniform over the copy surface but must be positioned to eliminate reflections and lens flare.

The two photoflood bulbs used for the lighting should be placed at a distance from the copy to provide even illumination while not subjecting the copy to excessive heat. This distance varies with the illumination power of the type of bulbs being used. For example, when using 250-watt, 3200-degree Kelvin photoflood bulbs, a bulb-to-copy distance of 16 to 22 inches is appropriate. For bulbs of lesser wattage, different distances can be tried and a choice can be made by examining the developed slides. The Kelvin-degree designation for the bulbs is an indicator of the color temperature of the light being produced. Consult the manufacturer's instructions

FIGURE 8-11 A copystand with a lighting system attached to the baseboard. Because this copystand was designed to photograph very large copy, the lighting system has four lamps (two on each side) to illuminate the baseboard area evenly.

as to the color temperature of the light source that should be used with your film.

The angle of illumination is just as important as the intensity and proper distance of the light source from the copy. This angle should be approximately 45 degrees from the horizontal surface on the right and left of the copystand (see Figure 8-13). If the angle of illumination is too high, the lights will be reflected on the copy surface or will create *hot spots*, which are areas of too-intense light that ruins both color and image clarity. For these same reasons, focused-type flood lamps *should not be used* for copy photography because the light they reflect is not uniform enough to produce acceptable images (see Figure 8-14).

FIGURE 8-13 Position the lights on the left and right sides of the baseboard at an angle approximately 45 degrees from the horizontal, and at a distance of approximately 16 to 22 inches from the center of the baseboard.

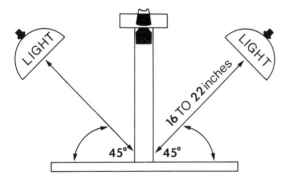

FIGURE 8-14 Focused-type bell-shaped flood lamps, such as the kind used for outdoor lighting, *are not suitable* for copy photography because the focused light causes uneven illumination in the slide image.

PHOTOGRAPHING FLAT COPY

When the camera, copystand, and lighting system have been set up, the flat copy can be positioned and photographed.

Assemble and align the background and overlay sheets of the flat on the copystand base by lining up their overlapping registration marks. Then place a T square across the copystand base to help align the copy in the viewfinder during focusing and composition. The lower edge of the reassembled flat is then butted against the T square shaft (see Figure 8-15).

Look through the camera viewfinder and slide the flat and T square to a position on the baseboard where the image appears centered in the viewfinder. At this point, if the camera and support arm are at the top of the vertical support shaft, the entire flat as well as part of the T square shaft and part of the copystand baseboard will be visible in the camera viewfinder (see Figure 8-16).

The next step is to release the setscrew on the camera support stage

FIGURE 8-15 Position a T square across the baseboard to help align the copy image in the camera viewfinder.

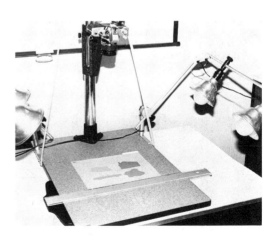

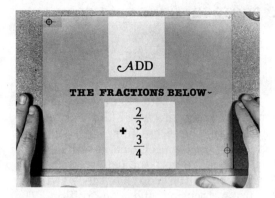

FIGURE 8-16 If the camera support arm and camera are at the top of the vertical support shaft of the copy-stand, the entire flat as well as part of the T square shaft and part of the surrounding baseboard will be visible in the camera viewfinder.

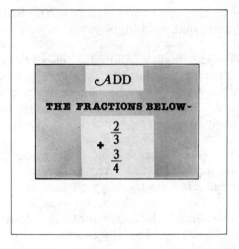

FIGURE 8-18 When the flat-copy image completely fills the viewfinder to all four edges, the camera is at a proper distance to take the picture. Check for type alignment with the horizontal edges of the viewfinder. Any flaws in the camera alignment or lighting will show up in the final slide.

and slowly slide the camera and stage toward the baseboard. Keep checking the slowly enlarging image of the flat in the viewfinder, and stop sliding the camera down when the background sheet of the flat fills the viewfinder from edge to edge both vertically and horizontally (see Figures 8-17 and 8-18).

At this point, tighten the camera support-stage setscrew, and focus the camera lens until the image is clear. Before photographing the flat, make sure that the acetate overlay does not

FIGURE 8-17 To enlarge the image of the flat copy appearing in the viewfinder, release the camera support stage and move it and the camera *down*, in the direction of the baseboard.

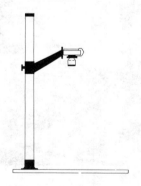

lift at the corners or buckle at the center. The moderate heat of the photo-flood bulbs that reaches the overlay can cause curling and buckling, and this in turn will produce fuzzy, out-of-focus type.

The best way to overcome this problem is with a sheet of *matte-surface glass* or plastic that is usually called *nonglare*, or *no-glare*, *glass*. This material is used to frame pictures that have a glossy, reflective surface. An 11-by-14-inch sheet can be purchased at a large art supply store, picture-framing store, or camera supply shop. If the glass is not sold separately, it can sometimes be purchased in combination with an inexpensive picture frame, and then the glass can be removed for this photographic application.

After adjusting the camera-to-base distance as described earlier, focus the image of the flat to clarity, and then place the sheet of matte glass over the flat and refocus to ensure clarity. At this point, you may set the camera shutter speed, take a light meter reading, and set the f/stop on the camera lens aperture ring. Before taking an exposure, look through the viewfinder once again to make sure that the type lines on the flat are exactly parallel to the top and bottom edges of the viewfinder outline, and that there are no disconcerting stray reflections on the surface of the matte glass or the flat beneath it.

Remember that you will be photographing exactly what you see.

EXPOSURE BRACKETING

A traditional method of obtaining the best combination of exposure and color content in a slide is to produce several slides of the same subject at different camera settings and then choose the best. Bracketing a series of three exposures for each frame, and keeping a record of each, will enable you to determine the best exposure combination of shutter speed and f/stop, as well as being an indicator of meter accuracy in relation to this photography process.

For example, at a shutter speed of 1/60 of a second, the camera meter will perhaps indicate an aperture setting of f/5.6. Take an exposure at these settings and then, *keeping the same shutter speed*, take an exposure one f/stop above the meter-indicated setting (in this case, f/8) and one f/stop below the meter setting (f/4). If the camera lens you are using has the capability of f/stop settings between the marked f/stops, you may wish to bracket your exposures ½ f/stop above and below the meter-indicated setting.

When the bracketed exposure slides are developed and mounted, compare them by projection and select the best exposure–color saturation combination. Then consult the recorded exposure information for that slide and use that information for future exposures. For example, you may find that the best exposed slide was produced at one f/stop under that indicated by the camera meter. Therefore, consistently setting the aperture one f/stop under the meter indication (regardless of the fact that this number will change from frame to frame) for all future exposures, a uniformity of exposure quality can be established.

SHUTTER SPEED
AND f/STOP SETTINGS

There is a range of shutter speeds and f/stop settings that, for purely mechanical reasons, produces the best exposure results in the flat-copy photography process. Your camera will undoubtedly have a larger range of exposure capabilities, but some of these settings should be avoided because they have the potential to generate image problems.

Shutter speeds of *less* than 1/60 of a second should be avoided whenever possible. The risk of camera or copystand vibration causing blurred images at slower shutter speeds is quite pronounced. Shutter speeds of *more* than 1/250 of a second should also be avoided. Although there is no risk of vibration-clarity problems at very fast shutter speeds, they create the necessity of using very wide aperture settings, which can affect image quality.

Using a very high shutter speed will usually necessitate setting the lens aperture at, or very near, wide open (the lowest f/stop and largest diaphragm opening). Depending on the type of lens, this can cause image problems. Some camera lenses experience a loss of image sharpness near the edges of the film frame when their apertures are wide open. Other lenses will cause straight lines to curve or become distorted near the edges of the film frame.

A wide-open aperture setting also greatly reduces the depth of field of the lens. This means that focusing will become a more critical factor, and there will be a greater possibility of image sharpness problems than if the lens is used at a higher f/stop.

The depth of field of a camera lens is related to the aperture setting and its effect on focus. For example, if photographing an object that is 7 feet away from the camera, using an aperture setting of f/16, everything within a zone of 5 feet to approximately 12 feet from the camera will be in focus. However, if an aperture setting of f/2.8 is used at the same distance of 7 feet, the zone of sharp focus is reduced to approximately $6\frac{1}{2}$ feet to $7\frac{1}{2}$ feet. At f/16 the zone of sharp focus is about 7 feet deep.

However, when the aperture is opened to f/2.8, the zone of sharp focus is reduced to only about 1 foot deep (see Figure 8-19). The depth of field will vary with the type of camera lens and its internal design; however, most lenses have a depth-of-field scale printed on the lens barrel. For more specific information on depth of field, consult your camera or lens manual, or a reference text on technical photography.

The depth-of-field capability of the camera lens has a direct application to flat-copy photography. By using slower shutter speeds, and using higher ASA film speeds, smaller apertures (higher

FIGURE 8-19 The depth of field, or zone of sharp focus, appearing in a picture is controlled by the aperture setting of the camera lens. In this example, both pictures were taken at the same distance, with the lens focused on the middle chess piece. In the top photograph, the camera lens was set wide open (in this case, f/1.7) when the exposure was made. Note that the near and far chess pieces are out of focus. This is an example of shallow depth of field. In the bottom photograph, the exposure was made at a slower shutter speed with a much smaller aperture setting (in this case, f/11). The near and far chess pieces are in sharper focus. This is an example of increased depth of field.

f/stop numbers) can be used. Smaller apertures increase the depth of field of the lens, which, because of the short distance between the camera and the copy, was quite small to begin with. For example, at a camera-to-copy distance of 2 feet, an aperture setting of $f/2.8$ will produce a zone of focus ranging from approximately 1 foot 11 inches to less than 2 feet 1 inch.

However, at the same camera-to-copy distance, 2 feet, an aperture setting of $f/16$ produces a zone focus ranging from 1 foot 9 inches to over 2 feet 2 inches. Obviously, the use of higher f/stops decreases the chances of a slight focus error ruining a slide (see Figure 8-20). Therefore, the use of apertures that are $f/4$ or larger is *not* recommended unless absolutely necessary.

COMMON IMAGE PROBLEMS AND THEIR SOLUTIONS

Problem: Off-Center Image (Figure 8-21)

An off-center image in a slide occurs when the lines of type do not

FIGURE 8-21 An off-center image caused by improper framing of the flat copy in the camera viewfinder.

have an equal border of distance around all four sides. Usually, one border on either the left or right side, or on the top or bottom, is too narrow. Although this problem does not necessarily affect the readability of the slide, the overall

FIGURE 8-20 During flat-copy photography, the use of a higher f/stop aperture setting on the camera lens is recommended for increased depth of field. This extra depth of focus is good insurance of image sharpness, especially if the flat is made up of several layers of cut paper with acetate overlays.

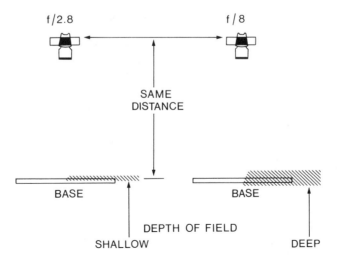

imbalance caused by a narrow border makes it difficult for the viewer to concentrate on the information.

Solution

Greater care should be taken when aligning the image of the flat copy in the camera viewfinder. It is quite easy to forget to establish equal borders around the type copy when your attention is on focusing, meter readings, and so on.

Problem: Nonparallel Type (Figure 8-22)

This problem occurs when the flat copy is not in proper alignment with the camera. The resulting slide has lines of type in the image that are not in parallel alignment with the upper and lower edges of opening in the slide mount.

Solution

If the flat copy was aligned properly on the copystand baseboard with a T square, the problem would then be a misalignment of the camera support

stage. To check the camera support stage, place the copystand on the floor or on a low table and look from directly above it at the position of the camera and support stage in relation to the copystand baseboard beneath. The camera support-stage arm should be exactly perpendicular to the front edge of the copystand baseboard. If it is not, loosen the setscrew holding the camera support arm to the vertical shaft, and swing the support structure until it is exactly perpendicular to the baseboard front edge (see Figure 8-23).

Problem: Nonparallel Image Sides (Figure 8-24)

Nonparallel sides are an image distortion caused by an improper camera-to-copy angle. Only the horizontal, longer pair of sides of the image are affected by this problem. Sometimes the distortion is so slight that it goes unnoticed until the slides are projected. This can also be the cause of a loss of type sharpness on one side of the image.

FIGURE 8-22 A slide in which the lines of type are nonparallel to the horizontal edges of the slide frame opening. This flaw is caused by improper framing of the flat copy in the camera viewfinder.

FIGURE 8-23 If nonparallel-type lines occur in a slide or series of slides even though the flat copies were aligned properly on the copystand baseboard (with the aid of a T square), the problem will then be related to a misalignment of the camera support stage. The camera and support-stage arm (when viewed from above) must be perpendicular to the front edge of the copystand baseboard.

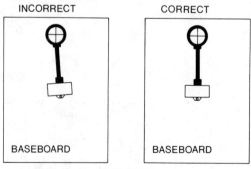

TOP VIEW

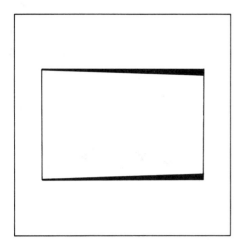

FIGURE 8-24 A slide in which the image has non-parallel sides, resulting in a "wedge" shape, is caused by an improper camera-to-copy angle.

Solution

The front parallel angle between the camera and the baseboard must be checked and corrected. As mentioned earlier in this chapter (and illustrated in Figures 8-4, 8-5, and 8-6), face the top of the camera at eye level and make sure that the camera body and lens are exactly parallel to the baseboard surface (see Figure 8-25).

FIGURE 8-25 The front parallel angle between the camera and the baseboard must be checked and adjusted if necessary to ensure that the film plane is parallel to the baseboard.

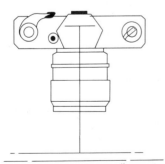

Problem: Hot Spots and Reflections (Figures 8-26A and 8-26B)

Hot spots are areas, usually near the edges of the film frame, that appear much brighter than the area in the center of the frame. *Reflections* are white streaks, blurs, or shapes that bleach out

FIGURE 8-26A, B Image problems caused by improper lighting adjustments.
Top: Hot spots caused by the lights being too near the edges of the flat copy.
Bottom: Reflections or bleached-out areas of the image caused by the lamp angle being too high on that side of the flat copy.

(A)

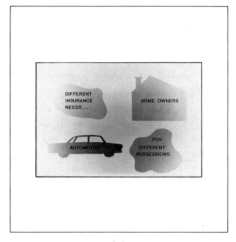

(B)

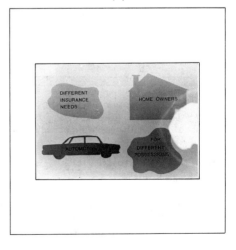

or obliterate parts of the color and image. *Both* of these problems are caused by improper lighting angles or by light sources that are too near the copy.

Solution

The occurrence of both hot spots and unwanted reflections can be prevented by very careful observation through the camera viewfinder. Always double-check the extreme right and left sides of the viewfinder image for a crescent-shaped white streak, which indicates that the angle of the lamp on that side is too high. Keep in mind that *both* the right and the left light sources should be at the same angle to the baseboard and the *same distance to the center of the copy.*

If one light source is nearer to the copy than the other, the nearer side will be lighter. This will cause hot spots and may also fool the camera light meter into giving an *f*/stop reading that is too high (see Figure 8-27).

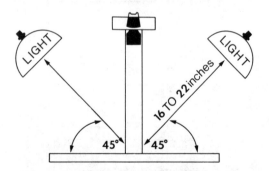

FIGURE 8-27 To avoid hot spots and reflections in the photographed image, be sure to keep the angles and distance of illumination at the proper adjustments.

Problem: Overextended Field of Image (Figure 8-28)

Unlike any of the preceding image problems, the overextended field of image is a purely mechanical problem

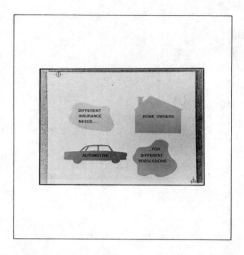

FIGURE 8-28 In this slide, the flat-copy image does not completely fill the frame, thus exposing part of the baseboard and the register marks on the extreme edges of the overlay. If this image flaw occurs even though everything seemed correct through the viewfinder when the image was photographed, the cause of the problem is a discrepancy between the viewfinder image and the field of coverage of the lens.

that is not caused by any fault of the photographer. The main symptom of the overextended field is seen in the developed slides. The slides exhibit an area that is larger than the flat copy, so that part of the copystand baseboard is seen around the edges of the slide, *even though this area did not appear in the camera viewfinder when the slides were exposed.*

Solution

An overextended field of image occurs when the camera lens covers a larger visual area than can be seen in the camera viewfinder. In an SLR camera, the light and image that passes through the camera lens is reflected to the viewfinder focusing screen through a system consisting of a mirror and a complex prism. When an exposure is made, the mirror panel within the camera rapidly swings out of the light path as the shutter curtain at the back of the camera opens to expose the film to light.

With some SLR cameras, the internal design demands of the various mechanical systems within the camera necessitate the use of a mirror that is slightly smaller than the area of visual coverage of the lens. The result is a discrepancy between what is seen in the viewfinder and the total, actual image that appears on the film frame. This discrepancy usually takes the form of a *larger* area of image coverage than was seen through the viewfinder.

The only method of correcting an overextended field of image is a trial-and-error approach. This approach is the only practical one insofar as the size of the field discrepancy will vary depending on the make and model of the camera, as well as the focal length of the lens. The best practice here is to shoot a set of slides starting with one that has the image of the flat copy *apparently* filling the viewfinder to all four edges. Then, with each successive exposure, move the camera ½ inch closer to the copy and refocus. The distance required to correct the lens-viewfinder discrepancy is usually minimal, seldom over an inch or so.

Problem: Curved, Straight Lines (Figure 8–29)

Like the problem of the overextended field of image described earlier, *curved, straight lines* are a purely mechanical image distortion. The problem here centers on the translation of straight lines and lines of type in the flat copy to curved lines that bow out at the center of the slide and tend to draw together toward the edges of the film frame area. This symptom is usually quite subtle, and because it is difficult to see through

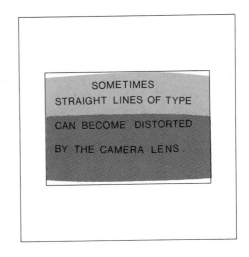

FIGURE 8–29 A slide in which lines of type or straight lines in the design appear slightly curved, although these lines were undistorted in the original flat copy. This flaw is caused by the camera lens, which is producing a linear distortion in the photographed image.

the viewfinder, it first becomes apparent when the slides are projected.

Solution

Curved, straight lines are a lens aberration that bends and distorts the light rays and, therefore, the image passing through the lens to the film. Linear distortion usually occurs when the lens is used with the aperture set at near or wide open. By setting the aperture at the high end of the scale (f/8, f/11, f/16, or higher), the light rays are channeled through the center of the lens, and this usually reduces or eliminates the linear distortion experienced at the large apertures.

In order to use high f/stop apertures and still produce properly exposed slides, it will be necessary to use slower shutter speeds and possibly a higher ASA film speed. If the linear distortion still persists at high f/stop apertures, replacing the lens should be considered.

Problem: Shadowed Type
(Figure 8-30)

Shadowed type appears as a darkened or smudged area in and around individual letters, or as a double edge or shadow edge to a letter. The shadowed-type effect usually occurs intermittently around the surface of the flat or in a single small area, rather than uniformly to all the letters and words.

Solution

Shadowed type is caused when the acetate overlay on which the pressure sensitive type is placed is not in consistent and uniform contact with the background color sheet beneath it. The result is an area or areas of the acetate that are raised, and the type on them casts a shadow on the background sheet. The best insurance against these raised acetate areas is the matte-surface glass sheet described earlier. The purpose of the matte-surface glass sheet is twofold. First, it reduces the occurrence of reflections on the surface of the flat copy while being photographed. Second, it provides a consistent and uniform

FIGURE 8-30 A close-up of part of a line of type with a shadow appearing behind the letters. This flaw is produced when the acetate overlay is photographed while not being in completely flat contact with the background sheet.

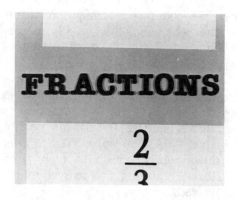

surface pressure on the flat copy and keeps the acetate overlay from raising or buckling.

Place the matte-surface sheet over the positioned and aligned flat copy on the copystand baseboard, and press the glass sheet down gently at the edges to ensure proper contact before photographing. If the shadow persists, check to see whether the copystand baseboard itself has a flat, level surface.

A FINAL WORD

Most image problems that develop during the photographing of a module can be traced to a forgotten step or a neglected adjustment. When faced with an image problem in the processed slides, always look first for a simple adjustment or a forgotten production step, and only after eliminating these, examine the possibility of mechanical failure.

The best way to ensure a minimum of image problems—or, for that matter, most problems in general—is to establish a rigid system for each of the steps taken to create a module. If necessary, write these steps down and consult this list for the first few modules until you have committed it to memory.

Always take good care of your tools. Whether it be an expensive camera or an inexpensive felt-tipped marker, treat all materials and equipment with respect. Store equipment away from dust and humidity, and store equipment and materials used for one part of a process away from the materials used for another so that you will always be able to locate specific tools quickly.

Do not waste time by trying to force a tool or material designed for one purpose to do another. Unfortunately, the "make-do" materials almost always look that way. These simple precautions and a step-by-step approach to each phase of production will consistently reward you with time and work saved and a successful, professional product.

GLOSSARY

Angle of illumination The angle in which two photoflood bulbs are placed to the right and left side of the copystand base to illuminate the flat copy for photographing. The proper angle of illumination is 45 degrees above the horizontal plane of the copystand baseboard.

Camera mirror In SLR cameras, a small mirror that directs the image passing through the camera lens to a glass prism that directs it to the photographer's eye. When an exposure is made, the mirror swings out of the way allowing light to pass through—past the shutter door at the back of the camera—to the film.

Camera prism In SLR cameras, the *pentaprism* is part of the camera viewfinder system. This prism transmits the light rays—passing through the camera lens and reflected to the prism by the camera mirror—to the photographer's eye (see *camera mirror*).

Camera tripod socket A threaded coupling in the baseplate of the camera body that allows it to be attached to a tripod or copystand with a threaded bolt.

Copystand A rigid support device consisting of a flat baseboard, a vertical support column, and a camera support-stage arm. The copystand allows the suspension of the camera over the flat copy for photographing under conditions of controlled lighting, minimum camera vibration, and simplified viewfinder framing.

Copystand baseboard A flat support board, usually made of wood or particle board, on which the flat copy is placed for photographing, and to which the vertical support column is attached.

Copystand camera support-stage arm An adjustable support arm that suspends the camera over the baseboard and flat copy.

Copystand vertical support A rigid metal support, usually tubular and approximately 2 feet in height, that holds the copystand camera support-stage arm and the baseboard in parallel alignment.

Curved, straight lines The symptoms of this image problem are that straight lines or lines of type in the flat copy are rendered curved in the slide image. Curved, straight lines are caused by a lens aberration that bends and distorts the light rays, and hence the image, passing through it to the film.

Depth of field The term applied to the relationship between focus and aperture in a given camera lens. The depth of field is a zone of sharp focus that is produced by the aperture setting at any focus point. This zone of focus increases in depth with a higher aperture (*f/* stop) setting and becomes more shallow as the aperture is opened up.

Distance of illumination The distance from the center of the flat copy to each light bulb on the left and right of the baseboard. The bulb-to-copy distance varies with the power of the bulbs and can be determined by examining test exposures made at varying distances. When using 250-watt, 3200-degree Kelvin bulbs, a distance of 16 to 22 inches between the bulb and the center of the copy can be used.

Exposure bracketing The practice of taking several exposures using the same shutter speed, and under the same lighting conditions, but increasing or decreasing the lens aperture by $\frac{1}{2}$ or 1 *f/*stop for each successive exposure. The purpose of exposure bracketing is to produce several exposures from which the best, in terms of color and brightness, can be chosen.

Focused-type flood lamp A bell-shaped electric light bulb with a lens built into the front of the bulb to focus the light on an intense spot. This type of bulb is not recommended for flat-copy photography, as the light is too focused. The focused-type flood lamp should not be confused with nonfocused flood lamps that have a frosted lens and produce a more uniform illumination suitable for flat-copy photography.

Gooseneck tube A thin, flexible metal tube with a threaded adapter on one end that allows it to be coupled to an electric bulb socket. Gooseneck tubes allow the socket and bulb attached to them to be placed in many different positions in relation to a desk or working surface.

Hot spots Areas of intense illumination that partially bleach out the image near the edges of the slide frame. Hot spots are caused by a photoflood bulb's being too near the side of the flat copy during photography.

Kelvin degrees A numerical scale used to designate the color temperature of a light source. Some color films designed for use with artificial light will have a Kelvin-degree designation determined by the manufacturer.

Lighting system The illumination source for flat-copy photography. The lighting system either is attached directly to the copystand or can be a free-standing separate system of photoflood bulbs.

Matte-surface glass Sometimes referred to as nonglare or no-glare glass. This material has a much less reflective surface than the conventional window or picture-framing glass sheets. Although primarily intended for picture-framing purposes, matte-surface glass has useful applications in flat-copy photography.

Nonparallel image sides Two narrow wedge-shaped areas that appear along the top and bottom edges of the film frame. The wedge-shaped areas reveal the copystand baseboard beyond the edges of the flat copy and are caused by a nonparallel camera-to-copy alignment.

Nonparallel type A slide in which the lines of type in the image are not in a parallel relationship to the upper and lower edges of the cutout opening of the slide mount. Nonparallel type is usually caused by improper positioning of the flat copy when photographing it.

Off-center image A slide whose type and image content is not centered in the middle of the cutout opening of the slide mount. Off-center images are usually caused by improper positioning of the flat copy when photographing it.

Overextended field of image A slide whose image area covers more than the total size of the flat copy and extends into the copystand baseboard area, even though properly framed in the viewfinder when the exposure was taken. This effect is caused when the camera lens covers an area that is larger than that appearing in the viewfinder.

Photographic enlarger A darkroom device that projects the photographic negative onto sensitized paper for development into the positive print. Some enlargers have a removable head, which allows the enlarger baseboard and vertical support to be used as a copystand.

Reflector dish A round, dish-shaped enclosure made of polished metal. The dish has a threaded opening at the bottom, which allows it to be threaded to a standard light bulb socket. The reflector dish helps to produce a more uniform illumination for the flat copy.

Shadowed type A dark smudge or shadowed edge appearing around some letters or words in the slide image. Shadowed type is caused by the acetate overlay buckling or lifting slightly away from the background sheet and causing a soft-edge shadow to appear on the background. If this problem is not detected prior to photographing the flat, the flaw will appear in the developed slide.

Zone of sharp focus See *Depth of field.*

9
THE AUDIO
PORTION

THE AUDIO PORTION

The audio portion of the sound-slide module has two vital functions with regard to the educational success goal of the unit.

The first of these functions is the obvious one of *explanation*. The visual portion of the module is not, nor was it ever meant to be, completely self-sufficient in terms of the information presentation.

The audio portion does much more than merely repeat the written information appearing in the visual or describe the image. The audio portion clarifies and enlarges upon the visual presentation. The viewer's eyes are led and directed through the presented image. Selected parts of the visual image can be emphasized by pauses in the audio portion, as well as changes in the inflection of the narrator's voice.

The second vital function of the audio portion of the module involves *pacing*. Because the amount of information varies from frame to frame, the narration of the module, by causing the viewer to follow the information at a preset pace, establishes an even information flow. This information flow pace discourages the viewer from rushing through or skipping over information presented in the visual, which may be vital to the understanding of the module as a whole.

NARRATION AND THE SCRIPT

The two principal ways of presenting the audio-narration of the module are by using either a live instructor or a cassette tape (the use of a cassette tape recorder for sound-slide modules has been established as a standard in the media industry). Actual methods of recording the audio-narration of the module are covered later in this chapter.

The obvious advantage of a recorded narration is that an instructor does not have to be present when the module is being used. Thus there is greater flexibility as to where and when the module will be presented, as well as allowing the student-viewers to replay all or part of the module. The availability of a recorded narration also permits an individual to study the entire module without impeding the progress of the rest of the study group or class.

The foundation of the narration is the script. Spontaneous narration, even for very informal subject matter, should be avoided for reasons that will become apparent. The narration can and should be presented in an *informal-sounding* and conversational manner, but it must be based on an accurate and detailed written script. As explained in Chapter 1, each frame of the module builds on the information presented in the preceding one.

Spontaneous narration does not promote the logical progression and increase of information with each additional frame. Even an experienced educator who thoroughly knows the module subject and is familiar with the process of extemporaneous speaking will experience difficulties with smooth and continuous information flow when attempting to produce a spontaneous narration.

Before beginning the recording process, the script should be reread and compared with the finished slides to make sure that the sequence is in proper order and that, in the process of producing the visuals, no information has been changed or omitted.

Even though a complete and detailed script has been prepared before the planning and creating of the visuals, it is good practice to review the narration part one final time before the recording process so that there will be no stumbling blocks in the logical information flow. Potential stumbling blocks for the viewer can be avoided by observing the following procedures:

1. Make sure that all technical terms are fully explained. If you don't know whether a viewer has prior knowledge of a term, explain it anyway.

2. Try to read the narration and compare it with the visual portion by using the general vocabulary of a viewer who is completely unfamiliar with the subject. Try to target any general descriptive language for the general education and sophistication of the viewer audience.

3. Make sure that the narrative is always directly related to the visual and that only the information present in the visual is given.

4. Eliminate any superfluous dialogue or time-wasting introductory terms or phrases in the narration, such as "Here we have . . ." or "Now we come to . . ." or "As you can see here . . ."

5. Make sure that the narration follows the information in the visual logically and does not skip about the image. For example, if three written statements are given and are to be repeated by narration, begin with the top statement in the visual and work down.

6. Do not break a sentence or statement between frames unless the visuals are clearly related and carry the idea.

7. Do not send the viewer back to an earlier frame in the module. If you wish to repeat a point or reinforce information, show the visual again.

8. Whenever possible, avoid phrases that force the viewer back to earlier parts of the module. Phrases such as "As you may remember . . ." or "As we studied earlier in frame six . . ." will ruin the logical flow of the module.

The elements of this checklist may seem rather simplistic, but in the process of producing the visuals and trying to match them properly to both the script and the final learning goal of the module, it is easy to overlook a flaw that can cause trouble later.

If a problem does become apparent during this final proofreading, it is still not too late to make corrections or adjustments. Even if the problem is a serious one, an extra frame or two can be added to cover a weak area in the module.

THE NARRATOR

The best narrator is the author-designer of the module. This person will be most familiar with not only the subject but the arrangement of the information flow. The module author will also be familiar with the proper pronunciation of all the technical terms. If a person other than the module author is to read the narration, he or she should check the pronunciation of all technical terms or unfamiliar words.

Before recording the narration, it is good practice to try at least one "dry run" through the script from beginning to end. This is useful for two reasons. First, it allows the narrator to become familiar with the *pattern* of words and sentences. Even if the narrator is the author of the module and is therefore completely familiar with its contents, he or she will find that the written words produce a pattern that differs from that of the spoken words. In addition, some word combinations or sentences that have a complex structure are difficult to read aloud the first time without pauses. These pauses might confuse the module viewer and should be eliminated from the recorded narration. The best way to eliminate pauses in speech or false starts is by simply practicing the narration a few times.

The second reason for the trial narration is that it establishes a time period for the entire module. A module time length can be determined by noting on a clock (or a stopwatch if one is available) the length of time it takes to read the entire module narration aloud, with approximately *five seconds* of blank time between the end of each frame statement and the beginning of the next. These five-second blanks represent the time that will be given the module user

to advance the projector to the next frame of the module when given an audible signal to do so.

Begin a narration timing by marking down the exact time of day or activating a stopwatch, and then read the module narration aloud. Read the statements in a calm, even voice of normal volume. Do not rush through the statements or, conversely, read them at a slower than normal pace.

Your speech should sound clear, and because you are reading a script, somewhat formal. However, it is quite possible to inject a relaxed, conversational tone into your speech. Remember that your normal speech, coupled with the visual presentation for any particular frame, will be more than sufficient to hold the viewer's attention without lecturing or overemphasizing words.

Overemphasizing words by reading sentences too slowly is a common problem for the inexperienced narrator. In normal conversational speech, the listener automatically pays more attention to words that are singled out of the flow of information by either saying them louder than normally or inserting a verbal pause before and after them.

When the narrator reads the module script at too slow a pace, the viewer-listener is confused because undue emphasis is being placed on too many words in each statement. This causes the viewer-listener to confuse the information value of the module's statement.

By keeping a normal tone and pattern of conversational speech, the narrator can emphasize specific words or phrases by the selective process of inflections on the verbal sounds that are used in everyday conversation.

Having made one or more narration trial runs, a time period for the entire module has now been established and is important for several reasons.

First, the length of time that the module runs, in minutes, should be marked both on the module storage box, the cassette tape that contains the audio-narration, and on a copy of the written narration script which should be included with the slides and tape. The module presentation length, or *running time*, is valuable information for the instructor who may wish to utilize the module during a limited amount of classroom time. Students also need to know the running time so that they can effectively fit the module into a study schedule.

Having an accurate record of the module running time is also important when actually recording the audio-narration, because thirty-minute, sixty-minute, and ninety-minute cassette tapes are available. With an established module running time, the cassette-tape length that is closest to the actual module running time can be chosen for the narration. (The cassette tape and the recording process will be described in detail later in this chapter.)

When reading the narration, it is important to avoid paraphrasing or embellishing. Even a single additional word can confuse the module user, especially if technical or complex written information appearing in the visual is being repeated by the narrator. For example, assume that the following printed set of statements appears in a visual:

> *Do not* mix water into acid.
> *Always* mix acid into water.

However, the narrator unintentionally embellishes the script (which calls for simply repeating this information) by saying, "Don't mix water into acid, but always remember to mix acid into water." The addition of the superfluous words *but* and *remember to* in the second statement does nothing to en-

hance the content of the frame and can confuse the viewer, who will probably be silently reading the statements along with the narrator. The extra words cause breaks in the flow of the viewer's concentration by presenting verbal information that does not appear as written words in the visual. Even the use of the contraction *don't* for *do not* can cause a break in viewer concentration. The narrator should always repeat *only* what is written in the script.

Avoid using more than one narrator for a module unless a difference in voices will aid the viewer's understanding of the subject being presented. For example, if presenting a dialogue between two persons as part of a module, the use of two different narration voices can help the viewer understand the information being exchanged or offered. Otherwise, multiple narration voices will cause confusion.

Finally, always supply a typewritten copy of the narration script with the narration tape and slide set for each module. This will be very valuable if the tape is damaged or lost, or if a recorded word or phrase is unclear to the viewer, allowing direct reference to the narration-script.

RECORDING THE NARRATION

As mentioned earlier, the use of a cassette tape recorder for audio-visual materials that have a separate sound track, such as sound-slide modules and filmstrips, has been established as a standard in the media industry. The choice of this recording device is based primarily on its excellent sound quality and compactness, as well as its relative inexpensiveness when compared with other, more complex, recording equipment. The cassette recorder is quite simple to use, and the cassette tape is small and easy to store either separately or in a slide-module storage box.

Another useful feature of the cassette tape, especially if it is to be used by persons who are unfamiliar with recording devices, is that the tape is self-loading. There are no tape reels or intricate tape threading involved in either the recording or the playback function.

Cassette tapes are available in time lengths designated C-30, C-60, and C-90. The numbers indicate the cassette's total minute running time. To determine the running time available for one side of the cassette, divide the designation number in half. Therefore, C-30 tapes have a fifteen-minute running time per side.

The C-90 tapes (forty-five minutes per side) *are not* recommended for narration recording. The C-90 tapes usually contain a thinner recording tape to facilitate the extended recording time. This thinner tape is more subject to mechanical problems in the recorder, such as jamming and slipping. In addition, some cassette recorders do not have a motor that is strong enough to turn the spools of a C-90 cassette at recording and playback speed, causing distortions in the recorded sounds.

On the average, most sound-slide presentations do not run longer than one-half hour. However, if a longer narration time is required, a second cassette can be added to the module.

Tape Preparation

When a cassette tape length has been chosen for the module and the narrator has had the opportunity to practice reading the script a few times, the actual narration recording can begin.

First, prepare the cassette tape for recording by manually advancing the tape in the cassette a few inches until the leader ends and the actual recording tape

appears in the small opening at the front of the cassette (see Figures 9–1A and 9–1B). This adjustment is done by holding the cassette with the front opening toward you. The tape should be entirely on the left spool (during recording and playback, the tape runs from the left spool to the right). The tape spool can be seen in the small clear plastic window built into the top of the cassette for this purpose. Then, by using your finger tip or a small piece of cardboard, turn the right spool in a *counterclockwise* direction until the leader, which is clear or colored tape, passes by and the actual recording tape runs across the front of

FIGURE 9–1A The tape cassette is a spool of narrow recording tape encased in a plastic carrier. Seen from the top are two gear openings that engage the drive mechanism of the tape recorder. A small, clear window allows for the viewing of how much tape is on each spool. The tape runs from left to right, so the left spool should be full when you begin recording.

FIGURE 9–1B The front of the cassette reveals a series of openings that give access to the recording and playback heads of the recorder. A length of clear leader can be seen running across the openings.

the cassette. The color of this recording tape is usually brown. The cassette can then be loaded into the recorder in accordance with the manufacturer's instructions (see Figures 9-2 and 9-3).

The Audible Advance Cue

The audible advance cue is an integral part of the narration recording. It indicates to the viewer of the module that the commentary for a frame is over

FIGURE 9-2 Before inserting the tape into the recorder, it is necessary to advance the tape manually past the leader strip, which cannot be recorded on. This can be done by inserting a finger tip into the right gear opening (the empty spool) and rotating the gearwheel counterclockwise until the recording tape (usually brown in color) advances past the openings in the front of the cassette.

FIGURE 9-3 If you find that rotating the gearwheel with your fingertip is too difficult or time consuming, try a small tapered piece of cardboard or the top of a ball point pen.

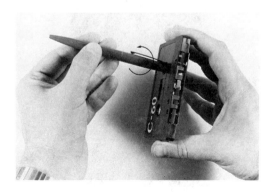

and that it is time to advance the projector to the next frame. The advance cue is a clear sound that is given on the tape a few seconds after the narration for a frame ends. After the cue sound is given, a pause of blank tape for another few seconds occurs (allowing the viewer to advance to the next slide), and then the narration for the next frame begins.

The advance-cue sound does not have to be louder than the general volume of the narration. The sound should, however, be distinctive, pleasant, and unmistakable to the user of the module. A bell or chime sound can be used, or a soft whistle or click. The sound cue does not have to last long if it is distinctive; and the narrator should produce the sound because this will eliminate the need to give a silent indication to a second person when the cue is called for. The method of producing the audible cue can be as simple as tapping a water glass or ceramic bowl with a pencil, or as elaborate as a battery-operated chime or other device.

As mentioned earlier, the narration pause takes approximately five seconds between frames, and it is during this pause that the audible advance cue is placed. The sequence of narration—pause ... cue ... pause ... narration—would be as follows: Narration for the frame ends (the tape continues to run), a pause of approximately two seconds; the audible cue is given, another pause of approximately two seconds; the narration for the next frame begins. The length of the pause between frames can be altered to suit the module designer's preference, but it is preferable that the pause not be cut below three seconds at the minimum or allowed to exceed ten seconds at the maximum. The reasons for this limitation range are that at less than three seconds between frames, the module user may have difficulty in advancing the frame in time to catch the beginning of the narration for the next frame.

At the other end of the spectrum, a pause of longer than ten seconds between frames may prompt the module user to begin reading or interpreting the visual information in the next frame before the narration begins, thus increasing the chance of confusion.

Regardless of the time span chosen for the pause between frames, the narrator should utilize a clock with a sweep second hand to help keep all the pauses between the frames of the module consistent.

Some General Suggestions

Depending on the manufacturer, cassette tape recorders have different control placements, methods of cassette loading and recording, and playback adjustments. Therefore, the manufacturer's instructions for these functions should be consulted. Some general suggestions for better narration recording follow.

When recording the narration, it is good practice to place the recorder to the left or right side of the narrator with a single page of script directly in front of him or her. This will allow the narrator free access to the recorder and will eliminate the need to hold the script in the hands, which can cause distracting sounds that will be picked up by the recorder. For a similar reason, the script placed in front of the narrator should consist of only a single page at a time.

As the reading of each page has been completed, the recorder can be stopped for a few moments while another page is being placed in front of the narrator, thus eliminating the sound of paper shuffling (see Figure 9–4).

FIGURE 9-4 By placing the script one page at a time in front of the reader-narrator during recording, the noise made by papers being shuffled or moved about will not be picked up on the sound track.

If the cassette recorder being used has a hand-held microphone rather than one built into the recorder case, the narrator should be careful not to hold it too close when speaking, as this will produce sound distortions. The narrator should also hold the microphone at a fixed position and not shift it or wave it around (see Figures 9–5 and 9–6).

FIGURE 9-5 When using a hand-held microphone, hold it steady and not too close to your mouth, as this will cause distortions of your voice.

FIGURE 9-6 Holding the mike steady and at a proper distance of approximately 10 inches from your face, read each segment of the script in a normal tone and volume.

FIGURE 9-7 After you have recorded one side of the cassette to your satisfaction, that side can be "locked" against accidental erasure or rerecording by removing the small plastic tab on the back *right-hand side of the cassette* with side 1 being upright. The tab on the left-hand side will render side 2 of the cassette (the down side) nonrecordable. If you wish to defeat this provision after the tabs have been removed, place a piece of tape over the opening that controls the side of the cassette you wish to record on again.

RECORDING THE SECOND SIDE

By recording the second side of the cassette, certain procedures can avoid the time-consuming and clumsy problem of having to rewind the cassette after each time the module is used. Having a duplicate narration on each side of the cassette, the module user merely has to advance the tape to the end of that side of the cassette when the narration ends. The next module user merely has to load the cassette with a full spool on the left side in order to be at the beginning of the narration.

The production of a second-side narration is quite simple. After the narration has been completed on one side of the cassette, press the *fast forward* button on the recorder and transfer any remaining tape to the right cassette spool. Remove the cassette from the recorder and turn it over. *Remember to advance the tape manually past the leader before reinserting the cassette into the recorder.* The reinserted cassette should have all of the recording tape again on the left spool. At this point, the narration can be repeated exactly as before.

After the second narration has been completed, both sides of the tape should be played back and compared with the narration-script for accuracy. The cassette tape should then be removed from the recorder, and the two small plastic tabs on the right and left back edges of the cassette should be broken off (see Figure 9-7). The tabs can be removed with a penknife or other pointed instrument. The removal of the tabs renders the cassette incapable of being recorded again or accidentally erased by the module user.

MUSIC

The selective use of music can, like the narration, play an integral part in the successful information flow of the module.

Music can be supplied by a record player or by a second cassette recorder and be played at the same time that the narration is being recorded.

When recording the narration together with background music from a record player or another tape recorder, be sure to adjust the music sound level so that it does not drown out the spoken words. For this purpose, too, a second cassette recorder, used during the narration recording to supply the music, is superior to a record player because the recorder allows compilation of music from several different records on a single tape. Therefore, the use of a prerecorded music tape eliminates the need for the narrator to change records or search for specific record bands during the recording of the narration. The final result is a blend of music and spoken words on a single tape.

If the module sound portion is to be composed solely of music, or if the music portion and spoken portion are kept separate, a second recorder can be dispensed with in favor of direct recording of the music portion from a record player onto the narration tape. However, where music and spoken words are mixed (the technical term for this is *voice-over*), a second recorder with a selected and prepared music sound-track works best.

THE MODULE PACKAGE

The elements of the module—the slides in an appropriate magazine, the cassette tape of the narration, and a typewritten copy of the narration script—should all be placed in a container or clearly marked storage box.

To avoid confusion when several modules are being used at the same time, it is good practice to place identifying labels on the slide magazine as well as on the cassette. The module can then be filed by whatever system is preferred (see Figure 9-8).

FIGURE 9-8 A module package consisting of slides in an appropriate magazine, a cassette narration tape, and a written copy of the complete script in a labeled storage box. It is good practice to place identification labels on the cassette and on the slide magazine.

GLOSSARY

Audible advance cue A soft, pleasant, and distinctive sound that is included in the recorded narration of a sound-slide module. The cue indicates to the module user that the narration for a frame has ended and that it is time to advance to the next frame.

Audio portion The narration or sound track of the sound-slide module. The audio portion is

usually recorded on a cassette tape (see *cassette tape*).

Cassette recorder A tape recorder that uses cassette tapes.

Cassette tape A small, self-contained package of recording tape designed to be used with a cassette tape recorder. Available in thirty-, sixty-, and ninety-minute tape lengths, cassette tapes are a preferred medium for sound-slide modules because of their compactness, relative inexpensiveness, and easy loading for recording and playback.

Module package The elements of a sound-slide module: the slides in an appropriate holder or magazine, the cassette tape containing the narration, and a typed copy of the narration script. Sometimes called a *storage box*.

Narrator A person who reads and transcribes on recording tape, the verbal portion of the module.

Pacing The technique of presenting the audio portion of a module over a preset period of time to lead the module user through the information at a speed that is judged best to promote comprehension and retention.

Pause A length of recording tape that is left blank to produce a soundless period of time in the narration of a module. A pause in the narration gives the module user time to take notes, compute answers, or, when combined with an audible advance cue, change the module frame.

Prerecorded music tape A tape of selected music recorded in advance and utilized during the recording of the narration tape as background music.

Proofreading The process of rereading and checking the information content, grammatical structure, and pronunciation of technical words or phrases in a narration script prior to recording.

Running time The total length of time of a recorded tape.

Script A frame-by-frame written transcription of the narration of a module.

Spontaneous narration A narration that is not planned or written out in advance of the recording process. Spontaneous narration is usually counterproductive to clear information flow in a sound-slide module and is not a recommended procedure.

Spool A wheellike holder on which is wound a length of recording tape or film.

Tape leader A length of protective tape at the beginning and end of a recording tape or film.

Voice-over A recorded narration in which the spoken words are superimposed on background music.

10
THE OVERHEAD
TRANSPARENCY

THE OVERHEAD TRANSPARENCY

The overhead transparency, although a very useful instructional tool, is not directly related to the sound-slide module system. The justification for this chapter is that the methods of producing an overhead transparency, with regard to the layout of the visual design and the graphic materials used, are very similar to the layout and materials involved in creating a flat copy for a sound-slide module.

The overhead transparency is actually a giant slide that is produced by hand rather than by a photographic process. No photographic film or photography processes are necessary. The medium of presentation is an overhead projector.

The overhead transparency system has several distinct advantages and disadvantages when compared with the sound-slide module system. One of its principal advantages is that it can be projected using much brighter room light levels than those necessary for a slide or filmstrip frame. This can definitely help viewers who must take notes or answer written test questions during projection. Another advantage is that through the process of *selective disclosure*, parts of a single transparency may either be revealed or concealed as the narration or discussion of the frame content progresses. This selective disclosure process saves a great deal of production time by allowing one transparency to impart a series of related information statements that would normally be spread over several sound-slide module frames.

The overhead transparency system is an excellent medium of instruction for large groups because the *short-throw projector lens* produces a large, screen-filling image while allowing both the projector and the instructor-operator to remain at the front of the room. Because the transparencies are large, they can be written on *while* being projected. The narrator or lecturer can also use a pencil to point to a specific item on the transparency, and this action will be translated to the projected image so that everyone can see it.

Overhead transparencies may have overlays built into them to allow the addition of information to the frame content *while* it is being projected. These multiple overlays are very valuable when presenting a series of concepts or statements on a related visual theme.

When compared with the sound-slide module system, the overhead transparency system has the following disadvantages. It is primarily designed to accompany a lecture or narration given by a live instructor. There is no viable way to package an overhead transparency module or combine it with a recorded narration tape in order to eliminate the need for an instructor-operator's being present when it is being used.

Another disadvantage of the overhead system is that although the newest projectors are smaller and lighter than those formerly used, they are still much more bulky and clumsy to transport than a 35-mm slide projector or audio-visual viewer.

Finally, because of the disadvantages already mentioned, the overhead transparency system does not lend itself well to student self-use, which is one of the principal values of the sound-slide module.

THE OVERHEAD TRANSPARENCY FORMAT

The overhead transparency consists of a thin, stiff cardboard frame with outside dimensions of 10½ by 12 inches and a cutout image area of 8 by 9¾ inches (see Figure 10-1). This cardboard frame holds a sheet of clear acetate or plastic on which the visual is placed. The clear sheet measures 8½ by 10½ inches and is taped to the transparency frame with cellophane or masking tape to keep it rigid during projection. The total usable projection area of the overhead is, technically, the size of the cutout.

However, to ensure absolute clarity in the projected image, the type or illus-

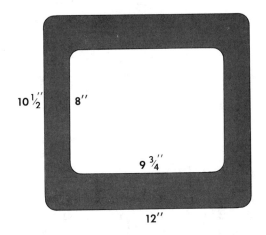

FIGURE 10-1 An overhead transparency frame resembles a giant version of a 35-mm slide frame. The overhead transparency frame is usually made of thin, stiff cardboard with outer dimensions of approximately 10½ by 12 inches. The interior cutout is approximately 8 by 9¾ inches.

trative material on the clear carrier should not be closer than ¼ inch from the interior cutout edges. This area of usable space on the clear carrier sheet measures 7½ by 9¼ inches, and all the elements of the visual should be fitted within this area (see Figure 10-2).

FIGURE 10-2 The area of usable space in relation to the total cutout area size is 7½ by 9¼ inches. Type or illustrative material should not be permitted to come closer than ¼ inch from any edge of the cutout.

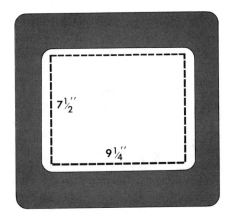

Graphic Materials

The overhead transparency is projected in a manner similar to that of a 35-mm slide. Intense light from the projector or bulb passes through the transparency to a lens system that projects the focused image on a screen.

Any parts of the transparency image that are opaque or too dense to permit the passage of light will project as black, that is, as an unlit area or shape on the screen. This effect is perfectly acceptable for both type and outlines of areas if this is the kind of projection effect desired by the designer.

All opaque mapping tapes, India ink and permanent marker, and most kinds of transfer type will project as shadow black (see Figure 10-3). Transfer type of the kind used in the layouts for a slide frame will usually transmit very little light and will therefore project as shadow black regardless of the actual color of the letters. Even white transfer type will usually project as shadow black (see Figures 10-4A and 10-4B).

However, the overhead system can and will project in color any graphic material that is transparent enough to

let light pass through it. To this end, a number of specially designed tapes, markers and pencils, shading sheets and

FIGURE 10-4A The overhead transparency is placed on the light table of the overhead projector. The bottom of the transparency is placed toward the screen, allowing the instructor to read or point to the information on the transparency while facing the audience. The projected image appears behind the instructor, and to one side.

(A)

FIGURE 10-4B Any type or graphic material that does not transmit light will project as shadow black. Even white type, if it is opaque, will project as black. Projectable colored type and tape, as well as markers, are also available.

(B)

FIGURE 10-3 A simple overhead transparency made of press type on an acetate carrier sheet.

pattern sheets, and transfer-type alphabet sheets are available. All of these materials are transparent and projectable and are available in a wide range of colors. Most manufacturers of regular opaque transfer type or other graphic materials will probably have a product line of projectable, color graphic materials.

Large areas of shadow black may be introduced to the projected image by the use of opaque black photographic masking tape or cut and positioned pieces of opaque shading film, which can be burnished down directly on the clear sheet.

THE LAYOUT

Unlike the flat-copy layout for a slide frame, which consists of a clear acetate overlay placed on a cut-paper background sheet, the overhead transparency image is all contained in the clear carrier sheet. All illustrative or pictorial images that are to be part of the frame, as well as type, graphs, colors, and so on, must be placed on the clear carrier sheet.

This factor can be somewhat limiting with regard to pictorial images that the designer may wish to incorporate into the overhead transparency. Because opaque images of any kind will not project in the overhead system except as silhouettes, the cutout photographs or other paper-based artwork cannot be used. Therefore, all artwork, such as pictures, graphs, diagrams, or other representational images will have to be drawn on the clear carrier sheet in either transparent or opaque media.

Because no background sheet is necessary in the preparation or use of an overhead transparency, a simple *grid page* can be placed beneath the clear carrier sheet as a guide for the layout of the type and illustrations. The grid page takes the place of the cardboard format guide that is used to balance the layout of the sound-slide flat copy.

A grid page with $\frac{1}{4}$-inch squares on its surface is available in the form of a self-adhesive sheet from most manufacturers of pressure-sensitive type or graphic materials. A grid page with $\frac{1}{4}$-inch squares can also be obtained from a large stationery store or outlet that carries accountants' supplies. The dimensions of the grid page should be those of a standard sheet of typewriter paper, $8\frac{1}{2}$ by 11 inches. A larger grid page can be trimmed to the proper size, or a grid can be measured and drawn on a sheet of typewriter paper.

A cardboard overhead transparency frame is placed over the grid page. When aligning the grid page, make sure that the edges of the cutout in the transparency frame fall exactly on the lines in the grid page. Then, using a black marker or pen, trace the outline of the cutout on the grid page (see Figures 10–5 and 10–6). After the transparency frame opening has been traced onto the grid sheet, remove the cardboard frame. Then, using a ruler and a *red* marker or pen, draw a rectangle that measures $\frac{1}{4}$ inch in on all sides from the outline of the transparency frame cutout previously drawn. This red rectangle marks the *area of usable space* within the overhead transparency frame. All type and illustrative material should be kept within the red rectangle when preparing the layout (see Figure 10–7).

The grid page can be taped down at the corners to a working surface or desk top, and an acetate sheet can be positioned and taped down on top of it. The

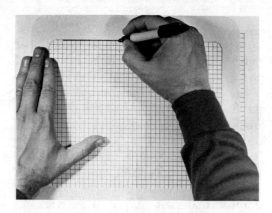

FIGURE 10-5 To make a grid-page guide for overhead transparency layouts, place a transparency frame over a ruled sheet that has ¼-inch squares. Be sure that the edges of the transparency frame cutout align as closely as possible with the lines on the ruled page. Then, holding the transparency frame in place, draw the outline of the cutout with a felt-tipped marker.

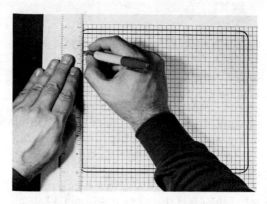

FIGURE 10-7 Next, measure and mark in red a new border that falls ¼ inch in from the heavy outline on all sides. All type and illustration matter should be kept within this red rectangle.

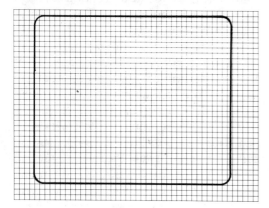

FIGURE 10-6 This heavily marked outline represents the total size of the transparency frame opening.

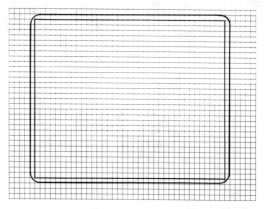

FIGURE 10-8 A sheet of clear acetate is taped directly over the newly completed grid page, and type can be applied where desired.

parallel vertical and horizontal lines in the grid take the place of any slip-sheets that would be used to align letters or lines of type (see Figures 10-8 and 10-9).

TYPE

As mentioned earlier, regular opaque transfer type can be used in the overhead transparency layout if it is understood in advance that these letters will project as shadow black. Smaller type sizes than would be used in the layout of a slide frame can be used in the overhead transparency.

Letter sizes ranging from 12-point to 48-point type can be used. Transparent projectable letters in various colors and sizes are also available from most manufacturers of transfer type.

Type alignment and application is the same as that of the overlays for slide flat copies. Make sure, however, that the

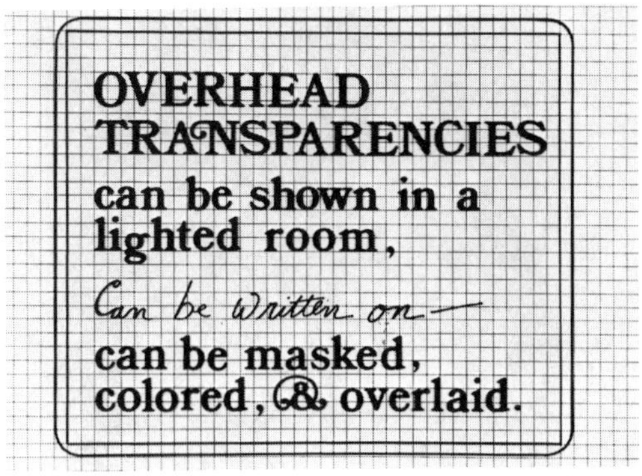

OVERHEAD TRANSPARENCIES
can be shown in a lighted room,
Can be Written on
can be masked,
colored, & overlaid.

FIGURE 10-9 Type, ruled lines, and other illustrative material can be applied to the acetate without the use of a slipsheet as a guide. As can be seen here, the bottom or top of the type letters can be placed along any horizontal line, with parallel lines of type being produced automatically.

carrier sheet is very clean and free of lint, dust, or fragments of transfer type because these will project along with the rest of the image.

Other Graphic Materials

Clear projectable tapes in a wide range of sizes and colors are available for charts and graphs and for underlining or placing behind words. Specially prepared marking pens and pencils in a number of projectable colors are also available for mechanical and freehand drawing on the transparency.

The lines made by some kinds of markers and pencils can be removed from the clear carrier sheet if they are gently rubbed with a tissue or soft cloth. These materials give the lecturer the option of writing directly on the transparency while it is being projected, and then cleaning off the markings and thus returning the transparency to its original state.

All type, tape, markings, and pictorial material should be kept on one side of the clear carrier sheet. The side on which the type and other materials are placed is kept face up when the transparency sheet is mounted into the frame holder and projected.

MOUNTING THE TRANSPARENCY

The cardboard transparency frame is used as a rigid support for the carrier sheet that contains the projectable image. The transparency can, however, be projected without the transparency frame if necessary.

The principal functions of the transparency frame are (1) it protects the edges of the carrier sheet and facilitates handling; (2) filing information or other directions can be written on the frame; and (3) if overlays for the transparency are to be used, the frame acts as a hinge support and alignment base.

Transparency frames may differ slightly, depending on the manufacturer. Although virtually all transparency frames are made of thin cardboard stock, some frames are of the book type and others are simple, single units.

The book-type transparency frame has a left and a right half that are held together with tape or paper hinges (see Figure 10-10). The transparency is placed between the leaves on one side and taped down with masking tape (see Figure 10-11). The leaves of the frame are then closed and taped or stapled into place (see Figure 10-12).

The single-unit transparency frame consists of a simple cardboard frame. The transparency is taped to the back of the frame with $\frac{1}{2}$-inch-wide strips of masking tape. The frame is turned over and placed on the projector, with the taped side down (see Figures 10-13 and 10-14). Whichever kind of transparency frame is used, the results in terms of projection of the image will be identical.

When mounting the transparency to

FIGURE 10-10 A book-type transparency frame consists of two thin frames held along one edge by tape hinges.

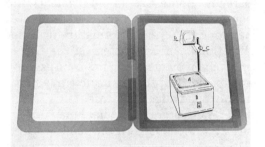

FIGURE 10-11 The transparency is taped to the inside of one frame. Double-sided tape may be used, as this will hold the two frames together when they are folded over.

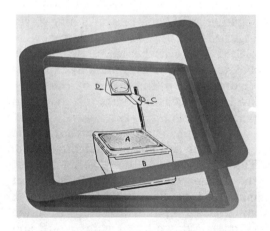

FIGURE 10-12 When the transparency has been taped to the inside of one frame, the other side of the frame is folded over like a book and is taped or stapled as necessary.

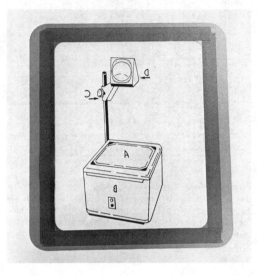

FIGURE 10-13 A single-cardboard transparency frame is the most commonly used. The transparency is taped to the back of the frame with strips of masking tape, and the frame is turned over and placed taped side down on the projector.

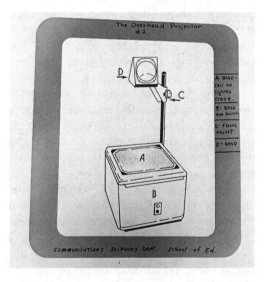

FIGURE 10-14 The transparency frame has plenty of room for notations and identification.

the frame, make sure that the carrier sheet does not buckle near the edges or crease across the image area, as this will cause projected-image clarity problems.

OVERLAYS

Additional clear overlay sheets containing pictorial and written information can be attached to the transparency frame. The overlay sheets are attached to the frame with masking tape hinges and can be easily flipped over onto the mounted transparency during projection (see Figure 10–15). This process allows the instructor using the transparency to automatically add or subtract selected information contained in the overlays, without the necessity of removing the transparency from the projector and substituting another.

Although the acetate used to create the base transparency and the overlays is clear, more than three sheets placed on each other will diffuse and diminish the projected image. Therefore, a good formula to follow when incorporating overlay sheets in a transparency is to avoid using more than *two* overlays unless absolutely necessary.

The overlay sheets are attached to the *front* of the transparency frame so that they are face up and easily accessible while the transparency is being projected. Each overlay should be attached *separately* to one of the frame edges, and small tape hinges can be used for this purpose (see Figures 10–16 through 10–19).

To help ensure accuracy of the image alignment, the overlays should be prepared at the same time as the main transparency. After the main transparency has been mounted in the transparency frame, the overlay sheets can easily be positioned, aligned, and taped to the edges of the frame.

FIGURE 10-16 If more than one overlay sheet is used, they should be attached separately to different edges of the frame.

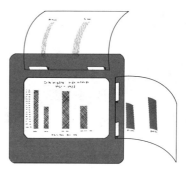

FIGURE 10-17 The use of overlays permits the adding of information to a basic image. However (as shown here), overlays can also be used to build up a total picture progressively.

FIGURE 10-15 Overlay sheets are attached to the front of the transparency frame with tape hinges.

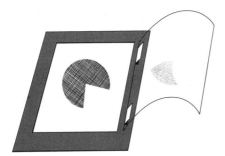

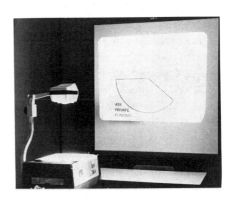

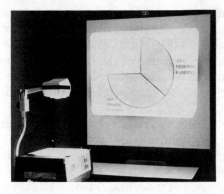

FIGURE 10-18 Each additional overlay adds a selective piece of information at the instructor's chosen pace.

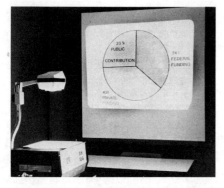

FIGURE 10-19 When the last overlay is flipped onto the image, all the information contained in the transparency is projected on the screen.

SELECTIVE DISCLOSURE MASKS

Selective disclosure masks, as the term implies, allow the partial disclosure of the transparency image through the medium of the opaque masks that block part of the projected image. The selective disclosure mask is made of a thin sheet of cardboard, cut to the desired shape, and fitted over the transparency. The mask can be fitted to slide out of the way, or it can be equipped with tape hinges similar to those of an overlay sheet. The masks have no set shapes

or sizes but are custom made to fit whatever part of the image is desired. It is preferable, however, that the mask be in some way attached to the transparency frame. This ensures that the mask will always align with the image quickly and properly, and it reduces the risk of losing the mask or confusing masks for different transparencies.

Selective disclosure masks fall into two main categories in terms of their construction, *hinged masks* and *sliding masks*.

Hinged Masks

Hinged masks act like small doors that are cut out to fit over the image part that is to be held back from projection. In addition to two small masking tape hinges used to hold the mask to the transparency frame, a small pull-tab of tape should be placed on one edge of the mask so that it can easily be picked up. Hinged masks can be used to cover part of the projected image or the entire image area either singly or in combination (see Figures 10-20, 10-21, and 10-22).

Sliding Masks

Sliding masks are designed to reveal part of the transparency image starting from one edge of a windowlike area whose size increases as the mask is being slid away from the transparency frame.

Because the sliding mask must be completely movable, it is held in alignment with the transparency and frame by two guide tracks made of strips of thin cardboard mounted on the edges of the transparency frame.

The first step in the production of a sliding mask is to cut a thin smooth sheet of cardboard to cover the transparency image completely and extend $\frac{1}{2}$

FIGURE 10-20 Hinged masks act like small doors and allow part of the projected image to be held back. The hinges are masking tape, and an extra tab of tape is attached to the edge of the mask to make it easier to pick up. This is an example of a partial mask.

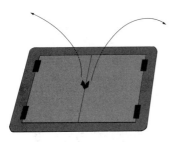

FIGURE 10-21 An example of a full mask with two hinged openings.

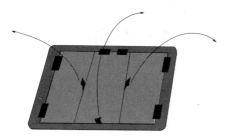

FIGURE 10-22 An example of a full mask with three hinged openings. The mask doors can be virtually any size or shape desired, as long as they can be attached to the transparency frame or each other.

inch on all sides onto the transparency frame. Position the mask over the transparency and frame, and temporarily hold it there with two small pieces of masking tape (see Figure 10-23).

Next, using a slightly thicker sheet of cardboard, cut *four* strips that are as long as the longer edges of the mask sheet cut earlier (approximately $10\frac{3}{4}$

FIGURE 10-23 To make a sliding mask, first cut a sheet of thin cardboard that is $\frac{1}{2}$ inch larger on all sides than the transparency frame opening. Fit the mask over the frame and hold it temporarily in place with small pieces of tape.

inches per strip). Two of the cardboard strips should be $\frac{3}{4}$-inch wide, and the other two strips should be $1\frac{1}{4}$-inch wide (see Figures 10-24 and 10-25).

After the strips have been measured and cut out, place a strip of double-sided tape on one side of each of the $\frac{3}{4}$-inch-wide strips. Then position one of the $\frac{3}{4}$-inch-wide strips, with the taped side down, on each side of the mask sheet and press down along the strip so that it adheres firmly to the transparency frame (see Figure 10-26).

After the $\frac{3}{4}$-inch-wide strips have been securely taped down, place another strip of double-sided tape on the upper face of each strip. Next, position a $1\frac{1}{4}$-inch-wide strip over each $\frac{3}{4}$-inch strip so that $\frac{1}{2}$ inch of the upper strip overlaps the mask-sheet area. Press down each $1\frac{1}{4}$-inch-wide strip so that it adheres firmly to the $\frac{3}{4}$-inch-wide strip beneath (see Figure 10-27).

A permanent guide track has now been created for the mask sheet. Finally, remove the small pieces of masking tape that were used to hold the mask sheet in place, and put a small masking-tape tab on one or both free edges of the mask sheet. These tabs are grasped when pulling the mask (see Figures 10-28, 10-29, and 10-30).

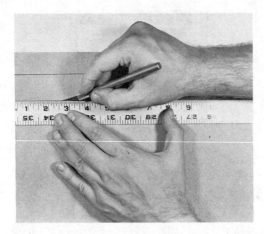

FIGURE 10–24 Measure and mark four rectangular strips on another sheet of thin cardboard. The strips should all be the same length as the longer edge of the mask sheet. Two strips should be ³/₄-inch wide, and two strips should be 1¹/₄-inch wide. Cut these out with a razor knife and a metal or metal-edged ruler.

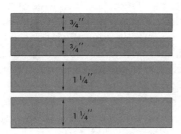

FIGURE 10–25 The two ³/₄-inch-wide strips will be attached to the frame first. Place strips of double-sided tape on them.

FIGURE 10–26 Place the ³/₄-inch-wide strips on either side of the mask sheet, and press them down so that they will firmly adhere to the transparency frame.

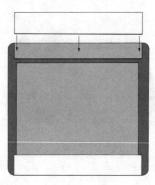

FIGURE 10–27 Next, using double-sided tape, tape down the two wider strips on top of the ³/₄-inch-wide strips. The 1¹/₄-inch-wide strips will overlap the mask along the two longest edges.

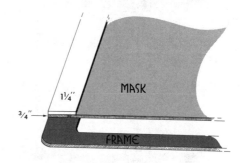

FIGURE 10–28 The mask sheet should slide back and forth freely in the channel made by the two strips of cardboard mounted on each side.

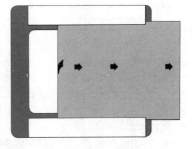

FIGURE 10–29 The sliding mask in this horizontal format allows selective disclosure of the frame contents from left to right during projection.

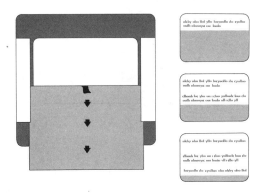

FIGURE 10-30 The sliding mask in this vertical format allows selective disclosure of the frame contents from top to bottom during projection.

THE OVERHEAD PROJECTOR

With regard to image projection, the overhead projector and the slide projector function on the same level. Light produced by a high-intensity bulb (usually fan cooled to reduce the risk of temperature damage to the transparency) passes through the transparency to a lens system that projects the enlarged image.

The main difference between the two types of projectors is that since the overhead transparency is much larger than a 35-mm slide, it has to be positioned on the projector by hand. There is no mechanical provision on the overhead projector for the changing of transparencies (see Figures 10-31A, and 10-31B).

The overhead projector consists of four major parts: the base, the light table, the support-stage arm, and the lens head (see Figure 10-32).

The base of the overhead projector is a boxlike container for the projector bulb and cooling fan. The top surface of the projector base is the light table. The light table consists of a heat-resistant glass or plastic Fresnel lens with a glass

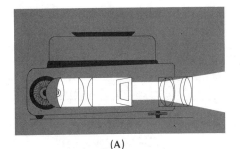

(A)

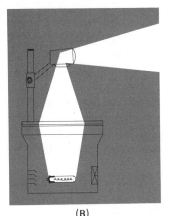

(B)

FIGURE 10-31A, B (A) In a slide projector, the light path is straight from the bulb through the transparency and through the focusing lens to the screen.

(B) In the overhead transparency projector, the light path is straight through the transparency to the lens head where the light is bent by a mirror and lens system to project at a right angle to the screen.

This system allows the overhead transparency to lie flat on the projector light table, to be pointed to or written on during projection.

plate over it. This lens, which is flat, spreads the light of the projection bulb evenly over the entire surface of the transparency, which is placed on top of the light table for projection. The lens head situated on the end of the support-stage arm is positioned directly over the light-table surface and directs the light coming through the transparency at a right angle so that the image can be seen on a flat, vertical surface such as a projection screen. The projected image is brought into sharp focus by increasing or decreasing the distance between the light table (with the transparency on it) and the lens head. Most types of overhead projectors have a fine-focus adjustment ratchet wheel or knob that allows the lens head to be raised or lowered in controlled degrees for this purpose.

Finally, the overall size of the projected image is controlled by the distance between the projector and the screen. The farther the projector is placed from the screen, the larger the projected image will be. The optical system of most overhead projectors allows them to project an image that will fill a 72-inch-square projection screen from only a few feet away. This enables both the projector and the instructor using it to remain at the front of the room (see Figures 10–33 and 10–34).

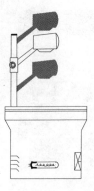

FIGURE 10–33 The focusing of the projected image is achieved by raising or lowering the lens head in relation to the transparency on the light table.

FIGURE 10–34 The overall size of the projected image is controlled by the distance between the projector and the screen. By increasing the distance (B) the image size (A) is also increased, and vice versa. Because of the wide angle of projection, the projector need only be a few feet from the screen to fill it with a projected image.

FIGURE 10–32 The overhead projector consists of four major parts: A, the light table; B, the base; C, the support-stage arm with focusing adjustment wheel; and D, the lens head.

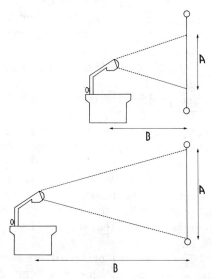

GLOSSARY

Book-type transparency frame An overhead transparency frame that has a left and right half held together by a paper-tape hinge similar to the leaves of a book. The base transparency sheet is aligned and sandwiched between the two leaves, which are then closed and taped or stapled to produce a finished, mounted transparency.

Clear carrier sheet The sheet of acetate that, with the addition of type or visual images, becomes the overhead transparency. This term also refers to the original transparency to which the overlays are to be added.

Fresnel lens A flat glass or plastic plate with tiny concentric embossed rings radiating from the center to the edges. A Fresnel lens can magnify images or evenly transmit light from a point source into an illumination area.

Grid page An $8\frac{1}{2}$-by-11-inch paper page that is ruled in $\frac{1}{4}$-inch squares (usually in light-blue ink). The grid page is used to guide the placement of type and illustrations on a sheet of clear acetate placed on top of it, which will be made into an overhead transparency.

Hinged masks Selective disclosure masks, made of thin sheets of cardboard, that are held in alignment with the transparency image by the use of masking tape hinges that attach the mask to the transparency frame edge. The mask is lifted and folded back to reveal the part of the image beneath it.

Multiple overlays Sheets of clear acetate that contain additional visual information and are attached to an overhead transparency on the transparency frame with tape hinges. An overlay can be folded over and placed on the base transparency to incorporate its visual information into that of the base transparency while being projected.

Opaque A substance that does not allow light to pass through it.

Overhead projector A device used to enlarge and project overhead transparencies (see *Fresnel lens; overhead projector base; overhead projector bulb; overhead projector lens head; overhead projector light table; overhead projector support-stage arm*).

Overhead projector base The boxlike base of the overhead transparency projector that houses the projector bulb and cooling fan. The top of the projector base is the *light table*, upon which a transparency is placed for projection.

Overhead projector bulb A high-intensity incandescent bulb that provides the illumination for the projection of an overhead transparency.

Overhead projector lens head A compact optical package consisting of lenses and a mirror that focus and project the illuminated transparency image onto a vertical viewing surface, such as a projection screen. The distance between the lens head and the surface of the light table where the transparency is placed (which is adjustable) affects the focus of the projected image.

Overhead projector light table A glass plate built into the top of the overhead projector base, upon which the transparency is placed to illuminate it for projection. Beneath the light-table glass plate is a Fresnel lens that provides even illumination from the projector bulb.

Overhead projector support-stage arm A vertical arm, usually metal, that is approximately 16 inches high and holds the *projector lens head* in alignment above the *projector light table* to permit proper projection. By increasing or decreasing the distance between the light table and the lens head, focus clarity is achieved.

Overhead transparency A large, usually handmade slide that is mounted in a cardboard frame and projected by an overhead transparency projector.

Overhead transparency frame A cardboard frame that has outside dimensions of approximately $10\frac{1}{2}$ by 12 inches and an aperture (cut out opening) of approximately 8-by-$9\frac{3}{4}$ inches. The overhead transparency is mounted in the frame to hold it rigid and flat during projection and to facilitate easy handling and filing-storage.

Projectable graphic materials Specially manufactured graphic materials such as type, mapping tapes, markers and pencils, and shading films that are designed to produce images that are transparent or can transmit light and therefore be projected. Most projectable graphic materials are available in a wide range of colors.

Selective disclosure mask An opaque sheet of

paper or thin cardboard that is used to hold back from projection selected areas of the overhead transparency. The use of selective disclosure masks permits the inclusion of several information elements in a single transparency which can be introduced to the projected image when desired (see *hinged masks; sliding masks*).

Shadow black A blank area or shape on the projected overhead transparency image caused by the presence of opaque type or materials in the transparency. A projected silhouette.

Sliding masks Selective disclosure masks made of thin sheets of cardboard that are held in alignment with the transparency image by the use of cardboard guide tracks attached to the transparency edges. The transparency image beneath the mask is revealed for projection when the mask is slid out of the way, along the guide tracks.

Short-throw projector lens A projection lens that produces a large, screen-filling image with the projector in which it is set at a relatively short distance from the screen. Short-throw projector lenses are very useful when operating a projector in a small room or area, or when it is necessary for the projector and the instructor to be near the front of the room.

Tape hinges Short pieces of cellophane or masking tape affixed along the seam between two pieces of paper, cardboard, or other such material. Tape hinges allow two or more sheets to be attached and folded over without the tape's being visible on the outside edges of the fold.

11
PRESENTATIONS
AND EVALUATIONS

PRESENTATIONS AND EVALUATIONS

Now that a sound-slide module has been designed and produced, it must be utilized effectively if it is to realize its potential as a teaching tool. The production and completion of the steps in the fabrication of a module are only the first part of the sound-slide module's useful life.

Although a sound-slide module may all but present itself, it is not a totally autonomous system that is guaranteed to be successful under any conditions. Many factors can influence the effectiveness of a module. Some of these factors may be related to nonapparent weaknesses in the information flow, whereas others may be related to the environment in which the module is presented or used.

For example, a module may be more effective when it is presented to a group of people rather than a single individual, or vice versa. Therefore, the mode of presentation chosen for a module, as well as the environment in which the presentation is made, has a profound effect on the way a viewer will receive and retain the information being offered.

Another influential factor is of course the willingness, attention, and enthusiasm of the viewer using the module, which will vary from individual to individual. However, despite any possible limitations in a viewer's perceptual processes, certain universal educational factors must be considered and reviewed periodically if a module is to succeed in being a valuable learning tool.

The key to understanding the effectiveness of a module will primarily be in the form of *viewer feedback*. Viewer feedback includes not only measurable learning responses to the module information (such as in tests and reviews) but also general responses (such as in viewer attention and interest exhibited while using the module).

The module designer should try to elicit responses from the module user whenever possible. The type of comments sought should cover not only the subject of the module and its understandability but other factors of the presentation as well, such as the pace of the narration and information flow. Although most modules are not entertainment oriented, comments about the visual attraction or attention-getting effectiveness of the graphics should also be elicited and evaluated.

Sometimes a well-thought-out module will fail because of minor technical problems relating to the narration, or perhaps because of something as simple as one badly designed frame. These flaws may be immediately apparent to the module user but not at all apparent to the designer, and it is here that viewer feedback may prove most valuable.

If a module constantly fails or produces very uneven results in the viewer's understanding and retention, but no obvious flaw can be discovered, a *reevaluation analysis* will be necessary.

The reevaluation analysis should be undertaken at regular intervals in any case with all complete in-use modules. Areas to reevaluate within the module should cover the vocabulary, the explanation of technical terms, the pace of the narration and information flow, and the timeliness and overall quality of all the illustrative materials, as well as the general value and relation that the module has to other modules that contain parallel or enlarged areas of specific information on the subject that the viewer may need or want to use.

When reevaluating a failing module, you should realize that some subjects or areas, in both abstract information and physical skills, simply cannot be effectively taught by a sound-slide module no matter how well it is prepared or presented. However, because the module designer or author is usually familiar with the subject matter being translated to the sound-slide format, most module failings can be traced to one of the problems described earlier, rather than a misapplication of a subject into the sound-slide medium.

When a problem has been located and defined, it can often be corrected without dismantling or scrapping the entire module. An amount of altering or substitution of visuals or changes in the narration tape will usually improve the module's effectiveness.

The sound-slide module is meant to be a flexible, adaptable learning system capable of being changed and redirected as the needs of the module user develop and change.

PRESENTATION METHODS

Sound-slide modules can be presented to large groups of viewers with a conventional slide projector and cassette tape player. Any limitations involved in this type of presentation would be environmentally oriented. An example of an environmental limitation on a large-group audio-visual presentation would be the number of persons that could be fitted comfortably into a given room or area. Another example of an environmental limitation would be the sound system. The cassette tape player must have the volume to fill the presentation room or area with a loud enough and clear enough sound track so that everything can be heard and understood.

If a module is to be used constantly with large groups of viewers, you may wish to consult a representative of an electronics store or music store about an additional amplification device for the cassette player to ensure clear, loud sound.

Although a single viewer or a small study group of two to four viewers can also use a separate projector, screen, and tape player, it is much more efficient and space saving to use a compact viewer unit. A *compact viewer unit*—or *table-top viewer* as these are sometimes called—consists of a televisionlike cabinet with a built-in screen approximately 1 square foot in size. A circular slide magazine is placed on the top of the unit that engages the slide-changing mechanism, the controls for which are located on the front of the unit. A cassette playback mechanism is also built into the table-top viewer, making it a complete presentation unit (see Figures 11-1 and 11-2).

The table-top viewer unit is both compact and light in weight, making it valuable in small-area situations as well as being useful for traveling media presentations. Some table-top viewer units also have a recording capability that allows for the production of the narration and sound track as well as its playback when completed. These units function the same way that a separate cassette tape recorder does, with a microphone and sound-level meter usually provided as part of the total equipment package.

The most technically advanced version of the table-top viewer currently available consists of a *silent electronic*

FIGURE 11-2 Portable table-top playback units are available from several manufacturers. These have a tape playback and a built-in screen. More-advanced models have recording and electronic pulse capability, providing a unit that can be used to create as well as present a sound-slide module.

pulse that can be added to the narration tape. This electronic pulse will automatically advance the module to the next slide frame after the narration for the preceding frame has finished, without the module user's having to press the advance button.

The electronic pulse, therefore, eliminates the need for an audible advance cue of any kind. The module user simply loads the slide magazine and advances to the first frame of the module. The electronically pulsed narration tape is then loaded and the playback button pressed. The module will then run automatically through from beginning to end without the module user's having to touch the unit at all.

The more advanced table-top viewer models are of course more expensive than a simple playback unit. However, the availability of recording the electronic pulse capabilities can prove to be well worth the additional expense.

Single-viewer sound-slide presentation equipment that is nonportable is also available for permanent or semipermanent media installations. These *carrel* units usually consist of a small desk

FIGURE 11-1 Different types of commercial playback units are available for single-person or small-group presentations. Here, a playback unit has been built into a carrel study space with a small desk such as would be found in a library, media resource center, or training area.

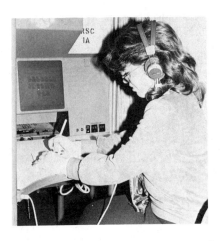

FIGURE 11-3 Carrel units can be used in conjunction with headphones, allowing many units to be used in close proximity without disturbing each other.

or enclosed cubicle space with a built-in viewer–playback unit. Carrel units, like the portable table-top viewer units, can be used with headphones so that a number of playback units can be operated in an enclosed area without distracting the module user with background noise. The headphones also allow the playback units to be operated in a library environment without disturbing others (see Figure 11-3).

PORTABLE, LARGE-GROUP PRESENTATION UNITS

As mentioned earlier, sound-slide presentations to large groups can be made with the use of a slide projector and cassette tape player. The only technical limitations with regard to the maximum number of persons able to attend are the size of the area available and the amount of volume that can be produced by the playback unit.

Some specially designed, portable, large-group presentation units have a slide projector and cassette playback mechanism built into a single case. These suitcase-sized presentation units are

easier to carry than several separate components; setup is quick and simple; and the tape playback part of the unit has a greater volume capability as well as a much larger speaker than a smaller, separate cassette player (see Figure 11-4). As in the case of the table-top viewers, the portable, large-group presentation units are available in different models ranging from playback-only units to models that have recording and electronic pulse capabilities.

When traveling with either a table-top viewer or a large-group presentation unit, it is always a good practice to carry at least one spare projector bulb and a 10-foot electrical extension cord along with the regular equipment. A duplicate cassette tape of each module narration should also be taken along as insurance against damage to the original narration tape through accident or overuse.

FIGURE 11-4 A portable, large-group presentation unit consists of a slide projector and an amplified cassette playback housed in a suitcase-sized carrier. More-advanced models have a recording and electronic pulse capability.

SOPHISTICATED
PRESENTATION METHODS

As we have seen throughout this book, the sound-slide module as a medium of educational communication is filled with potentials for creativity and innovation. These potentials apply to the methods of presentation as well as to the design and fabrication of a module.

Sophisticated presentation methods using highly specialized audio-visual equipment can elevate and magnify the sound-slide system into the area of multimedia communications. Techniques such as *rear-screen projection, dissolve units*, and *multiple-projector presentations* offer a wide range of special effects designed to enhance a sound-slide presentation so that it will be a visually striking experience.

Although an in-depth analysis of sophisticated electronic hardware is beyond the scope of this book, and the specialized equipment already mentioned is not required for the presentation of a sound-slide module, a brief discussion of these tools and techniques is in order, if only to demonstrate the level to which a sound-slide module may be taken if necessary.

Those readers of this book who are or will be involved in the application of sound-slide systems to advertising, sales, public relations, industrial statistics, or even fine arts will certainly find many valuable possibilities in specialized presentation techniques.

Rear-Screen Projection

Rear-screen projection utilizes a special screen material that *transmits* the projected light instead of *reflecting* it. The projector is positioned *behind* the screen rather than in front of it. The

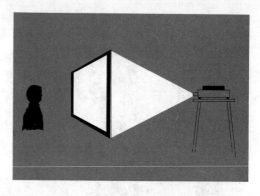

FIGURE 11-5 The rear-screen projection method utilizes a special screen that transmits, rather than reflects, projected light. The projector is positioned behind the screen. This projection system allows persons to move past the projected image without disturbing it with cast shadows.

screen material is stretched on a wood or metal frame and is free-standing to avoid the possibility of struts or supports creating shadows in the image area (see Figure 11-5).

This system of projection is very useful for trade shows and continuously running exhibits where numerous persons will be constantly passing in front of the screen (making conventional projection impossible).

The main drawback of the rear-screen projection system is that the very nature of the screen makes a certain amount of image diffusion unavoidable. Therefore, the edges of type and other pictorial matter are slightly less sharp when compared with regular front-screen projection. To avoid viewer confusion due to loss of image sharpness, larger type should be used in the preparation of slides that will be shown in rear-screen projection systems.

Dissolve Units

A dissolve unit is a compact electronic device that is used in conjunction with two projectors that are designed to be compatible with it. The dissolve unit controls the flow of electrical current to

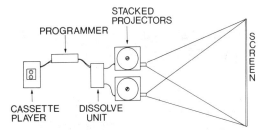

FIGURE 11-6 A simple two-projector setup. The cassette player (with a silent pulsed tape) directs the programmer, which in turn controls the dissolve unit. The projectors are stacked on top of each other in a special rack. The projector images are aligned so that they fit exactly on top of each other on the screen. In the newest equipment, the programmer has been incorporated into either the playback unit's functions or the dissolve unit's functions, eliminating the programmer as a separate unit altogether.

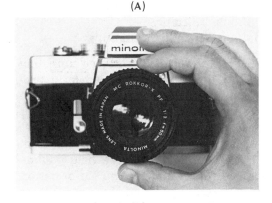

(A)

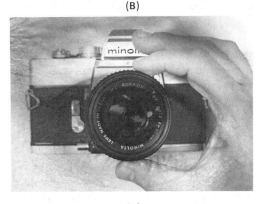

(B)

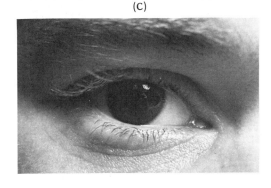

(C)

FIGURE 11-7A, B, C The dissolve unit provides a progression from one slide image to the next in a smooth fade in, fade out. The screen is not blacked out as with a conventional projector cycle. The length of the fade-in, fade-out cycle can be varied to produce striking, cinematic effects.

the projector bulbs during the slide-changing cycle of each projector. The projectors are set up so that their projected images exactly overlap each other on the screen (see Figure 11-6).

Under the control of the dissolve unit, the projectors "take turns" showing their slides. The image from one projector slowly fades to black while the image of the other projector slowly increases to full intensity. For a brief moment in the cycle, both projector images are superimposed. Then the new dominant image becomes apparent to the viewer.

The fade-in, fade-out slide change produced by the dissolve unit is extremely attractive and attention getting. The screen is never completely dark, and there is no sharp visual cutoff between slide images such as that produced by the conventional slide projector cycle.

The dissolve unit determines which projector to fade in and which to fade out through impulses directed to it by a *programmer* unit, which is connected to a cassette playback unit. The electronic pulses recorded on the narration tape are sorted by the programmer, which then directs the dissolve unit as to which projector to operate (see Figures 11-7A, 11-7B, and 11-7C). The projectors can be either placed side by side or stacked one over the other by using a bracket support available for this purpose.

Multiple-Projector, Multiple-Screen Presentations

The presentation package consisting of two projectors controlled by a programmer and dissolve unit, and a single screen, can also be multiplied. Two or more screens, each with an attendant set of controlled projectors can also be used. Visual information can be held on one screen while images and information continue to appear and change on others (see Figure 11–8). Obviously, there are many possible combinations of special visual effects, and representatives of large photographic equipment or audio-visual equipment supply companies will be able to explain the functions and applications of these various units.

Most Americans have now achieved a high degree of visual sophistication due to their extensive exposure to a variety of popular media. Therefore, the educator-communicator—regardless of the field of specialty—needs modes of

FIGURE 11–8 Multiple-projector, multiple-screen presentations can use three or more screens and as many as six, eight, or ten projectors controlled through computer programming.

information presentation that can tap and exploit the viewer's already-existing media receptability. The sound-slide system is one such information presentation medium that can, if approached with creativity, imagination, and enthusiasm, yield valuable and productive results.

GLOSSARY

Carrel unit A semipermanent cubicle installation usually consisting of a small desk, a chair, and a built-in sound-slide viewer, tape recorder, record player, television, or other piece of audio-visual equipment.

Dissolve unit An electronic device used in conjunction with two compatible slide projec-

tors. The dissolve unit controls the flow of electrical current to the projector bulbs during the slide-changing cycle. The slide projectors, whose images are overlapped, take turns fading in and fading out their slides, producing a brief superimposition effect and a smooth change from one image to another. The dissolve unit is directed by a programming unit that interprets the silent electronic pulses present on the narration tape (see *programming unit*).

Environmental presentation limitations Physical limitations on the number of persons able to attend a sound-slide presentation, such as the size of the room, the size of the projection screen, and the maximum volume of the cassette player.

Failing module A sound-slide module that produces uneven and little or no results in the areas of viewer understanding or knowledge retention.

Large-group presentation unit A portable suitcase-shaped carrier containing a slide projector and cassette tape player. Some large-group presentation units are available with recording and silent electronic pulse capabilities (see *silent electronic pulse*).

Multiple-projector, multiple-screen presentation A sound-slide presentation that consists of two or more pairs of projectors and two or more screens utilizing dissolve and programming units.

Presentation mode The method by which a sound-slide module is presented, dictated by the number of persons who will view the module and the environment or area in which it will be shown. For a large group of people, the presentation mode would be by projector and amplified sound system. For a small group or a single viewer, the presentation mode would be by a table-top viewer.

Programming unit Used in conjunction with a dissolve unit and matching projectors. This device interprets the silent pulses present on the narration tape and directs the dissolve unit accordingly as to which projector image to fade in and which to fade out.

Rear-screen projection A free-standing projection screen made of a light-transmitting, rather than reflective, material. The slide projector is located behind the screen for projection, allowing people to walk or stand in front of the screen while an image appears on it.

Reevaluation analysis A periodic analysis of the content of a sound-slide module with regard to the timeliness of the information, narration pace, vocabulary, and explanation of technical terms and overall quality.

Silent electronic pulse An inaudible electronic signal that can be added to a narration cassette tape, with a specially designed recording device. When played back through a compatible presentation system, the silent pulse will trigger an automatic slide advance wherever it is placed on the narration tape.

Slide-changing cycle Within the slide projector, the mechanical action of returning a slide to the tray magazine, advancing to the next slide, and moving the new slide into position for projection.

Sound amplification device An electronic device, such as a public-address system, into which a cassette player can be linked to increase the maximum amount of volume available.

Table-top viewer A light weight, portable viewer for sound-slide modules. A table-top viewer consists of a televisionlike cabinet with an approximately 1-square-foot screen. The viewer is equipped with a slide-changing mechanism and a cassette tape playback unit. Some table-top viewers are available with recording and silent electronic pulse capabilities (see *silent electronic pulse*).

Viewer feedback Information about the effectiveness and usefulness of a sound-slide module taken from actual users of the module.

INDEX

Slides, image problems (continued)
hot spots and reflections, 143, 149, 150
nonparallel image sides, 148–49
nonparallel type, 148
off-center image, 147–148
overextended field of image, 150–51
shadowed type, 152
marking mounts for identification and
storage, 134–35
master set, importance of, 125–26
plastic file pages, 126
processing of, 132–33
projector magazine, 133–35
proportions of image compared to those of
flat copy, 20–21
push processing described, 131
storage of, 133–35
Slipsheet (*see* Overlay)
SLR (single lens reflex) camera, 118–20
Snitch file (*see* Art and Illustrations)
Sound slide presentation methods, 185–90
Stencil knife:
blade set into drawing compass as a circle
cutter, 83–85
described, 23–24
silhouetting, uses of in, 72–73
Storyboard:
background color themes for frames, 14–15
color, in backgrounds, 14–15
color-coding graphic information for
emphasis, 12–14
felt-tipped pen or marker, use of, 14
split-screen effect in frame design, 12–14
storyboard, pad, 11–14

Tape:
cassette audio (*see* Audio portion of the
module)
charting, cutting, application, and uses of,
92–94
double-sided, use of, 69–71
masking, photographic quality, 111–12
Texture sheets, 105–9
Touch-up process for cut photographs, 73–74
Tracing a photograph onto the acetate overlay,
102–3
Transfer type (*see* Type, pressure sensitive)
Transparent triangle (*see* Overlay)
T square:
in application of pressure-sensitive type to the
acetate overlay, 44–48
definition of, 21
format guide, use of with the, 61–62

T Square (continued)
in production of format guide, 21–24
Tungsten light-type film (*see* Film)
Tungsten photoflood bulb (*see* Photoflood
bulbs)
TV planning pad, 11–14
Tweezers, used for application of charting
tape, 93–94
Type:
burnisher, 25–27
pressure sensitive:
application process to the acetate overlay,
43–48
burnishing process, described, 33–34
colors, symbols and illustrations available,
37–38
columns, application of on the overlay,
52–54
cracks and chips, repair methods, 33–34
crowded type, 30–31
described, 25
erasure of pencil guideline, 33
felt-tipped marker or pen, 14, 56, 58, 61
guideline for application process, 27–28
line spacing on the overlay, 49–52
manufacturers' brand names, 35–36
overspaced type, 30–31
point size range, defined, 34–35
problem letters, 31–32
removal from acetate overlay, 47–48
removal from a paper surface, 28–30
spacing lettering, 30–31
storage and shelf life, 38
styles, defined, 36
tracing letters or words in pencil, 31–34
56–58
transfer process described, 27–30
verticality of letters, 32–33
word centering on overlay, 54–59
superimposed on full-frame photograph,
15
Typewritten slides (*see* Slides, black and white)

Vertical slipsheet (*see* Overlay)

X-Acto brand hobby knife, 23–24

Zip.A.Tone brand texture sheets, 108
Zone of sharp focus of camera lens, 146–47